APPROACHES TO PAUL

APPROACHES TO PAUL

a student's guide
to recent
scholarship

Magnus Zetterholm

Fortress Press

Minneapolis

APPROACHES TO PAUL
A Student's Guide to Recent Scholarship

Cover photo: Fragment of a twelfth-century Byzantine
plaque with a representation of St. Paul © Werner
Forman / Art Resource, NY
Cover design: Micah Thompson

Library of Congress Cataloging-in-Publication Data

Zetterholm, Magnus, 1958-
  Approaches to Paul : a student's guide to recent
scholarship / Magnus Zetterholm.
        p. cm.
  Includes bibliographical references and index.
  ISBN 978-0-8006-6337-7 (alk. paper)
  1. Bible. N.T. Epistles of Paul--Theology--History.
  2. Judaism (Christian theology)--History of doctrines.
  3. Jews in the New Testament. I. Title.
  BS2655.J4Z47 2009
  225.9'2--dc22

                                          2008044041

The paper used in this publication meets the minimum
requirements of American National Standard for Information Sciences — Permanence of Paper for Printed
Library Materials, ANSI Z329.48-1984.

Manufactured in the U.S.A.

13 12 11 10 09 1 2 3 4 5 6 7 8 9 10

In memory of my parents

Gunn Zetterholm
1923–1984

Nils Zetterholm
1920–1992

CONTENTS

The study of Paul involves a paradox that is rather unique in the field of religious studies. On the one hand, Pauline theology, carefully extracted from the apostle's literary production, is one of the cornerstones upon which the Christian church is built. Several important Christian doctrines—"righteousness through faith alone" being the most famous one—represent a very precise understanding of what Paul intended to communicate to his audience. Thus, with regard to certain aspects of vital importance for the Christian church over the centuries, there has been a rather general agreement on what Paul meant. The vast majority of Pauline scholars have commonly agreed that Paul broke radically with Judaism and that he ceased observing the Jewish law in a Jewish way. According to this understanding, the historical Paul clearly lived in a state of opposition to Judaism.

On the other hand, among scholars who generally share this overarching perspective on Paul, there has simultaneously been a considerable disagreement over what Paul really wanted to say. Scholars have developed various strategies for coming to terms with apparent inconsistencies in Paul's thinking. In recent decades, the situation has become yet more complicated: an increasing number of scholars have begun to question one of the few areas where up to now there has been a fairly widespread consensus: *Paul's relation to Judaism.*

Since the beginning of the 1980s, Pauline scholarship has experienced a virtual explosion of interpretations that aim at explaining Paul *without assuming a radical break with Judaism.* Some scholars even believe that Paul continued to observe the Torah after his transforming vision of the risen Christ and that he believed that only non-Jews should refrain from Torah observance. If this is true, it seems to mean that the church will need to revisit some of its fundamental doctrines.

Pauline scholarship today may best be described as including two fundamental approaches to Paul that are really impossible to reconcile: one that assumes that Paul broke with Judaism, and one that presumes that he remained within Judaism. Within both these paradigms there are considerable variations. With Pauline studies we are entering a world where almost nothing seems certain any longer, and the focus of this book is precisely this variation of perspectives and mutually irreconcilable readings of Paul. Thus, the reader who expects to find in this book the ultimate answers to the question of who Paul really was will be disappointed. With regard to the historical Paul, I am afraid that this book provides very few absolute answers. Rather, the aim of the present study is to point to the questions and to perhaps contribute an explanation as to why Pauline scholarship has developed in this peculiar way.

This book focuses on the significance of the underlying assumptions in Pauline scholarship. For that reason it is perhaps only fair that I give an account of some of my own. In general, I approach the issue of Paul and Judaism from a secular perspective. This means, for instance, that I am not affiliated with any religious community. I generally lack theological convictions and consequently have no theology to defend. Having said that, it should be clear that I do not mean to suggest that this state of affair guarantees scholarly objectivity or freedom from influencing biases—only that my biases are of a different kind. It will probably become clear in the book that I side with those scholars who regard Paul as a part of first-century Judaism. I firmly believe that trying to understand Paul as *connected* to Judaism, rather than in *conflict* with Judaism, is a better perspective when searching for the historical Paul.

I am quite aware that recognizing the connection between the traditional Christian teaching on Paul and the crimes committed against the Jewish people throughout history has led me to take this position. I must confess that I find it strange that so much Pauline scholarship, even in a post-Holocaust perspective, still insists on showing the inferiority of Judaism in comparison to Christianity. However, the most decisive reason for assuming a Jewish Paul is, in my view, the history of Pauline scholarship itself. Considering the historical situation in which the Christian anti-Semitic discourse emerged and how this emergence led to the formation of a pattern of thought within Western civilization that emphasized the opposition between Judaism and Christianity, I find it hard to take seriously this *theological* pattern as a fundamental point of departure for a *historical* study of Paul. Thus I am convinced that Pauline scholarship needs to explore other interpretive keys than the dogmatically motivated dichotomy between Judaism and Christianity.

Part of my agenda certainly is to invite new generations of Pauline scholars to engage in such an enterprise, which I believe in no way constitutes a threat to Christian theology. The only threat is to certain preconceived ways of creating theology that, from a Jewish perspective—*Paul's* perspective—would appear hopelessly disconnected from the historical roots of the Christian church.

Publishing books is rarely a one-person show. Behind the scene, several people are usually involved in various ways and deserve the gratitude of the author (who gets all the royalties). So also in the case of this book: as always, Karin, my best colleague and my partner in life, has been a keen discussion companion also with regard to this project. She has read and commented on various versions and provided all other kinds of support that have made it possible for me to bring this project to an end. In addition, I am indebted to Sven Heilo, Bengt Holmberg, Mark Nanos, and Birger Olsson, who have all read the whole or parts of the manuscript and suggested important improvements. The same is true for Neil Elliott at Fortress, who together with Marissa Bauck and the rest of the Fortress staff have turned this project into a really pleasant publishing experience.

I have benefitted from two sabbaticals at Yale University. During my first visit, in 2004–2005, I first began planning this book, which I am now about to complete during my second visit, this present semester. Thus, I wish to express my gratitude, especially to Dale Martin in the Religion Department and to Harold Attridge at Yale Divinity School, for allowing me to be part of the intellectual milieu of this fine institution.

Financial supporters indeed belong to the circle of those who deserve my gratitude. Parts of the book were written when I was a Research Fellow at the Swedish Research Council during the spring semester 2009. In addition, I received a generous scholarship from The Lars Hierta Memorial Foundation in 2007. For this important form of assistance I am truly grateful.

Finally, I have dedicated this book to the memory of my parents as a small token of appreciation for an upbringing characterized by the constant challenge to question authorities and those who claim to possess the absolute truth. In the end, that is, of course, what scholarship really is about.

ABBREVIATIONS OF SOURCES

'Abod. Zar.	*'Abodah Zarah (Tosefta)*
'Abot	*'Abot (Mishnah)*
A.J.	*Antiquitates judaicae/Jewish Antiquities (Josephus)*
B.J.	*Bellum judaicum/The Jewish War (Josephus)*
C. Ap.	*Contra Apionem/Against Apion (Josephus)*
CIJ	*Corpus inscriptionum judaicarum (Epigraphica)*
Civ.	*De civitate Dei/The City of God (Augustinus)*
1 Clem.	*1 Clement (Apostolic Fathers)*
CPJ	*Corpus papyrorum judaicorum (Papyri, Ostraka)*
Dom.	*Domitianus (Suetonius)*
Hist. eccl.	*Historia ecclesiastica/Church History (Eusebius)*
Jub.	*Jubilees (OT Pseudepigrapha)*
Magn.	*To the Magnesians (Apostolic Fathers)*
MAMA	*Monumenta Asiae Antiqua (Epigraphica)*
Med.	*De Medicina/On Medicine (Celsus)*
1QS	*Serek Hayaḥad/Rule of the Community (Qumran)*
Sanh.	*Sanhedrin (Mishnah)*
Sat.	*Satirae/Satires (Juvenal)*
Spec.	*De specialibus legibus/On the Special Laws (Philo)*

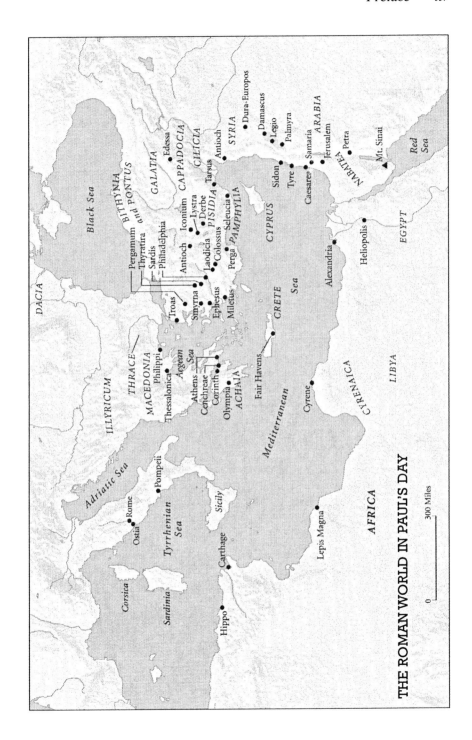

THE ROMAN WORLD IN PAUL'S DAY

1

PAUL AND HISTORY

Introduction

With regard to Pauline scholarship it is probably no exaggeration to suggest that Paul's relation to Judaism aptly frames the most important discussions of the twentieth century. Thus an overwhelming amount of current "approaches to Paul" are related to the issue of the extent to which Paul remained within a Jewish religious context. While very few scholars in the beginning of last century seriously questioned that Paul was the founder of Christianity and that he himself had abandoned Judaism, the situation in the beginning of the twenty-first century is remarkably different. In contemporary discussions on Paul, the traditional perspective, characterized by an almost absolute contradiction between Paul and Judaism, is challenged by scholars who maintain that Paul, to some extent, remained within Judaism. A small number of scholars go even further, arguing that Paul even continued to observe the Torah after his earth-shattering vision of the risen Christ. In their view, Paul was as Jewish as any Jew in antiquity. The current situation could hence be described as two extreme positions framing a middle position that is criticized from both ends—and for quite different reasons.

It is rather obvious that the recent development of localizing Paul within a Jewish context has caused tensions within the scholarly community. For historical reasons, the bonds between biblical studies and Christian theology have been strong, and even in a post-Enlightenment context, this situation prevails. Even though there has been a similar process with regard to Jesus, who in the beginning of the twentieth century was commonly viewed in contrast to Judaism, but who is now firmly localized within first-century Judaism,[1] the hesitation to accept a Jewish Paul has been more substantial.

Given the prominence of the doctrine of "righteousness by faith," especially within the Reformation churches, this hardly comes as a surprise. Traditionally, Christian *faith* has been constructed over and against Jewish *works-righteousness*. As a consequence, Paul has, from a Christian perspective, been seen as the main advocate of the "law-free" gospel. In the course of history, Judaism has become the dark background against which Christianity has been able to shine forth so much more brilliantly. However, the idea that Paul remained within Judaism is often perceived as threatening not only from a Christian perspective; a Jewish Paul is hardly a winning scenario from a contemporary Jewish viewpoint either. Because of the rather complex relations between Judaism and Christianity throughout history (which themselves are partly the result of the Christian interpretation of Paul), Paul has also commonly been seen from a Jewish perspective as constituting the clear demarcation line between Judaism and Christianity.

It is accordingly easy to understand why the resistance to the idea of seeing Paul as a representative of the Jewish faith and tradition has been, and still remains, powerful. However, the complex relation between scholarship and theology (Jewish and Christian) and the historical relations between Judaism and Christianity strongly suggest that prescientific assumptions, which have gradually come to be regarded as irrefutable truths, may be involved in the traditional historical construction of Paul. The idea that the image of Paul as depicted by church tradition represents the most plausible historical reconstruction can consequently be called into question.

To a considerable degree, many recent approaches to Paul aim at precisely this question. By deconstructing the view of Paul that has emerged in a dialectical relationship between the academy and the church throughout history, scholars critical of the "Lutheran" Paul intend to find a more historically accurate view of the apostle. As has been pointed out by Heikki Räisänen (whose work will be scrutinized in chapter 4), even scholars who generally share the view that Paul broke with Judaism have been unable to reach a consensus on Paul. "It is symptomatic that the followers of the apostle have hardly ever been able to agree on what he really wanted to say," Räisänen states.[2] Räisänen himself believes that because Paul is so inconsistent, he cannot be understood in a proper way. Other scholars have rather criticized the overarching traditional perspectives and argued that Paul can be made intelligible from assumptions other than the Lutheran ones. They argue, in fact, that from these new assumptions a *more* coherent picture emerges. In any case, it is evident that the way in which Paul is being viewed is strongly connected to the general assumptions scholars use in their work.

Paul, Apostle to the Gentiles

Paul's letter to the Romans is an excellent starting point for introducing the interpretive problems of Paul's relation to Judaism. The letter, composed in the mid-50s CE, when Paul resided in Corinth, is regarded as perhaps his most important work, and it has exerted an enormous influence on the theological development of the Christian church. The Reformation theology of Martin Luther, for instance, is to a great extent based on Romans. The prologue (Rom 1:1-5) constitutes a comprehensive summary of Paul's understanding of the gospel of Jesus Christ and his own role in the cosmic drama in which he finds himself deeply involved:

> Paul, a servant of Jesus Christ, called to be an apostle, set apart for the gospel of God, which he promised beforehand through his prophets in the holy scriptures, the gospel concerning his Son, who was descended from David according to the flesh and was declared to be Son of God with power according to the spirit of holiness by resurrection from the dead, Jesus Christ our Lord, through whom we have received grace and apostleship to bring about the obedience of faith among all the Gentiles for the sake of his name.[3]

Romans undoubtedly contains material pertaining to many of the complex questions the Christian church has wrestled with in course of history. Does faith or works justify a person? What is the role of Judaism in the Christian civilization? Has the role of the chosen people been transferred from the Jews to the Christians? Who is the true Israel? What is the relation between the Jewish law, the Torah, and grace?

The letters of Paul, with the exception of Romans, are addressed to communities founded by Paul himself and usually deal with local problems in the community. According to Acts, Paul undertook three extensive missionary journeys in Asia Minor and founded several communities where he resided for some time and then moved on. By writing letters, he answered questions and set about correcting matters he regarded as unsatisfactory. Because of this, it is quite difficult to reconstruct a systematic theology with the Pauline letters as a point of departure. Most of the letters at best offer limited glimpses of what Paul thought about certain matters. At times it is hard to know what he deals with, as we lack knowledge about the specific background situation of a letter. Regarding First Corinthians, for instance, we know it was a response to a query from the community in Corinth, but that letter is not extant. That is to say, we know the answers Paul gave, but not the questions posed.

When it comes to Romans, the situation is somewhat different. The Roman community was not founded by Paul, but probably by Jewish followers of Jesus who had migrated to Rome already during the 40s. This might be the reason why we find a more coherent theological survey in Romans than in the other letters. Paul's plan to extend his missionary endeavors westwards, toward Spain, has commonly been regarded as the reason why Paul wrote the letter. Because of this missionary plan of his, some scholars have assumed that he needed Rome as a base and composed the letter as a presentation of himself and his theology.[4]

The Elusive Paul

The nature of Paul's letter to the Romans has led some scholars to regard it as Paul's spiritual testament.[5] More recently, however, many scholars believe that Paul also wrote Romans in order to come to grips with local problems within the Roman community.[6] The fact that the overall purpose of the letter is not altogether clear brings a central problem within the field of New Testament scholarship to the fore—a problem it shares with all historical research—namely *that there are many historical issues that cannot be determined only from the ancient texts*. It is possible to understand Romans as a purely theological treatise with no direct bearing on the local situation in Rome, but it is also possible that Paul composed the letter as an answer to specific problems that had come up in the community. The reader here confronts two different perspectives that considerably influence the overall interpretation of the letter.

The same is true regarding the question of the recipients of the letter. The Roman community was made up of both Jews and non-Jews who were followers of Jesus. But which group is Paul addressing? Is he speaking only to the non-Jewish part of the community, or to the community as a whole? The identity of the addressees is, in fact, crucial when determining Paul's relation to Judaism. In Romans 7:6, he writes: "But now we are discharged from the law, dead to that which held us captive, so that we are slaves not under the old written code but in the new life of the Spirit." Does this mean that Paul claims that the Torah is no longer in force with respect to himself and to all other Jewish followers of Jesus? This is the conclusion if we presume that he is addressing the Roman community *as a whole*, that is, both Jesus-believing Jews and Jesus-believing non-Jews. The fact that Paul includes himself— "now *we* have become free"—indicates that he actually regards himself as "free" from the law.

But let us return to the prologue of the letter where Paul states that through Jesus, "we have received grace and apostleship to bring about the obedience of faith among *all the Gentiles* for the sake of his name, including yourselves who are called to belong to Jesus Christ." Here Paul emphasizes his special mission—to reach out to non-Jews. Does this mean that the recipients of Romans are specifically the non-Jews in the community and that the purpose of the statement in Romans 7:6 is not at all to define the relation of *every human being* to the Torah? Is it possible that Paul in Romans 7:6 is only defining the relation of the *non-Jew* to the Torah, and that he employs a rather common rhetorical figure when he includes himself?

It is evident that many non-Jews harbored a keen interest in Judaism prior to becoming involved in the Jesus movement. We know from the Jewish historian Josephus (*B.J.* 7.45; *C. Ap.* 2.282), for instance, that Judaism was rather fashionable in Rome at that time and that non-Jews adopted Jewish customs and manners. Interested non-Jews, so-called God-fearers, took part in the activity of the synagogues, and it is very likely that it was from this group that the first adherents to the Jesus movement were recruited.[7] If this is the case, we must assume that they, to some extent, had adapted to a Jewish way of life. They celebrated the Sabbath, ate Jewish food, said Jewish prayers, and they perhaps even thought they enjoyed a special status in relation to the God of Israel by imitating a Jewish way of life.

Many Jews probably did not mind non-Jews turning to the God of Israel or letting themselves be influenced by the Torah. The notion that some non-Jews also had a place in the world to come was no alien idea in ancient Judaism. Quite contrary to what is often assumed, Judaism did not generally claim the exclusive right to salvation. But the Torah was understood by some as a means for only the Jewish people to keep its special relation to the God of Israel alive. Thus it is possible that Paul, instead of working out a general way of salvation for humanity, in fact only attempted to correct what he considered to be a misconception among first-century Jesus-believing non-Jews.

A similar complex of problems appears in another Pauline letter, Galatians, which is of equal importance regarding Paul's relation to Judaism. In contrast to Romans, the purpose of which, as we have seen, is somewhat unclear, there is no doubt that Galatians was written to address a specific situation and with a special aim. Paul was furious with the Galatians, because he suspected that individuals proclaiming a different gospel from his had influenced them. The problem in Galatia seems to have been that non-Jewish followers of Jesus had been subject to persuasion to convert to Judaism. It is, however, unclear what lies at the bottom of this. Perhaps these opponents of Paul were Jesus-believing, Jewish missionaries asserting that a non-Jew had to become a Jew in order to be included in the salvation by Jesus Christ. Acts 15 hints that such ideas were in circulation. Luke, the author of Acts, mentions that "certain individuals came down from Judea and were teaching the brothers, 'Unless you are circumcised according to the custom of Moses, you cannot be saved'" (Acts 15:1). In 15:5, Luke further states that "some believers who belonged to the sect of the Pharisees stood up and said, 'It is necessary for them to be circumcised and ordered to keep the law of Moses.'"

Another possibility is that the Jesus-believing groups were victims of pressure from local *Jewish* groups without any direct connection to the Jesus movement.[8] The Jewish communities were often subject to locally issued regulations concerning the relation to the official civic religion. In antiquity, political and religious powers were indissolubly united and exacted loyalty to the politico-religious system on part of the populace. Jews as a rule were exempt from the obligation to participate in Greco-Roman religious feasts and other such rites, however; as these were irreconcilable with the Jewish faith.[9] Non-Jews, on the other hand, taking part as interested guests in synagogue activities, no doubt also fulfilled the religious obligations incumbent on them by state decree, and most of them probably did not consider this a problem. Many God-fearing non-Jews simply included the God of Israel in their pantheon, side by side with all the other gods. In the non-Jewish world, among Greeks and Romans, the idea of worshipping only one single god was considered peculiar and, on the whole, unnecessary.

We must presume that this was accepted by the Jewish communities living, as they were, under the constant threat of having their special rights abolished. The suspicion that they had caused non-Jewish inhabitants in a city to neglect their civic religious obligations could easily result in reprisals from the authorities charged with safeguarding proper relations with the gods. Maintaining the sensitive balance between the Jewish and the non-Jewish worlds was thus of advantage to each and everyone. In this respect, the Jesus movement seems to have differed from other Jewish groups, for it stipulated that non-Jewish adherents must refrain from what was considered "idolatry," that is, involvement in Greco-Roman religion. Considering the conditions in society, this is likely to have created a complicated political situation for all Jewish groups in the area. Hence, it is in fact possible that the demands in Galatia for a regular conversion to Judaism emanated from Jewish groups that otherwise had nothing to do with the Jesus movement.

Regardless of the individuals behind the demands, Paul reacts most vehemently, and Galatians, as well as Romans, contains many Torah-critical statements. In Galatians 2:16a, Paul writes, "we know that a person is justified not by the works of the law but through faith in Jesus Christ." In Galatians 3:13a, he maintains, "Christ redeemed us from the curse of the law," and in Galatians 5:4 he thunders: "You who want to be justified by the law have cut yourselves off from Christ; you have fallen away from grace." Here the matter *seems* clear-cut: Paul has dissociated himself from one of the most central tenets of Judaism, the Torah, and replaced it with Christ. Those who seek their righteousness in the Torah are foredoomed to failure and barred from grace. Paul really *seems* to have abandoned Judaism and instead created a new religion.

This is exactly the way scholars have traditionally assessed it, and there is a good deal of truth in Brad Young's description of the situation:

> The consensus of scholarship has come to view [Paul] as a Hellenistic Jew who departed radically from his Judaism. Scholars view him as being influenced by his upbringing in the Stoic environs of Tarsus and various streams of thought flowing forth from paganism, Greco-Roman culture, popular Hellenistic philosophy, mystery religious cults, and Gnostic systems. Seldom is the origin of Paul's faith seen as rooted in Pharisaism.[10]

Paul is commonly thought to have left Judaism because he had realized that the Torah represents a person's ambition to become righteous by means of his or her own efforts. Such an endeavor is not only impossible, as no one can keep the entire Torah all the time, but it also represents the cardinal sin—self-righteousness. On this view, when Jesus appears to Paul on the road to Damascus (Acts 9:3-9), Paul is struck by the insight of the basic fault of Judaism and converts to Christianity. "The one who is righteous will live by faith," has often been regarded as the all-embracing conflict between Jewish self-righteousness obtained by keeping the precepts of the Torah, and Christian faith in Jesus as a basis for an attributive, undeserved righteousness, on the other. Strangely enough, Paul quotes a Jewish text, in fact from the prophet Habakkuk, who wrote: "Look at the proud! Their spirit is not right in them, but the righteous live by their faith" (Hab 2:4). When Paul formulates what would later become the cornerstone of the Protestant churches—righteousness by faith alone—he accordingly refers to the very Jewish tradition with which he is presumed to have broken. Righteousness, forgiveness, and atonement are, of course, all central Jewish concepts, and when Paul attempts to explain how this righteousness by faith alone functions

(Romans 4), he selects one of the prominent figures of *Judaism,* Abraham, as an example.

Paul and Judaism

In the beginning of the twentieth century, a number of scholars pointed out that the image of Judaism commonly held up as a contrasting picture beside Christianity was historically dubious. They insisted that ancient Judaism was *not* a religion in which the believer merited salvation by keeping a set of peculiar precepts. The image of Paul as the hero of the Christian civilization who liberated Christianity from the burden of Jewish law was called in question, but it was only in the 1970s that these ideas began to have a profound impact on New Testament scholarship. Yet, the idea that Paul in reality belonged to the Judaism of the first century remained the opinion of a minority, and to say the least, many scholars are still skeptical of the hypothesis that Paul did not abandon Judaism and create a new religion.

During the last decades of the twentieth century, a new trend in research was introduced with the aim of placing Paul in the context of the richly faceted Judaism of the first century. There are several reasons for this. The post-war insight among Christian scholars of the connection between the horrors of the extermination camps and the traditional anti-Semitism transmitted down the centuries by the churches initiated an incentive to reflect upon the part played by Paul in Christian theology. The declaration *Nostra Aetate,* issued by the Second Vatican Council (1962–1965), constituted a far-reaching attempt on the part of the Roman Catholic Church to clear away the foundation of a Christian theology formulated at the expense of the Jews. The emergence of an organized Jewish-Christian dialogue, with the ambition of discerning similarities and differences between the respective traditions, resulted in a reappraisal of their own religious tradition. Jewish scholars, with knowledge and points of reference that differed from those of the traditional New Testament scholars, started to become seriously interested in the study of the New Testament. As a result of research in the field of the historical Jesus, an increasingly Jewish portrait of him emerged, a portrait that has become more and more accepted. Finally, general hermeneutic reflection has played an important part. The emergence of

textual theoretical perspectives, which have made the process of interpretation as such problematic, as well as the relation between the text,
the reader, and the original intention of the author, have been especially
important.

The Aim and Outline of this Book

For the present we can thus note that there are two diametrically
opposed basic perspectives regarding the understanding of Paul's relation to Judaism. It is evident that it is possible to understand Paul as the
one who broke with Judaism. For a long time, this has been the obvious point of departure for the majority of Pauline scholars—and probably still is. However, it is also possible to see Paul as the representative
of a universalistic, messianic, Jewish movement, for which the main
problem was the salvation of the non-Jews. An increasing number of
scholars are now addressing issues pertaining to Paul's relation to
Judaism from the basic assumption that Paul was as Torah-observant
as any other Jew during the first century. Thus we can see Paul as the
reformer of a particularistic Judaism and the creator of a universalistic
Christianity, in which the demands of the Torah had yielded to grace.
But we can also view him as wholly true to his Jewish tradition, constantly occupied with formulating the theological basis for the relation
of the non-Jew to the God of Israel and a social theory for coexistence
between Jewish and non-Jewish followers of Jesus.

*From a historical point of view, both these perspectives cannot be entirely
correct.* The aim of this book is to attempt to explain how Paul's relation
to Judaism can be understood in two very different ways and to explore
which approach is likely to produce the most historically plausible picture of Paul and the development of the early Jesus movement. How
did the view of Paul originate that until very recently dominated New
Testament scholarship, and how have the new approaches developed
that now challenge the traditional image of Paul? As the relation of Paul
to Judaism apparently cannot be discerned unequivocally from the biblical text, it is obvious that factors outside the text have played a crucial
part. Thus an important question concerns the roles that social climate,
theological trends, and philosophical traditions may have played in the
evolution of the various images of the apostle.

It is quite obvious that such an account will be far from complete, and it is important to emphasize that the purpose of this book is not to present a comprehensive description of all Pauline scholarship. The focus here is how Paul's relation to Judaism has been assessed, especially the question of why certain specific interpretations originated, and the dependency of these interpretations on circumstances outside of the text. Even with this limitation in mind, it would be impossible within the scope of this book to cover all relevant research. Thus we will only be able to deal with a few representative works essential for the question of Paul's relation to Judaism, and the overall purpose is to point to certain tendencies particularly important for the development of various approaches to Paul. The selection of scholars who are used for instantiating a certain trend could thus have been done differently in some instances. Moreover, references to secondary literature are kept to a minimum. The relevant literature can easily be found through the bibliographies in the works under discussion, which I hope the reader of this book will find worthwhile to consult in the original.

The concentration on major currents within the discipline makes it important also to emphasize that this presentation to some extent represents a simplification and, of course, a subjective reconstruction of a development from certain points of view. It is important to bear in mind that the whole picture is much more complex, and there are always different angles that could have been taken into consideration.

A good starting point for this project is the so-called Tübingen School, which emanated from the radical German theologian Ferdinand Christian Baur (1792–1860). Baur personifies one of the first attempts to describe the development of Paul and the early church against the background of a specific philosophical tradition, and his work has exerted considerable influence on the research on Paul and the development of the early church. When dealing with the Tübingen School, there is every reason to look more closely at the way ancient Judaism was presented at the end of the nineteenth century, since this view had an enormous influence on New Testament scholarship. We will also search for the roots of the widespread contempt for Judaism and Jewish culture that marked the European cultural climate at the dawn of the twentieth century. This is the main concern of chapter 2.

In chapter 3, we will remain within the German cultural sphere and examine the development of the traditional view of Paul, here represented by the circle around Rudolf Bultmann and in the tradition of German Protestantism.

Chapter 4 deals with the so-called "new perspective on Paul" that emerged as the result of a strong reevaluation of ancient Judaism by the American scholar E. P. Sanders, who offered a fundamental settling of accounts with the image of Judaism that made up the foundation of almost all New Testament scholarship. Sanders's work led to a true explosion of studies on Paul, and various scholars called in question previously established conceptions of Paul and his relation to Judaism.

Some scholars, however, maintain that this "new perspective," though motivated by the understanding of how anti-Jewish thought-patterns and Reformation theology have influenced research on Paul, nevertheless repeats old paradigms, albeit in a new manner. For this reason, in chapter 5 we are going to look more closely at scholars who apply even more radical approaches to Paul, and in differing ways suggest that Paul can be completely located within the framework of first-century Judaism. Some even argue that Paul never abandoned Judaism or ceased observing the Torah.

Now scholarship quite often proceeds in an oscillating way. Thus scholars who maintain that the Reformation perspective nevertheless represents Paul more accurately than the more recent approaches have profoundly criticized the new perspective on Paul as well as the even more radical approaches. In chapter 6 we will take a look at scholars who, for example, call Sanders's new view of Judaism into question and argue that Luther should still have a word on the relation between Paul and Judaism.

The ongoing discussion on Paul and Judaism has also promoted different multidisciplinary approaches, and the discussion as such has led to an increased interest in Paul as an important figure within Western culture, not least within some philosophical discourses. The emergence of postcolonial perspectives has led to an increased interest in the political context of Paul's writings, and such perspectives have frequently been used in combination with more radical approaches to Paul. Scholars working with feminist perspectives have been forced to relate to an increasingly Jewish Paul, resulting in some self-critical discussions on underlying anti-Jewish currents within feminist inter-pretations. This will be our focus in chapter 7.

Finally, in the closing chapter, we are going to analyze the reasons for the elusive image of Paul and the many approaches that have emerged. To what extent is biblical scholarship governed by other aims than "the objective quest for truth"? What are the roles of normative theology, philosophical traditions, and anti-Jewish currents handed down from previous generations? Who is the "real" Paul: the founder of Christianity, or just one of many Jews imagining that the God of Israel, through Jesus Christ, also offers non-Jews a place in the world to come?

Before we start examining Paul and the different approaches con-cerning his relation to the Judaism he undeniably was born into, we need to briefly survey his life and literary production in order to indi-cate some areas where the contradicting perspectives on Paul are par-ticularly salient.

Paul—from Pharisee to Apostle

"I am a Jew, from Tarsus in Cilicia"

The sources of our knowledge of Paul are Acts, the second part of the double work of the evangelist Luke, written at the end of the first century, and Paul's own letters. As historical sources, Acts and the Pauline corpus are, however, not unproblematic. In Acts, the historiog-raphy is totally subordinate to the theological message. A prominent theme, for instance, is how the gospel is conveyed from Jerusalem to the center of the world, the city of Rome. In this drama, Paul is the hero. Onward, through incessant hardships, he battles unwearied for the truth of the gospel and finally reaches Rome thanks to divine intervention. The letters of Paul offer only a few biographical clues, and these are often included in highly rhetorical discourses. Of course, this does not pre-clude that they also contain historically correct information. Although many questions remain unanswered, and it is sometimes difficult to har-monize particulars in Acts with notices in the letters of Paul, it still seems possible to reconstruct at least the main outlines of the life of the apostle.

According to Acts, Paul came from Tarsus, a city located in present-day southeastern Turkey (Acts 21:39, 22:3). Tarsus was an important center of commerce and learning in the Roman province of Cilicia, established in the year 64 BCE, and had roughly half a million inhabitants. In Acts, Paul claims not only that he comes from Tarsus, but also that he is a citizen there (Acts 21:39), which is rather surprising. In the first place, most inhabitants in the Greco-Roman cities were not citizens in a strict sense, but either free inhabitants or slaves. Only a small group of men with political influence were citizens in the true sense of the word and could be elected for official assignments. Women from all groups were usually excluded from political life. Secondly, the considerable Jewish population did not enjoy citizenship as a group, since this would have implied participation in the official religion, something Jews were unable to do if they wanted to be true to their own religious tradition. As noted above, the Jewish population in the Greco-Roman cities usually enjoyed status as privileged inhabitants, with the right to exercise limited self-government and with no obligations to take part in the religious rituals of the city.

It is, however, possible that citizenship was conferred on certain individuals from Jewish families who belonged to the social upper crust in some Greco-Roman cities without demanding that they give up their Jewish identity. The statement in Acts concerning Paul's citizenship in Tarsus may therefore be correct and indicates that Paul came from a family of some standing. This is further emphasized by the fact that Paul not only claims to be a citizen of Tarsus, but also by birthright a citizen of the Roman Empire (Acts 22:25-28).

The question of Paul's citizenship is brought up in Luke's account of how Paul, during a visit to Jerusalem, was accused of having taught Jews not to observe the Torah any longer and of having brought Greeks into the temple (Acts 21:17-36). The intention of Luke is probably to claim that Paul was accused of bringing non-Jews into the section of the temple called the "the Court of the Israelites." Although non-Jews were permitted to enter the temple precincts, they were not allowed to advance further than the "the Court of the Gentiles." Luke describes how Paul was rescued by the Roman governor from being killed by an incensed mob. The governor arrested Paul, who then addressed the governor in Greek, referring to his relatively high social status, saying: "I am a Jew, from Tarsus in Cilicia, a citizen of an important city" (Acts 21:39).

This narrative is interesting, because it illustrates that apparently the idea of Paul relativizing the importance of the Torah was known at least when Luke wrote Acts, and if the account is historically reliable, already in Paul's lifetime. But it is worth noting that Luke relates these facts as false—in Acts, Paul is generally depicted as faithful to his Jewish tradition. The reason why Paul visits the temple, according to Acts, is to show that the accusations are unfounded: Paul observes and guards the Torah (Acts 21:24).

The rest of the narrative offers further important information about the background of Paul. In a peroration to the enraged crowd, Paul repeats that he was born in Tarsus, but adds that he was "brought up in this city" (Acts 22:3), that is, in Jerusalem, and that he had studied under Gamaliel. As opposed to the citizenship in Tarsus and Rome, which Paul never himself mentions, we have in Philippians 3:4b-6 an autobiographical note that may confirm Luke's account. Paul writes:

> If anyone else has reason to be confident in the flesh, I have more: circumcised on the eighth day, a member of the people of Israel, of the tribe of Benjamin, a Hebrew born of Hebrews; as to the law, a Pharisee; as to zeal, a persecutor of the church; as to righteousness under the law, blameless.

Besides referring to his Jewish identity in several ways, Paul here describes himself as a Pharisee. This agrees well with the statement given in Acts that he had studied under Gamaliel, who was a leading Pharisee. The Pharisees were a religious, and to a certain extent, political, party that emphasized the importance of continuous interpretation of the Torah. One problem that occupied the Pharisees was how to apply the Torah to new situations. Unlike the Sadducees, the Pharisees accepted the oral Torah, that is, all interpretations and adaptations of the biblical text, which were considered divinely inspired and just as binding as the original precepts. In the Gospels, especially Matthew, the Pharisees are portrayed as the main opponents of Jesus, but the evangelist's presentation of them as hypocrites and exponents of a rigid, petrified religion must be viewed as a caricature. The Pharisees represented a pious movement. They enjoyed wide popular support and were dedicated to an interpretation of the biblical texts that was anything but rigid and literal.

The fact that Paul was nurtured in an environment that saw new interpretations of the biblical texts as a natural part of the divine revelation is an important aspect when trying to understand his way of reasoning.

"As to zeal, a persecutor of the church"

In Philippians 3:6, Paul describes himself as having formerly been "a persecutor of the church," something he also does in Galatians 1:13 and 1 Corinthians 15:9. The translation is a little misleading. The Greek word *ekklēsia,* here translated as "church," actually only means "community." What Paul refers to was, of course, not a "church" in our sense, but a group of Jews who believed that Jesus of Nazareth was the Messiah of Israel. In Acts 6:8-15, Luke describes how Stephen, a Greek-speaking Jew involved in the Jesus movement, was falsely accused of having uttered blasphemies concerning "Moses and God" and for expressing disparaging words about the temple and the Torah. Before the High Priest, Stephen delivered a lengthy speech (Acts 7:1-53), which led his audience to become "enraged and [to grind] their teeth at Stephen" (Acts 7:54), and all "rushed together against him. Then they dragged him out of the city and began to stone him" (Acts 7:57b-58a). Here Luke introduces "a young man named Saul" for the first time, who is no other person than Paul, referred to by his Jewish name. Luke mentions that Paul thought the stoning of Stephen, the first martyr of the Jesus movement, was justified (Acts 8:1).

Luke then goes on to describe how the adherents of the Jesus movement in Jerusalem are sorely harassed and how Paul, as the one responsible for the persecutions, "was ravaging the church by entering house after house; dragging off both men and women" and "committ[ing] them to prison" (Acts 8:3). Luke continues relating how Paul was "breathing threats and murder against the disciples of the Lord" (Acts 9:1) and on his own initiative, procured a letter to the synagogues in Damascus, authorizing him to arrest adherents of the Jesus movement. The reason for Paul's powerful resistance to the Jesus movement is not altogether clear. The Pharisees, of course, represented basically an elitist movement, which to a certain extent opposed the kind of popular movements that Jesus and John the Baptist represented. But it does not seem that faith in Jesus as such was reason enough for persecuting those who professed such a belief. Both prior to and after Jesus, there were various movements in Israel with more or less explicit messianic claims. Josephus describes how local messianic movements appeared in connection with the death of Herod the Great in 4 BCE (*A.J.* 17.273-284; *B.J.* 2.57-65). The leaders of these movements were even proclaimed kings by their followers in a manner that, of course, brings to mind King David, the outstanding prototype of all messianism.[11] The same kind of movements appeared when the two Jewish wars broke out in 66–70 and 132–135 CE respectively. The leader of the second revolt, Bar Kochba, "Son of the Star," was believed to be the Messiah by his followers.

It seems that messianic claims were a political rather than a theological problem. It is possible that one reason why Paul felt it necessary to stop the spread of the Jesus movement had to do with the conditions of the Jews under Roman occupation. As a complicated web of religious and political aspects had led to the accusations, trial, and execution of Jesus, it is conceivable that Paul's resistance to the Jesus movement was motivated by a combination of religious and political factors. Potential messianic figures with widespread popular support constituted an obvious danger on different levels, not the least of which would be causing revolts that could awaken the sleeping watchdog—Rome. The complete crushing of all resistance during the Jewish Wars bears witness to the quite realistic misgivings that Rome was prone to act harshly against movements that could be seen as a threat. Jerusalem was conquered and laid waste in 70 CE. In 135, the city was turned into a Roman city to which Jews had no admittance, and the name of the Roman province, *Iudaea*, was changed to *Syria Palaestina*. The original Greek word, *phylistim*, can be derived from the Hebrew word *pĕlištîm*, which means "Philistines"—during the early Israelite kingdom the Philistines were one of the arch-enemies of Israel. In one blow "Israel" is changed into "the land of the Philistines" and the Jewish people became for a long time deprived of their cultic center.

"Who are you, Lord?"

According to Acts, Paul experiences something very unexpected on the road to Damascus, while on his way to arrest adherents of the Jesus movement. The antagonist in Luke's narrative is suddenly changed into the protagonist.

Luke writes that Paul, when he approached Damascus, was swiftly blinded by a light from heaven (Acts 9:3-9):

> Now as he was going along and approaching Damascus, suddenly a light from heaven flashed around him. He fell to the ground and heard a voice saying to him, "Saul, Saul, why do you persecute me?" He asked, "Who are you, Lord?" The reply came, "I am Jesus, whom you are persecuting. But get up and enter the city, and you will be told what you are to do." The men who were traveling with him stood speechless because they heard the voice but saw no one. Saul got up from the ground, and though his eyes were open, he could see nothing; so they led him by the hand and brought him into Damascus. For three days he was without sight, and neither ate nor drank.

Luke continues narrating how Paul miraculously regained his sight through a certain Ananias, who by divine revelation had learned that Paul had been chosen as an instrument in the plan of God for the salvation of the world. Ananias laid his hands on Paul, who then regained his sight, and as soon as he was baptized, he immediately started preaching in the synagogues that Jesus is "the Son of God" (Acts 9:20).

It is likely that Paul experienced something that resembles what in psychology of religion is called "a mystical experience." Characteristic of these experiences are the very elements mentioned in the account in Acts—light, voices, and a sense of transmission of knowledge. Such experiences are not unusual, and nothing indicates that it was different in antiquity. It is possible that Paul's involvement in the persecutions of the adherents of the Jesus movement created an interior psychological conflict that brought on a solution by means of an experience described in Acts and perhaps also in Galatians 1:15-17, where Paul may allude to the same incident that Luke describes:

> But when God, who had set me apart before I was born and called me through his grace, was pleased to reveal his Son to me, so that I might proclaim him among the Gentiles, I did not confer with any human being, nor did I go up to Jerusalem to those who were already apostles before me, but I went away at once into Arabia, and afterwards I returned to Damascus.

If Paul refers to the same experience, his way of narrating it indicates what it meant for his further activity. The significance of this for mystical experiences is that they are interpreted with the culturally conditioned cognitive patterns of the individual as a point of departure. In Paul's case, the prophetic vocation seems to have been the one nearest at hand.[12] Compare, for instance, Paul in Galatians 1:15-16 with the calling of Jeremiah as a prophet (Jer 1:4-5): "Now the word of the Lord came to me saying, 'Before I formed you in the womb I knew you, and before you were born I consecrated you; I appointed you a prophet to the nations.'"

It is also worthwhile to compare the description of the experience of Paul in Acts and Galatians with the visions of the two classical prophets Isaiah and Ezekiel (Isa 6:1-8; Ezek 1:4—3:15). This brings to the fore the question of how to deal with what happened to Paul on the road to Damascus. Traditionally, the description in Acts has provided the norm for a religious conversion. On the road to Damascus, the Jew Paul becomes a Christian. This, of course, corresponds to the notion that Paul abandoned Judaism. In a famous article that has exerted a strong influence on the research on Paul in several respects, Krister Stendahl called into question whether Paul really was "converted." Instead of speaking of Paul's "conversion," Stendahl insists, we should rather see his experience as the calling to a specific task—the mission to the non-Jews—in a manner resembling the calling of the classical prophets.[13]

In Acts 9:20-25, Luke reports that Paul ends up in Damascus after his experience, where he promptly starts preaching in the synagogues. According to Acts, this results in the decision of the Jews to get rid of Paul, and he is forced to escape to Jerusalem, where he tries to get in touch with the disciples. The latter are suspicious of Paul's recently acquired devotion to Jesus for obvious reasons. Paul himself refers to this incident in 2 Corinthians 11:32-33 and mentions that "the governor under King Aretas" had the city under close surveillance in order to apprehend him, which enables us to approximately date the incident. Aretas IV was king of the Nabateans from 9 BCE to 40 CE and may have taken control of Damascus in the year 37. Paul's flight from Damascus thus ought to have taken place during the period 37–40.

In any case, Paul is introduced to the apostles and can move about freely in Jerusalem. But even in Jerusalem his life is threatened and he has to flee to Tarsus. Here the account of Acts differs from Paul's own version in Galatians. In Galatians 1:17, Paul is extremely careful to emphasize that he, after his calling, "did not confer with any human being" and above all had no contact with the apostles in Jerusalem. He writes that not until three years later, after having sojourned in Arabia and Damascus, did he visit Peter in Jerusalem for fifteen days (Gal 1:18). Then, "still unknown by sight to the churches of Judea that are in Christ," Paul traveled to Syria and Cilicia, which probably means Tarsus (Gal 1:21-22).

It is possible, but perhaps not very probable, that Paul developed his theology in splendid isolation from the apostles in Jerusalem. Galatians was written in a situation where Paul's missionary activity was indeed threatened. He may possibly have felt abandoned by the leadership of the Jesus movement, and this may have influenced the way he presented his relation to them. Galatians contains rather sarcastic references to Peter, John, and James and also bears witness of a split between Paul and Peter, which may have involved James too (Gal 2:11-14). A more deep-seated conflict between Paul and some of the leaders could perhaps also have contributed to his wish to dissociate himself from them. The note in Acts 9:27 that Paul at an early stage visited the apostles in Jerusalem for that reason seems plausible, even though Paul later emphasized his independence from them.

On the other hand, the description in Acts 9:20 of how Paul started working as a missionary immediately after his calling should perhaps not be taken at face value. If Paul really had a transforming mystical experience, he must have undergone a rather long process of resocializing, including the social as well as cognitive aspects. This probably took place in Damascus, and in this case it must have been here that Paul started the process of working over his experience in depth. In that process, his Pharisaic training must have stood him in good stead.

According to Acts, the lynching of Stephen (Acts 6:8–8:1) resulted in a far-reaching persecution of the adherents of the Jesus movement in Jerusalem, and all except the apostles dispersed (Acts 8:1). Some of them managed to reach Antioch in the Roman province of Syria (Acts 11:19). That some of the refugees ended up there is not very surprising—Antioch was a true world metropolis with excellent overland communications and, in addition, a large Jewish population.

Luke's assertion in Acts that it was in Antioch that the message of Jesus was first preached to non-Jews as well seems plausible. He writes that those who first reached Antioch "spoke the word to no one except Jews. But among them were some men of Cyprus and Cyrene who, on coming to Antioch, spoke to the Hellenists also, proclaiming the Lord Jesus" (Acts 11:19-20).

This preaching most probably took place in a synagogue, where non-Jews also were present, which is how they too were reached by the message.[14] Josephus (*B.J.* 7.45) states that the Jewish communities in Antioch had a special attraction for the non-Jewish population, which is why we may assume that the God-fearers were especially numerous. We may also assume that there were different Jewish views on the proper degree of social interaction with non-Jews. Certain Jewish groups were probably critical of an overly intimate relationship between Jews and non-Jews. At the same time, it seems as though a relatively large part of the Jewish population welcomed contact with non-Jews, and in Antioch, as well as in other places, there was a pronounced trend among Jewish groups wanting to combine a Jewish life with Hellenistic culture. In short, there was a mutual interest in social contacts between Jews and non-Jews, and the synagogue was the natural meeting point. Thus the community in Antioch probably was an ordinary synagogue, where Jews generally welcomed non-Jews. As a result of the activities of the missionaries from Jerusalem, its members became convinced that Jesus was the Messiah of Israel and that the messianic age had arrived, which was why non-Jews could be included in the salvation by the God of Israel.

According to Acts, Paul became involved in the community in Antioch, thanks to a certain Barnabas, who brought him to Antioch from Tarsus, and they both functioned as teachers for a year (Acts 11:25-26). Luke tells that the Holy Spirit then announced that Barnabas and Paul were going to receive new assignments—Paul, the Pharisee and teacher, now became a missionary.

"Set apart for me Barnabas and Saul"

In the middle of the 40s, Paul started a large-scale missionary activity in the eastern part of the Roman Empire. Luke writes in Acts 13:2-3:

> While they were worshiping the Lord and fasting, the Holy Spirit said, "Set apart for me Barnabas and Saul for the work to which I have called them." Then after fasting and praying they laid their hands on them and sent them off.

The first missionary journey started from Antioch and went via Cyprus to the southern parts of present-day Turkey and was sponsored by the community in Antioch. In the beginning, Paul, together with a certain John, presumably acted as assistants to Barnabas on the mission journey. It is not yet a question of independent missionary work for Paul. Although the synagogues remained the centers of activity, some non-Jews were reached by the gospel of Jesus. On Cyprus, the trio met the Roman governor Sergius Paulus, who became a follower of Jesus (Acts 13:6-12). Luke claims that they "spoke in such a way that a great number of both Jews and Greeks became believers" (Acts 14:1).

However, the mission to the non-Jews, which seems to have held a prominent position from the very beginning, also caused problems. Even though everyone in the Jesus movement presumably agreed that non-Jews also had a place in the world to come, there was no agreement on *how* this should be realized. Luke writes, "certain individuals came down from Judea and were teaching the brothers, 'Unless you are circumcised according to the custom of Moses, you cannot be saved'" (Acts 15:1). According to those who represented this view, only Jews could enjoy salvation through the God of Israel.

There seems to have been quite a variety of Jewish views on the fate of non-Jews in the age to come. Some sectarians, such as the Qumran community near the Dead Sea, believed that everyone not belonging to their sect, Jews as well as non-Jews, would all perish in the final battle. The idea that the non-Jewish peoples all would either be annihilated or conquered by Israel in the last days can be found in the Bible. In Micah 5:10-15, the prophet says:

> In that day, says the LORD, I will cut off your horses from among you and will destroy your chariots; and I will cut off the cities of your land and throw down all your strongholds; and I will cut off sorceries from your hand, and you shall have no more soothsayers; and I will cut off your images and your pillars from among you, and you shall bow

down no more to the work of your hands; and I will uproot your sacred poles from among you and destroy your towns. And in anger and wrath I will execute vengeance on the nations that did not obey.

On the other hand, there are passages with an entirely different perspective, indicating that non-Jews will have a part in the final salvation, provided they turn to the God of Israel. In Isaiah 2:2-4, there is a majestic vision of a future existence in peace and harmony:

> In days to come the mountain of the LORD's house shall be established as the highest of the mountains, and shall be raised above the hills; all the nations shall stream to it. Many peoples shall come and say, "Come, let us go up to the mountain of the LORD, to the house of the God of Jacob; that he may teach us his ways and that we may walk in his paths." For out of Zion shall go forth instruction, and the word of the LORD from Jerusalem. He shall judge between the nations, and shall arbitrate for many peoples; they shall beat their swords into plowshares, and their spears into pruning hooks; nation shall not lift up sword against nation, neither shall they learn war any more.

Here it seems as if the non-Jewish peoples will have their share in the world to come in the same way as the Jewish people, but without first having to convert to Judaism. The text rather seems to presuppose a retained ethnic distinction, but ethnic uniformity—Jews and non-Jews shall all gather before God and keep his commandments.[15]

It is reasonable to assume that those Jewish communities that welcomed non-Jews as guests also believed that some non-Jews, in one way or another, would have a place in the world to come. The question of how this would be accomplished, and how Jews and non-Jews should relate to each other until the kingdom of God finally breaks forth in full power, was brought to the fore by the Jesus movement's belief that they were now living in the messianic age.

Luke mentions that uncertainty concerning these matters resulted in disturbances and discussions in Antioch, and the community decided to send a delegation to Jerusalem in order to have the issue settled by the apostles (Acts 15:1-2). This meeting, commonly called the "apostolic council," is usually considered to have taken place in the year 49 CE. It is probably the same gathering that Paul refers to in Galatians 2:1-10, where he mentions his visit to Jerusalem to meet with James, Peter, and John, to whom he presented his gospel.

In Acts, Luke offers a more exhaustive account of what Paul merely touches upon, namely the decision of the apostolic council that non-Jews in the movement did not have to become Jews, and that they were not formally obliged to observe the Torah, only a minor set of rules, the so-called apostolic decree (Acts 15:19-20, 28-29, 21:25). The council also decided that Peter should carry out the mission to the Jews, whereas Paul became responsible for preaching the gospel to the non-Jews. It seems that Paul's opinion that non-Jews could become members of the Jesus movement without first having to convert to Judaism had been favorably received in the leading circles of the movement.

This, however, did not mean that all problems were solved. In Galatians 2:11-14, Paul tells of a schism between himself and Peter, the so-called Antioch incident—another illustration of how the same text can lead to quite different interpretations. Paul writes that he presented his view of the gospel at a meeting with James, Peter (also called Cephas), and John and that they all took his hand as an acknowledgement that they belonged together (Gal 2:1-10). In the following verses he continues:

> But when Cephas came to Antioch, I opposed him to his face, because he stood self-condemned; for until certain people came from James, he used to eat with the Gentiles. But after they came, he drew back and kept himself separate for fear of the circumcision faction. And the other Jews joined him in this hypocrisy, so that even Barnabas was led astray by their hypocrisy. But when I saw that they were not acting consistently with the truth of the gospel, I said to Cephas before them all, "If you, though a Jew, live like a Gentile and not like a Jew, how can you compel the Gentiles to live like Jews?" (Gal 2:11-15)

A common interpretation of this passage is that the community in Antioch had given up the Jewish food precepts and that this was what the emissaries of James reacted against.[16] The traditional interpretations usually assume that Paul had abandoned Judaism and no longer observed the Torah. However, as we have indicated above, such a basic supposition is far from self-evident—it is not at all certain that Paul's intention was that all Jews in the Jesus movement should stop observing the Torah. Furthermore, if the non-Jewish adherents of the Jesus movement were recruited from the group of non-Jews that already took part in the activities of the synagogue, it is, as noted above, likely that they previously had adapted a Jewish lifestyle, especially with regard to food.

Other interpretations conclude that the problem was how Jews and non-Jews convened. Generally speaking, this is more likely. Many suggestions in this direction, however, presuppose that Jews considered non-Jews "intrinsically impure," or that the problem concerned ritual impurity issues.[17] But ritual impurity was generally connected with the temple in Jerusalem and really had no bearing on non-Jews.[18] Non-Jews were, in fact, considered neither ritually defiling, nor intrinsically impure.[19]

On the other hand, non-Jews, and for that matter Jews as well, might be considered *morally* impure. Regarding non-Jews, the problem was mainly their involvement in Greco-Roman religion, which from a Jewish perspective was regarded as "idolatry."[20] As we noticed above, it is likely that, for sociopolitical reasons, Jewish communities accepted that non-Jewish guests also took part in the official religion. This implies that the community members probably were used to turning a blind eye at the involvement of non-Jews in Greco-Roman cults. It is also possible that they distinguished between cultic actions determined by the sociopolitical system, and those that were performed because of personal convictions.

The issue in Antioch may have revolved around Paul's understanding of how Jews and non-Jews should associate in the convental community. A point that Paul seems to have emphasized was that Jews and non-Jews in the Jesus movement enjoyed the same standing in relation to the God of Israel. In Romans 10:12, Paul writes, "There is no distinction between Jew and Greek; the same Lord is Lord of all and is generous to all who call on him." From a Jewish perspective, this was a rather revolutionary notion, not held even by everyone in the Jesus movement. Equally challenging was certainly Paul's idea that the non-Jewish Jesus-believers would be saved by inclusion into the covenant. But from a Jewish perspective, Paul's solution is logical, since most Jews seem to have believed that it was the covenant with the God of Israel that guaranteed the individual a place in the world to come.

Observing the Torah was a way of expressing a will to remain within the covenant that God made with the Jewish people at Sinai.

The problem for non-Jews was that the covenant was between the *Jewish* people and the God of *Israel* and thus presupposed Torah observance. Hence, the covenant with God implied salvation, but the covenant was only for Jews. This apparently caused a problem. With his Pharisaic training and ability to find creative solutions to problems that called for adaptation of the existing tradition, Paul, however, had found a "loophole in the law" enabling him to include non-Jews in the covenant providing salvation, *without first having to make them Jews.* Paul made use of the fact that the God of Israel had first made a covenant with Abraham (Genesis 15) before he was circumcised and long before the Torah was given at Sinai. In Romans 4:9-12 he argues:

> Is this blessedness, then, pronounced only on the circumcised, or also on the uncircumcised? We say, "Faith was reckoned to Abraham as righteousness." How then was it reckoned to him? Was it before or after he had been circumcised? It was not after, but before he was circumcised. He received the sign of circumcision as a seal of the righteousness that he had by faith while he was still uncircumcised. The purpose was to make him the ancestor of all who believe without being circumcised and who thus have righteousness reckoned to them, and likewise the ancestor of the circumcised who are not only circumcised but who also follow the example of the faith that our ancestor Abraham had before he was circumcised.

The example of Abraham shows, according to Paul, that an uncircumcised man also can be considered righteous and moreover enter into a covenant with God. This application of the passage about Abraham made it possible for non-Jews to be included in the covenant with the God of Israel, but with their ethnic identity unchanged.

Of course there were social separatist trends within first-century Judaism. The aim of a Jewish lifestyle is even, to a certain extent, to create a social barrier between the Jewish people and other people (see, for instance, Leviticus 18:24-30). But at the same time, we should not exaggerate the social consequences of this. In the Diaspora, the Jews had long since learned to survive in a society with values they did not share and religious cults they regarded as idolatry. Even though a certain degree of assimilation certainly took place, centuries of inter-relationship with the non-Jewish world had not caused the Jewish population to lose its distinctive religious and cultural character. On the contrary, Jewish identity in the Diaspora was well developed. Different Jewish groups, of course, had their own strategies for how to relate to the non-Jewish world. Certain groups were highly critical to social intercourse with non-Jews and lived in their own secluded parts of cities where they had minimal contact with non-Jews, but it is not correct to say that the Jewish population as a whole shunned social contacts with non-Jews.[21]

The problem in Antioch, then, was probably the degree of intimacy in social relations. If Paul argued that non-Jewish adherents of the Jesus movement had become included in the covenant through Christ and emphasized that Jews and non-Jews had the same status before the God of Israel, this probably had far-reaching social consequences. However, it probably did not affect the *food* they ate, but rather the *ritual* of community meals.[22] Such matters as the seating at the table and how wine and food were handled may have indicated to some Jews (like James) who did not share Paul's ideology regarding the equal standing of the non-Jews before God that the Jewish identity of the community was threatened. Accordingly, it is likely that it was solicitude for the Jewish adherents to the Jesus movement that caused James's reaction. Paul's comment to Peter that he lived "like a Gentile and not like a Jew" (Gal 2:14) could be taken as an ironic allusion to the criticism of the delegation, the tenor of which no doubt was that the Jesus-believing Jews in the community, because of their close dealings with non-Jews, challenged traditional social boundaries.

The delegation from James—the circumcision faction that Peter feared—seems to have recommended that the status of the non-Jews should be altered. The reason for this may simply have been an effort to try to get the ethnic identity and the social intercourse to correspond. If Jews and non-Jews socialized as if they belonged to the same ethnic group, James's representatives may have thought it best to have the non-Jews turned into Jews, in spite of the earlier agreement from Jerusalem. This does not necessarily mean that James had changed his mind on the general principle that non-Jews could be saved without becoming Jews, only that he disagreed with Paul on the implications for social interaction resulting from this theology. According to James, non-Jews could very well be connected to the Jesus movement, but only if the distinction between Jew and non-Jew was manifest also in social relations. Peter, however, seems to have chosen another way, namely to restrict commensality.

Both these solutions were impossible for Paul to accept for theological reasons. If non-Jewish men were circumcised, and both men and women were turned into Jesus-believing Jews, multitudes of peoples, would not flock to the house of God, as in Isaiah 2:3, but only the Jewish people. God would then be the God of the Jews only, not of the non-Jews, as Paul asserts in Romans 3:29-31.[23] Peter's solution of regarding the non-Jews in the movement as ordinary God-fearers was therefore not acceptable to Paul. Because of their faith in Jesus, these individuals, unlike ordinary non-Jews taking part in the activities of the synagogue, had become partakers in the covenant that grants salvation, and their standing before the God of Israel was consequently comparable to that of the Jewish people. This must, according to Paul's outlook, also be reflected in the social relations.

This suggested interpretation of the Antioch incident is possible and perhaps even feasible, but we must point out that there are many other ways of understanding what really took place in Antioch. The problem is that the text does not offer enough facts concerning, for instance, the relations between various groups, the identity of the members of the delegation, or who insisted on retaining circumcision for the reader to be able to form a univocal opinion of the historical course of events. The problem concerning the standing of the non-Jews and Paul's fury over the meddling from the outside and from Peter is however manifest.

For Paul, the Antioch incident marks the transition toward a more independent ministry. It shows that the early Jesus movement was far from homogeneous and also that the first period was characterized by profound conflicts. Divergent views on how non-Jews would be saved and on the relations between Jews and non-Jews existed side by side, and in spite of the importance Paul later enjoys, we must admit that during his lifetime, he represented the opinion of a minority, and was generally rather marginalized and had severe difficulties in legitimizing his standing as an apostle.

"If only I may finish my course"

After the Antioch incident Paul departed on two very extensive missionary journeys in present day Turkey and Greece. With the exception of First Thessalonians, written during the second journey, Paul composed all his letters during, or following, the third journey, undertaken around 53–58. Thirteen letters bear Paul's name, but for a majority of scholars it is evident that not all of them were written by Paul himself. Most scholars would agree that First Thessalonians was Paul's earliest letter, written around 50–51 during his sojourn in Corinth, but because of the content of Second Thessalonians, many scholars doubt that Paul really wrote this letter. If so, it was probably written shortly after First Thessalonians. Otherwise, the letter was probably written at the end of the first century, in a time of external hardships, which may be the reason why eschatological aspects are so strongly emphasized.

On the other hand, Galatians belongs to the letters that can safely be considered authentic. It was probably written during the period 53–55, when Paul resided in Ephesus. The two letters to the community in Corinth, both regarded as authentic, were also written by Paul in Ephesus, but somewhat later than Galatians, presumably around 55–57. Romans, which we dealt with in the introduction to this chapter, was probably written in Corinth about 56 or 57.

Philippians, Colossians, Philemon, and Ephesians constitute a separate problem. Their common denominator is that the author mentions that he is imprisoned, though not saying where or when. The question that arises is which imprisonment — or imprisonments — Paul refers to, as this is crucial for the dating of the letters. Different scholars here offer different answers. Some claim that they were written during an otherwise unknown imprisonment in Ephesus sometime between 53 and 56, others suggest they were written during his imprisonment in Caesarea about 58–60, and still others maintain that they were written in Rome 60–62. In addition, the matter becomes even more complicated as some scholars doubt that Ephesians was written by Paul, and some even question the authenticity of Colossians. If Paul is not the author of these letters, they too must have been written toward the end of the first century.

Regarding the so-called Pastoral Epistles (First and Second Timothy, Titus), practically all scholars agree that they were written after the death of Paul.[24] The developed hierarchical organization hinted at is a clear reason why most scholars conclude they were written around 100.

In order to be on the safe side, we should accordingly only regard First Thessalonians, Galatians, both letters to the Corinthians, Romans, Philippians, and Philemon as authentic. It seems unlikely that Paul wrote Ephesians and the Pastoral Epistles, but it cannot be completely ruled out that the he is the author of Second Thessalonians and Colossians.

The fact that there are New Testament letters claiming the nominal authorship of Paul, in spite of being written several decades after his death, does not mean they should be considered obvious falsifications. In antiquity, people had somewhat different views on authorship than we have today. It was, for instance, possible to let ancient heroic figures pose as authors of later literary works. The Wisdom of Solomon and the book of Baruch, included in the so-called deuterocanonical literature (Old Testament Apocrypha), are good examples of this. The book of Isaiah includes texts written several hundred years after the death of the prophet Isaiah. Many scholars believe that later prophets from the prophetic schools incorporated their texts in the book of Isaiah, as they considered themselves his ideological heirs. Regarding Ephesians and the Pastoral Epistles, the conditions may have been similar—individuals considering themselves to belong to a Pauline tradition wrote these letters in Paul's name. It is, however, important to bear in mind that their claim to represent authentic Pauline thoughts does not necessarily mean that this really was the case. When reading Ephesians and the Pastoral Epistles, one should be aware of the possibility that the authors represent an interpretation of Paul with which he himself would have felt uncomfortable.

Regarding the last period of Paul's life, we are entirely dependent on Acts. Even if we assume that Colossians, Philippians, and Philemon were written during this period, this is of no help, since these letters contain no direct autobiographical material. But in Acts, Luke gives a detailed account of how Paul traveled to Jerusalem, how he was accused of bringing non-Jews into parts of the temple out-of-bounds to them, and how he taught the Jews that they no longer had to observe the Torah. These accusations, according to Acts, resulted in what almost amounted to a riot, and Paul was arrested by the Roman governor. The governor, in turn, attempted to find out what this was all about by letting the chief priests and the Jewish Sanhedrin interrogate him. During this meeting, Paul managed to stir up a conflict between the Pharisees and the Sadducees, with the consequence that the governor again had to intervene and save him (Acts 23:1-10).

The governor decided to turn the case over to a higher authority, especially since Paul had referred to his Roman citizenship. Because of this, Paul was taken to the Roman procurator, Felix, in Caesarea. But as Felix wanted to remain on friendly terms with the Jews, he put Paul in custody, where he had to languish for two years until the successor of Felix, Porcius Festus, arrived. The latter, according to Acts 25:1-12, was called on by the chief priests and "leaders of the Jews" who presented accusations against Paul and were planning to assassinate him. Paul, on the other hand, persisted in claiming that he had "in no way committed an offense against the law of the Jews, or against the temple, or against the emperor" (Acts 25:8). Referring to his right as a Roman citizen to have his case tried by a higher authority, he appealed to the emperor, leaving the governor no other option than to transfer him to Rome.

After many hardships, Paul arrived in Rome and was met by fellow believers. He was placed in a kind of house arrest, but seems to have been allowed to receive everyone who wanted to see him. According to Acts, he stayed in Rome for two years "proclaiming the kingdom of God and teaching about the Lord Jesus Christ with all boldness and without hindrance" (Acts 28:31). Here, rather abruptly, Luke breaks off the narrative about Paul, but according to tradition (*1 Clem.* 5:2-7; Eusebius *Hist. eccl.* 2.25.5) Paul, and for that matter Peter, suffered martyrdom under Emperor Nero.

At the beginning of the second century, the Jesus movement was transformed and Christianity as we know it today appeared—as a non-Jewish religion where a Jewish identity was incompatible with being a Christian. In this non-Jewish part of the Jesus movement, which developed into the Christian church, the one-sided reading of Paul fitted like a glove. Eventually, the notion of the Apostle to the Gentiles arose, the man who repudiated his original religious identity in order to become the one who brought the salvation of the God of Israel, not to the Jews, but to the non-Jews, and at the same time banished everything Jewish to the rubbish heap.

We are now going to move forwards, almost two thousand years in time, and examine how this idea has been utilized and how the image of another, even more complex Paul, is gradually emerging.

2

THE EMERGENCE OF A PARADIGM

The Tübingen School and German Idealism

Hegel and Dialectics

The leading philosopher in nineteenth-century Germany was no doubt Georg Friedrich Wilhelm Hegel (1770–1831). In his early years, he studied theology at the University of Tübingen with the purpose of becoming a minister. While there, he was strongly attracted to mysticism, something that is also evident in his philosophy, which to a great extent is characterized by theological issues. From 1818 until his death he held a professorship in Berlin. In Tübingen, where he had started his academic career, his influence would eventually result in the emergence of one of the most radical theological schools the world had seen: the Tübingen School.

In view of the enormous influence that his ideas generally had, it is perhaps only natural that Hegel's philosophy had such an impact on the theological development in the nineteenth century. During his sojourn at the Berlin University, he gathered adepts from all over Europe. At the end of the nineteenth century, most leading philosophers were Hegelians.

Many theologians saw in Hegel's philosophical system new opportunities to recover ground after the humiliating defeat theology had suffered from the philosophy of the Enlightenment. Although the "absolute spirit" of Hegel was something quite different from the Christian God, Hegel regarded Christianity as the highest form of religion and even used basic Christian terms, though with a rather different tenor. The main reason why Hegel's philosophy became so popular was presumably that it comprised every aspect of the world, from the approach to knowledge to the enfolding of history—art, culture, religion, and the social structure of society.

The basis of Hegel's philosophical system is far-reaching rationalism. Thought and reality merge completely, but while Hegel's predecessors imagined a system consisting of immutable thoughts and an unalterable reality, Hegel conceived of thought as a continuous process toward higher and higher stages. This process, which according to Hegel is the process of reality, progresses due to the fact that every state brings forth its own negation, which then gives birth to a more complex unity. Every *thesis* generates its *antithesis*, and these two opposites are joined in a *synthesis*. This synthesis partially embodies elements from both thesis and antithesis, but does not quite obliterate those elements. It is important to note already that the synthesis represents a *higher order.*

The point of departure for Hegel is the most abstract conceivable notion, the term "being," which at the same time represents "the absolute." According to Hegel, the conception of "pure being" will turn into its opposite, that is, "nothing." When these two conceptions merge, the synthesis "becoming" appears, including elements from both the thesis "being" and the antithesis "nothing." In this manner, not only the formation of conceptions, but the entire development of the world evolves in dialectic triads, in which every new evolutionary stage turns into its opposite and then again merges with its own negation. In this way the evolution of the world rises to never-ceasing higher stages.

In Hegel's world nothing was better in former times. The past always represents a lower evolutionary form than the present, and the future always holds something better in store. The reason for this is that the dialectical process is not governed by chance. Behind the scenes, "the world spirit" acts, and evolution is in fact nothing but this spirit manifest in concrete form in history. While most people are unaware of this, a few, the geniuses and the heroes of history, are capable of actively taking part in the world evolution. The history of the world is thus a process run by reason, which in reality is the true lord of the world. Hegel's philosophy inspired a whole generation of young theologians, but hardly those who represented theological orthodoxy.

F. C. Baur and the Tübingen School

The Tübingen School is one example of what Hegel's philosophical system gave rise to, and it is closely associated with Ferdinand Christian Baur (1792–1860). Baur came to Tübingen in 1809 and studied philosophy for some years and then theology. Tübingen already housed a Tübingen School, which reached its peak during the first decades of the nineteenth century. It was founded by Ernst Gottlieb Storr, who died in 1805, but his work was carried on by Ernst Gottlieb Bengel, grandson of the famous biblical scholar Johann Albrecht Bengel (1687–1752), who had been Storr's mentor. Bengel came to exert great influence on the young Baur, who thus received his basic theological training within a relatively conservative, Lutheran theological tradition.

The aim of the Old Tübingen School was to create a scientific basis for the authority of the Bible by means of historical research. Storr wanted to prove the authenticity of the New Testament and show that divine revelation is not contradicted by reason. However, among the successors of Storr, a rather strong Kantian trait could be discerned, and a certain shifting of emphasis toward the ethical side of the Christian faith took place: the true nature of Jesus was demonstrated by the divine morality and the ethical truths revealed in his teaching. The Old Tübingen School was essentially nothing but a type of conservative Christianity trying to trim its sails to the new philosophical winds, without giving up its own supernatural foundation.

Baur graduated from the University of Tübingen in 1814 and made a living as a private tutor and teacher until he was offered a position as professor at the lower seminary in Blaubeuren.[1] Here he wrote his first book, *Symbolik und Mythologie, oder die Naturreligion des Altertums* ("Symbol and Mythology or Nature Religion of Antiquity," 1824/25). This examination of the nature of religion hardly seems inspired by Hegel—the work rather displays influences from Schleiermacher, Schelling, and Fichte. Baur's interest in Hegel only surfaced when he received the summons to take over the professorship in Tübingen in 1826 and was initiated by one of his soon-to-be famous disciples, David Friedrich Strauss (1808–1874).

Strauss studied in Tübingen between 1825 and 1829 and gradually became interested in the Hegelian philosophical system. He even moved to Berlin in order to attend Hegel's lectures and also met Hegel shortly before his death. Strauss remained in Berlin until 1832, when he returned to Tübingen to teach at the Protestant seminary for Württemberg theologians. After Hegel's death, Strauss attended the lectures on Jesus by Schleiermacher, who inspired him to undertake his own study of the life of Jesus. In 1835, his book, *Das Leben Jesu kritisch bearbeitet* (*The Life of Jesus*, ET 1846), was published. This book caused a seldom-seen sensation. The entire theological establishment was shaken to its very foundations and the book gave rise to a heated debate all over Europe.

Strauss's book constitutes the definitive antithesis of the Old Tübingen School, which strove to form a synthesis between the Jesus of scholarship and the Jesus of faith. *Das Leben Jesu* instead blasted an unbridgeable chasm between the historical Jesus and the Christ the Christians confessed. Strauss dismissed all rational and supernatural interpretations of the miracle narratives in the Gospels. According to Strauss, these were but myths created by the earliest disciples of Jesus. The publication of the book had far-reaching consequences for Strauss and he was immediately dismissed from his position in Tübingen. During this time, Baur kept a low profile. Although he shared Strauss's opinions, he understood that if he did not want to face the same fate as Strauss, he simply had to bide his time. Baur was encumbered enough by his friendship with Strauss, and the works he published were viewed by the critics as emanating from the same heretical tradition as *Das Leben Jesu*.

Thus one might say that the publication of Strauss's book was the starting shot of the *new* Tübingen School. In the course of more than a decade, the members of the group published works that in strong terms called in question traditional interpretations, but from the end of the 1840s, the members became more involved in defending their individual positions against attacks than accomplishing more research. Personal conflicts and bitter internal controversies also tore the group to pieces in the all-too-common manner found in academic circles even in our time. Baur's death in 1860 tolled the death knell of the Tübingen School, at least in the formal sense.

The importance of the Tübingen School for the discipline of New Testament exegesis can, however, hardly be overestimated. Through its programmatic emphasis on the inner-worldly perspective, where super-natural explanations had no place, the Tübingen School laid the foundations for modern biblical scholarship. Admittedly, some scholars had already hinted at this development, but mostly from theistic points of departure. The methodological starting point for the Tübingen School, however, was the dismissal of a transcendent God, active in history. Baur's ambition was to create an objective foundation for biblical scholarship. The Tübingen School is founded on anything but objective biblical scholarship, however. In Baur's case, speculative, philosophical idealism was crucial for his conclusions.

Baur and History—Jew versus Christian

In spite of its innovative perspective, Baur's Hegelianism had some rather unfortunate consequences for the development of the view of the relationship between Paul and Judaism. In 1845, he published his most important exegetical work, *Paulus, der Apostel Jesu Christi* (*Paul, the Apostle of Jesus Christ*, ET 1876), but as early as 1831 he had already set the tone in an article about the different factions in Corinth: "Die Christuspartei in der korinthischen Gemeinde" ("The Christ Party in the Corinthian Church). In 1 Corinthians 1:10 Paul exhorts the community to remain in accord and not split up into different groups, but to "be united in the same mind and the same purpose." In the following verses he wrote:

> For it has been reported to me by Chloe's people that there are quarrels among you, my brothers and sisters. What I mean is that each of you says, "I belong to Paul," or "I belong to Apollos," or "I belong to Cephas," or "I belong to Christ." (1 Cor 1:11-12)

It seems that the community had divided into four different factions, each championing its own leader. The question then arises as to what these groups represented and what their mutual relations were like. Baur claimed that there were in fact only two factions—one pro-Pauline non-Jewish party and one pro-Petrine Jewish-Christian party. To Baur, it seemed clear that the text revealed a basic antagonism between a Pauline, universal type of Christianity, for which the Torah had had its day, and a Jewish-oriented, particularistic type of Christianity, still bound by the

Torah. This perspective, the basic conflict between — in practice — Judaism and Christianity, became the keystone in Baur's idealistically inspired writing of history. These writings were developed into a comprehensive explanation of the history of the early church in, among other works, Baur's posthumously published lectures, *Vorlesungen über neutestamentliche Theologie* ("Lectures on New Testament Theology") 1864.

According to Baur, the embryo of the conflict between Judaism and Christianity is so fundamental that it is present even prior to Paul's emergence on the scene. Baur's basic assumption is that Christianity represents the "absolute religion" and that all messianic particularism was thwarted with the death of Jesus. Hence it is Stephen who represents the earliest formulation of the true nature of Christianity. The first disciples were loyal to their Jewish religion, and the only thing that distinguished them from other Jews, Baur maintained, was the belief that Jesus was the Messiah. The attachment to Judaism among the first disciples of Jesus, however, shows that Christianity was still undeveloped and rudimentary. When Stephen in his speech (Acts 7:1-53) confronted traditional Jewish religion, the Jewish reaction to this challenge was manifested in his lynching. The antagonism between Judaism and Christianity then becomes a fact.

Baur saw the same conflict manifested in Romans, and above all in Galatians, and noted the considerable difference between the descriptions of the apostolic council in Jerusalem in Acts and Galatians respectively. Baur was of the opinion that the account in Acts could not reflect the real historic circumstances, simply because the conflict between Judaism and Christianity was toned down. For this reason Luke could not be the author of Acts, and as the first era of the church definition was characterized by the deep antagonism between Judaism and Christianity, the harmonized account in Acts must represent a later period, probably the end of the second century.

Baur believed that the history of the church evolved in three phases, the first one ending with the fall of Jerusalem and the destruction of the temple in 70 CE. This period was characterized by the deep conflict between Judaism and the emerging Christianity. Judaism was about to turn into its own negation and became superseded by Paul's Christianity in which the gospel was substituted for the Torah. In fact, this conflict became crucial for Baur's dating of the books of the New Testament: texts that did not expose this conflict could not be from this early period. Regarding Paul, this meant that Baur only accepted four letters as authentic: Romans, Galatians, and the two letters to the Corinthians. Revelation, which Baur believed was written by the apostle John, also dated from this period, according to him. John, so Baur claimed, had come to Asia Minor to oppose Paul, which can be surmised from the reference to the Nicolaitans mentioned in Revelation 2:6 and 2:15. According to Baur, the Nicolaitans adhered to the Torah-free gospel and were thus free to eat food sacrificed to idols, which was precisely what the author of Revelation found so abominable.

The second period ran from the fall of Jerusalem to the end of the Bar Kochba uprising in 135 CE, when the Jewish people were expelled from Judea. In Baur's view, the Synoptic Gospels (Matthew, Mark, and Luke), Acts, Philemon, Philippians, Ephesians, and the letters to the Thessalonians dated from this period, during which Baur imagined that both sides strove to downplay the conflict. This is most clearly exposed in the account in Acts, which does not acknowledge any antagonism between Peter and Paul. The overall aim of Acts, according to Baur, was to obliterate the differences between the two apostles by depicting their respective spheres of activity as parallel: in the first part of Acts, Peter was portrayed as being as similar to Paul as possible; in the second part, Paul was characterized in a manner reminding the reader of Peter.

During the last period, from the 140s CE until the end of the second century, the separation of Christianity from Judaism reached its peak, and was reflected, for instance, in the Gospel of John, in which the Jews were made to represent unbelief personified. All threats against the universalism of Christianity—Judaism, Jewish Christianity, and Gnosticism—had been eliminated. The conflict between Peter and Paul was done away with as the church accepted the picture of the parallel apostolates in Acts. Instead of Paul *or* Peter, *both* were chosen. In the Gospel of John, the relation between the Father and the Son was described as the basis of love and constituted the merging of the divine and the human. All is consummated and Christianity has taken the place of Judaism as the highest form of religion, representing the concretion of the Hegelian "absolute spirit" in history.

Baur's hypothesis of the evolution of the early church is impressive— but not correct. As in the case of all historic reconstructions, the outcome is entirely dependent on the fundamental assumptions upon which it is based. Baur's dependence on Hegel leads to a deterministic view of history that affects, not least, the dating of the books of the New

Testament. Using the conflict between Judaism and Christianity as the only criterion for dating the texts simply does not work, and Baur's analysis is a fine example of reasoning in a circle: the books of the New Testament are used for reconstructing history, while the historical development at the same time constitutes the basis for forming a judgment for dating the respective text.

The most serious consequence of Baur's view of history is, however, that the conflict between Judaism and Christianity is forced on to a Procrustean bed in which Judaism *of necessity* is depicted as inferior to Christianity, *because it represents an earlier stratum—an antithesis—in the divinely controlled world order.* Baur thus conferred *scientific legitimacy* on this view of Judaism in its relation to Christianity. Strangely enough, Baur does not seem to have taken the consequences of his theoretical superstructure seriously. The evolution of world history in dialectic triads should, according to Hegel, result in the synthesis, including elements from both the thesis and antithesis simultaneously abolished and preserved. In the case of the history of Christianity, we would accordingly expect to find also Jewish-Christian influences in Christian theology. But with Baur, the synthesis bears close resemblance to the classic Lutheran picture of Paul. At the end of the day, the theological sympathies of Baur seem to rest precisely here.

Perhaps this is not so strange. As we will see, the idea of the state of opposition of Judaism to Christianity is not a new one, but has efficiently been passed on down the centuries. It is consequently no wonder that Baur drew the conclusions he did. In order to comprehend why this was so, we turn to the question why negative attitudes to Jews became such a prominent feature of the European cultural heritage. At the end of this extended discussion we will return to an evaluation of Baur's approach to Paul.

Anti-Semitism in Antiquity

Pre-Christian Attitudes

Is it possible to talk about anti-Semitism in antiquity? In a way it is, of course, anachronistic, since the term "anti-Semitism" was minted only at the end of the nineteenth century, probably by Wilhelm Marr, referring to the then current anti-Jewish campaigns in Germany. However, if "anti-Semitism" is taken to refer to specific views on Jews or special actions taken against Jews, motivated by fictitious or real characteristics of Jews that are unproportionally distorted and not leveled against other ethnic groups in the same manner, we must admit that anti-Semitism existed already in antiquity.[2] In the following survey I intend to employ the terms "anti-Semitism" and "anti-Jewishness" as synonymous, according to the definition above.

As early as the third century BCE, Greek authors in Egypt commented on the Jewish exodus from Egypt and various distinctive Jewish cultural features such as circumcision and the Sabbath celebration. Some of this material was included in a clearly anti-Semitic literary tradition handed down throughout history. To a certain extent, such manifestations can be explained by the general Greek attitude toward foreign peoples, commonly considered uncouth and barbarian, at best suitable as slaves to the superior Greeks. During the Greek expansion, not least under Alexander the Great, Greek immigrants established cultural centers — *gymnasia* — where the specific Greek culture was cultivated and conveyed to the new generations. But in the Greek attitude toward Jews in antiquity, there was also an almost mythical conception. Motives such as Jewish xenophobia, misanthropy, and lack of respect for the gods of the Greeks created a grotesque picture of the Jewish people as a constant threat against the civilized, that is, the Greek world, in a way without parallel among other peoples.[3]

In Rome, Alexandria, and Antioch, Jews and non-Jews had lived together for a long time, usually without any problems. Josephus relates, for example, that Jews were already part of the original population when Antioch was founded in 300 BCE, and indicates that they were recognized as a special group with special conditions (*A.J.* 12.119). If it was at all possible for Jews to live in the Greco-Roman cities, the civic authorities had to take into account that the overwhelming majority of the Jewish population was unwilling to compromise regarding their faith in the one God. In the Shema, for example, this was strongly emphasized: "Hear, Israel, the Lord, our God, the Lord is one" (Deut 6:4, my translation).

In Greek and Roman religion, on the contrary, the divine was manifested in many forms, and worshipping many gods was the natural religious expression. In addition to this, Greek, Roman, and other imported deities functioned well together as they basically belonged to the same religious system. Concurrent with the Roman conquest of new territories, foreign deities were adopted. In Rome itself, temples dedicated to Greek and Egyptian gods and goddesses were built.[4]

But it was, of course, quite inconceivable for a Jew who wanted to remain true to his or her religious heritage to take part in cults including other gods than the God of Israel. One might think that this should not create any problems, but an aggravating matter was that the Romans (and Greeks) imagined that good relations to the divine world—*pax deorum*—were maintained by the official cult.[5] Thus the entire well-being of a local city was dependent on the official religion. In practice, this meant that the individual inhabitant was expected to take part in religious feasts, and because there was no real distinction between politics and religion, one might say that loyalty to the political system was expressed through religion.

With this background, it is no wonder that tensions ensued between Jews and non-Jews in the great cities of antiquity, especially since the Jewish population could amount to as much as ten percent of the total population. In a city like Antioch during the first century CE, this meant that the majority of roughly 40,000 Jews were likely to refuse worshipping those gods who the non-Jewish population believed protected the city against natural disasters and plagues. When such things occurred— Antioch lies in an area often hit by earthquakes and flooding—it is easy to imagine who got the blame.

But Rome had really nothing to gain from trying to force the Jews to conform in religious matters, and as noted in the previous chapter, local regulations were normally issued giving them the right to practice their own religion and to be excused from participation in the official cult. Instead there were other opportunities for the Jewish communities to demonstrate their loyalty to the local city and to Rome, for example, by erecting monuments paying homage to the emperor.[6]

Nevertheless, during the first century CE, several serious events occurred when underlying anti-Semitic feelings led to disastrous consequences. During the summer of 38 CE, a period of disturbances began in Alexandria that lasted for several years. The provoking incident was a visit by the Jewish King Agrippa, who stopped in Alexandria on his way from Rome to his new kingdom in northern Israel. The royal visit probably gave rise to various nationalistic manifestations, provoking the non-Jewish population to start a true pogrom. Jews were burned alive or dragged through the streets until they died. Jewish homes and shops were pillaged, and in the synagogues, statues of the emperor, Gaius Iulius Caesar Germanicus—better known as Caligula—were placed. This, of course, made them useless as places of worship, but at the same time, the Jews did not dare to throw the statues out, as this could be regarded as a demonstration of unseemly disrespect against the emperor. In this delicate situation, this could be taken as a justification to continue the acts of violence.[7]

Only after the emperor was murdered in 41 CE could order be restored, and his successor, Claudius, issued an edict in which he confirmed the rights of the Jews to practice their own religion, but also warned them not to strive for more rights than they already enjoyed (*CPJ* 153; Josephus, *A.J.* 19.280-285). In Alexandria there had been a strong movement within the Jewish community demanding more influence, but endeavoring to combine Jewish identity with Hellenistic culture as well.

In connection with the Jewish War in 66–70 CE, new disturbances broke out in several places in Syria. Josephus (*B.J.* 7.46-53) describes how the loyalty of the Jewish population in Antioch was called in question: Jews were accused of planning to burn down the city, resulting in public executions. Jews were forced to sacrifice to Greek deities, and those who refused were killed. Order was not restored until Roman troops intervened. Rome could no doubt resort to strong measures against the Jews when necessary, for instance when they effectively and brutally quashed the revolt, captured and destroyed Jerusalem and the temple. In the aftermath of the war, prisoners were paraded around the eastern part of the empire, exposed in the theatres, and publicly humiliated. Coins celebrating the victory over the vanquished Jews were struck. This should, however, not be regarded as a sign of anti-Jewish sentiment; it was rather the normal Roman way of treating conquered enemies. In fact, it lay in Rome's interest to normalize the relations to the Jewish population as soon as possible.

This ambition, however, may have contributed to increasing the tensions between Jews and non-Jews. During the riots, both in Alexandria and Antioch, the Roman authorities intervened and prevented further violence. After the Jewish War ended in 70 CE (though the fortress Masada near the Dead Sea held out until 73), Josephus describes how the population in Antioch implored the Roman Emperor Titus to expel the Jews from the city. Titus refused and left, but when he returned shortly afterwards, he was invited to a public gathering, probably in the theater. In *Bellum judaicum* 7.110-111, Josephus writes:

> So relinquishing their first request the Antiochenes turned to a second, petitioning him [Titus] to remove the brazen tablets on which were inscribed the privileges of the Jews. But this too, Titus refused, and, leaving the status of the Jews exactly as it was before, he set out for Egypt.

It is easy to imagine that the relations between Jews and non-Jews were somewhat strained after that. Under the surface, the hatred against the Jews simmered, as they not only refused to worship the gods of the city and had caused the war, but also because they enjoyed support by the occupying forces.

It seems clear that the period during and after the Jewish War was troublesome for the Jews in both the land of Israel and the Diaspora. But at the same time, it is necessary to remember that this is not the whole truth. While a pronounced suspicion against the Jewish population certainly was prevalent, sometimes resulting in downright persecution, there are many examples of an opposing tendency. As we briefly touched upon in the previous chapter, it seems that Judaism attracted large groups of non-Jews. Again, concerning Antioch, Josephus (*B.J.* 7.45) writes that the Jewish population exerted considerable influence on non-Jews: "[the Jews] were constantly attracting to their religious ceremonies multitudes of Greeks, and these they had in some measure incorporated with themselves." In *Contra Apionem* 2.282, he claims that there is "not one city, Greek or barbarian, nor a single nation, to which our custom of abstaining from work on the seventh day has not spread . . . and many of our prohibitions in the matter of food are not observed."

Josephus no doubt shows a certain apologetic bias, but there is no reason to doubt the basic accuracy of his statement. The Roman authors especially confirm this non-Jewish interest in Judaism, which they found utterly contemptible and regarded as an improper cultural influence. The Roman author Seneca, for instance, gave vent to his misgivings in a statement quoted by the church father Augustine: "The customs of this accursed race have gained such influence that they are now received throughout the world. The vanquished have given laws to their victors" (*Civ.* 6.11). Similarly, the Roman satirist Juvenal heaped scorn on those whose fathers respected the Sabbath (*Sat.* 14.96-106): "They worship nothing except the clouds and spirit of the sky," he states and continues:

> They think there is no difference between pork, which their fathers abstained from, and human flesh. In time, they get rid of their foreskins. And with their habit of despising the laws of Rome, they study, observe, and revere the Judaic code, as handed down to Moses in his mystic scroll, which tells them not to show the way to anyone except a fellow worshipper and if asked, to take only the circumcised to the fountain. But it's their fathers who are to blame, taking every seventh day as a day of laziness and separate from ordinary life.

Josephus also reports that in connection with the outbreak of the Jewish War in 66 CE, the Jewish population in Damascus was brought together and slaughtered. However, when the non-Jewish men planned the massacre on the Jews, they had to keep their plan secret from their wives who could not be trusted, because, "with a few exceptions [they] had all become converts to the Jewish religion" (*B.J.* 2.559).[8]

In the aftermath of the first Jewish War, the non-Jewish population's interest in Judaism seems to have attracted the attention of the authorities. The historian Dio Cassius (67.14.1-2) recorded that Emperor Domitian had his cousin, the former consul Flavius Clemens, executed because of his interest in Judaism. Clemens's wife, Flavia Domitilla, also a relative of the emperor, saved her skin, but was banished. This incident is also mentioned by Suetonius (*Dom.* 15.1). Others who were accused of *atheism*, which in this context meant those who had neglected to participate in the official religion, had their property confiscated.

To sum up: non-Jewish interest in Judaism could be manifested in various manners. Some authors express admiration for Moses and some were generally impressed by the long history of Judaism. As we also noted in the previous chapter, it was common for people to worship the God of Israel together with their own Greek, Roman, Syrian, or Egyptian gods. To ordinary non-Jews in the Mediterranean world, this was a completely natural line to take toward deities. It also happened that non-Jews supported Jewish communities financially and were rewarded for this with honorary titles, something that must be understood in terms of the patron-client system so widespread in antiquity. An inscription (*CIJ* 766) mentions that a certain Julia Severa built a synagogue. That she most certainly was not Jewish is evident from another source (*MAMA* 6.263), where she is mentioned as a priestess of the local shrine. Some non-Jews converted to Judaism — Acts 6:5 mentions the proselyte Nicolaus from Antioch — and ceased in every respect to be non-Jewish (even though they may have been looked upon with some suspicion). The vast majority of "Judaizing" non-Jews, however, remained non-Jews and lived their lives, to some extent, in two worlds.[9]

All these often contradictory attitudes to Jews and Judaism are important when it comes to understanding the specifically Christian anti-Semitism at the beginning of the second century CE, and Peter Schäfer is probably correct in his conclusion regarding the Roman attitude to Judaism:

> Beginning with Cicero and Seneca, and reaching its climax with Juvenal and Tacitus, there is an ambivalence between dislike and fear, criticism and respect, attraction and repulsion, which responds to the peculiar combination of exclusiveness and yet success that characterizes Judaism in the eyes of the Roman authors. . . . On the whole, however, the pecularity of the Roman attitude toward the Jews seems better expressed by the term "Judeophobia" in its ambivalent combination of fear and hatred.[10]

Thus at the end of the first century we are facing a situation characterized by contradictory views and attitudes concerning Jews. While Judaism fascinated some non-Jews, others feared its negative influence. Rome protected the Jewish population from overly brutal abuse, but at the same time took steps to limit Jewish influence in society.

Jews were hated for starting the war in Syria, which led to disturbances and serious confrontations between Jews and non-Jews, but their religion was admired on account of its ancient traditions. This is the complex situation in which the Jesus movement stepped into the world stage and in this context the anti-Semitic discourse would find quite new ways.

Christian Anti-Semitism

While Jesus probably saw himself as a Jewish prophet, modeled to a large extent on the prophet Elijah,[11] with a message predominantly to the Jewish people only,[12] some of his followers also turned their attention to reaching non-Jews. The belief among Jesus-believing Jews that they now were living in the messianic age probably brought to the fore universalistic ideas from the Bible on the salvation of the non-Jews and gave rise to the mission to the non-Jews.[13] As we saw in the previous chapter, there were different opinions about what was going to happen to the non-Jews at the end of time. Some imagined that the non-Jewish nations would be vanquished by Israel or annihilated by God, while others thought that non-Jews also had a place in the world to come. Within parts of the Jesus movement a resolution was passed that non-Jews could be included in the salvation of the God of Israel by faith in Jesus without having to convert to Judaism.

As we noticed in the previous chapter, it was in Antioch that Jesus-believing Jews first turned to non-Jews outside Israel with the message of Jesus (Acts 11:19-21). The message that the death and resurrection of Jesus had opened a way for non-Jews also is likely to have attracted many God-fearers. In the Jesus movement, they would gain a well-defined place in the salvation history of the Jewish people without having to give up their non-Jewish identity, which would involve all manner of complications. In addition to this, Paul later emphasized that Jews and non-Jews had the same status before God, something that had far-reaching consequences for how Jews and non-Jews could interact within the Jesus movement.

One major problem, however, was the relation of the non-Jews to the official religion. We noted earlier that Jewish communities probably accepted that non-Jews fulfilled their religious obligations to the city and to the empire. But because non-Jews within the Jesus movement now had been more closely linked to the Jewish people and, through Jesus, were considered, at least by Paul, to have the same status before the God of Israel, their relation to the Greco-Roman cult represented a serious problem. A crucial issue was, for instance, whether a Jesus-believing non-Jew could be present when Roman religious ceremonies were performed. Could a non-Jewish believer in Jesus take part in meals where wine sacrificed to Roman gods was served? Was it possible to combine faith in Jesus with the holding of political offices, which probably involved sacrifices to Greco-Roman gods?

The principal response was that an individual believing in Jesus had to abstain from "idolatry." Hence, the non-Jewish adherents to the Jesus movement were obliged to adapt to the Jewish attitude toward gods other than the God of Israel. It is reasonable to assume that the movement developed several pragmatic strategies in order to cope with this. One was that Jesus-believing non-Jews in fact posed as Jews vis-à-vis the authorities. If we assume that, even prior to having come in contact with the Jesus movement, they had adapted a Jewish lifestyle, it is not inconceivable that they took advantage of this in order not to be suspected of neglecting their religious obligations toward society.[14]

Those who in this manner chose to solve potential conflicts with the majority society became, as a result, more intimately bound to the Jewish faction of the Jesus movement. At the same time, one must note that their religious identity appears in a somewhat obscure manner. In their relations to the authorities, they appeared as Jews because they behaved like Jews. They celebrated the Sabbath, they probably ate Jewish food, and took no part in the official religious cults. But at the same time, in relation to the Jewish Jesus movement, their non-Jewish identity was maintained—even accentuated. According to Paul, non-Jews are included in the salvation of the God of Israel precisely as non-Jews and should under no circumstances convert to Judaism (1 Cor 7:17-20).

We should, however, also take into account that the Jewish leadership of the Jesus movement probably tried to arrive at compromises, making it possible for some adherents of the movement to maintain contacts with the non-Jewish society. Paul, in fact, seems to have encouraged further contacts between Jesus-believing non-Jews and persons outside the Jesus movement. In 1 Corinthians 5:9-13, he writes:

> I wrote to you in my letter not to associate with sexually immoral persons — not at all meaning the immoral of this world, or the greedy and robbers, or idolaters, since you would then need to go out of the world. But now I am writing to you not to associate with anyone who bears the name of brother or sister who is sexually immoral or greedy, or is an idolater, reviler, drunkard, or robber. Do not even eat with such a one. For what have I to do with judging those outside? Is it not those who are inside that you are to judge? God will judge those outside. "Drive out the wicked person from among you."

On the other hand, Paul here seems to worry about social intercourse among those who belonged to the group but who did not live up to the moral norms of the movement, rather than general contacts with persons not belonging to the Jesus movement. Later on in the letter, Paul raised the issue of whether it was seemly for non-Jewish adherents to the Jesus movement to eat food that had been used in Greco-Roman sacrificial rituals. This probably meant most of the provisions for sale in the cities, for instance, meat. As with all religion in antiquity, Greco-Roman religion involved the sacrifice of animals, and all meat not consumed in course of the sacrifices was afterwards sold in the market. From the Jewish viewpoint such food had, of course, been offered to "idols." Paul's way of handling the issue can, however, be interpreted in such a way that he in principle did not object to consummation of such food. The issue is raised in 1 Corinthians 8:4-6:

> Hence, as to the eating of food offered to idols, we know that "no idol in the world really exists," and that "there is no God but one." Indeed, even though there may be so-called gods in heaven or on earth — as in fact there are many gods and many lords — yet for us there is one God, the Father, from whom are all things and for whom we exist, and one Lord, Jesus Christ, through whom are all things and through whom we exist.

As in reality no other God than the God of Israel exists, Paul insisted that idolatry in practice was impossible. The crucial issue was the attitude of the individual, not the ritual action, or, as in this case, the consumption of food offered to Greco-Roman gods. What seems to be the problem was if someone ate the food *considering it to be sacrificed to Greek or Roman gods*. Paul continues in 1 Corinthians 8:7-13:

> It is not everyone, however, who has this knowledge. Since some have become so accustomed to idols until now, they still think of the food they eat as food offered to an idol; and their conscience, being weak, is defiled. "Food will not bring us close to God." We are no worse off if we do not eat, and no better off if we do. But take care that this liberty of yours does not somehow become a stumbling block to the weak. For if others see you, who possess knowledge, eating in the temple of an idol, might they not, since their conscience is weak, be encouraged to the point of eating food sacrificed to idols? So by your knowledge those weak believers for whom Christ died are destroyed. But when you thus sin against members of your family, and wound their conscience when it is weak, you sin against Christ. Therefore, if food is a cause of their falling, I will never eat meat, so that I may not cause one of them to fall.

The principle seems clear: those who confessed faith in Jesus had to abstain from "idolatry." But completely in agreement with how the rabbis later reasoned in the Mishnah and Talmud, Paul went on by *defining* what was meant by "idolatry,"[15] and then specified the proper behavior. What Paul understood as "idolatry" was the conscious partaking in Greco-Roman cult, in which the individual regarded the rituals as a true expression of Greco-Roman religion. But if the individual, on the other hand, believed that no other god than the God of Israel exists, then he or she was principally free to eat any food whatsoever and take part in any social gathering that might involve Greco-Roman religious rituals. The only exception was that the person in question should make allowance for those who were unable to distinguish between the performance of empty rites and the true participation in Greco-Roman rituals. Hence, according to Paul, it was inappropriate to take part in meals that took place in Greco-Roman temples.

On the other hand, Paul seems to have considered it quite in order to accept dinner invitations from persons outside the Jesus movement. Paul gave the following piece of advice in 1 Corinthians 10:27-29:

If an unbeliever invites you to a meal and you are disposed to go, eat whatever is set before you without raising any question on the ground of conscience. But if someone says to you, "This has been offered in sacrifice," then do not eat it, out of consideration for the one who informed you, and for the sake of conscience — I mean the other's conscience, not your own. For why should my liberty be subject to the judgment of someone else's conscience?

It is rather likely that such gatherings included, for instance, libation offerings of wine, honey, or oil, as well as prayers. We can here note the same principle as Paul applied to meals in Greco-Roman temples: once a person knows what he or she is doing, everything is permissible, but all people do not know this, and a person should consequently sometimes abstain from certain food out of consideration of others.[16]

Just as there were different views within the Jesus movement on how non-Jews should relate to the Jewish people, there were most certainly different opinions regarding the relations of the non-Jewish Jesus believers to the Greco-Roman society. It is likely, however, that the Jewish part of the Jesus movement brought about adjustments to make it easier for non-Jews to become part of the movement, since the participation of the non-Jews may very well have functioned as a kind of legitimization of the belief of the movement that it was really living in the messianic age. If this was the case, non-Jews should be seen streaming to the God of Israel, and to the same extent as this was observed, the fundamental ideas of the movement would be substantiated. Hence there was every reason not to raise the bar of entry too high.

During the last decades of the first century, however, the non-Jewish adherents of the Jesus movement found themselves in an increasingly complex situation. As noted above, the Jewish War caused underlying anti-Semitic sentiments to surface. Although Rome protected the Jewish population against assaults, it also laid a special tax on them, the so-called *fiscus Judaicus*, that all Jews between the ages of three and sixty (or sixty-two) were liable to pay. The money was supposed to be used to defray the costs for building a temple to Jupiter Capitolinus, which had burnt down in 69 CE. In reality this meant that the Jews had to buy their religious freedom by contributing to a temple that, from a Jewish point of view, was the temple of an idol. At the same time, Rome intensified its ideological offensive against those who neglected to fulfill their religious obligations to the state. It was during this period that Emperor Domitian executed his cousin Flavius Clemens and banished the latter's wife, as mentioned above.

In this situation, the religious identity, or rather the lack of a well-defined religious identity, of the *Jesus-believing* non-Jews was brought to a head. Previously they could hide within the Jewish community and exploit the fact that the Jesus-believing Jews were part of first-century Judaism and as such exempt from participation in the official religion. Or they could enjoy social connections outside the movement and cope with any cultic matters in a responsible manner. In the relations to the authorities, this system probably worked rather well, and non-Jews could join the Jesus movement without encountering any major obstacles.

But in the aftermath of the war and the introduction of the special tax on Jews, the situation dramatically changed—now there was a very tangible price for their commitment to the Jesus movement, and this was not only a question of money. If the Jesus-believing non-Jews paid the tax, they would henceforth be regarded as Jews, enjoying the opportunity to avoid taking part in Greco-Roman religion while at the same time increasingly adopting a Jewish identity. It is quite likely that the Matthean community represents precisely this option as it seems that the community, in its original Jewish context, advocated Torah observance, circumcision of non-Jewish males, and generally took a negative stance toward non-Jews.[17] Thus it is quite possible that some non-Jewish Jesus-believers disappeared in communities like the Matthean one and became Jews.

However, parts of the Jesus movement had only recently agreed that the non-Jews were *not* to become Jews. In addition, to pose as a Jew in the current political situation could be downright dangerous and lead to persecution and even death. But the alternative—to break with the Jesus movement altogether and return to pagan society—was also fraught with considerable social complications. In *Bellum judaicum* 2.462-463, Josephus describes how the Syrians, on the eve of the outbreak of the Jewish War, kept an eye on those who sympathized with the Jews:

The whole of Syria was a scene of frightful disorder; every city was divided into two camps, and the safety of one party lay in their anticipating the other. They passed their days in blood, their nights, yet more dreadful, in terror. For, though believing that they had rid themselves of the Jews, still each city had its Judaizers, who aroused suspicion.

These Judaizers were probably non-Jews sympathizing with the Jews in their political ambitions to achieve independence from Rome or people who had adapted Jewish manners and customs. In both cases it is easy to see that situation worsened after the war, and those adherents to the Jesus movement who emphasized their non-Jewish identity ran considerable risk of getting into difficulties because of their former dealings with the Jews. They could also be accused of neglecting their religious obligations. The Roman author Suetonius (*Dom.* 12.2) describes being present "when the person of a man ninety years old was examined before the procurator and a very crowded court to see whether he was circumcised." This text is usually interpreted as an example of how the Roman authorities searched for Jews liable for paying the Jew tax. But as the man had long ago passed the upper age limit for taxation, *it is more plausible that the examination was done in order to ascertain if the man was non-Jewish and consequently, like Flavius Clemens, guilty of atheism.*

To sum up matters, we might say that the non-Jewish adherents to the Jesus movement were caught in a trap after the Jewish War, to the effect that both alternative lines of action could have disastrous consequences. This situation is probably what caused some non-Jewish members of the Jesus movement to attempt to find another solution, a third way, that eventually resulted in the separation between Jews and non-Jews. Since it was the Jesus-believing non-Jews' relation to Judaism that constituted the stumbling block, this could be overcome if they parted ways with Judaism, which in reality meant the Jesus-believing Jews.

Such an undertaking was, of course, not without dangers, as the legal status of the movement was dependent on the very presumption that the Jesus movement was basically a form of Judaism. The Jewish population, we recall, was excused from participation in the official cult, a fact the non-Jewish Jesus believers previously had taken advantage of. Without the protection afforded Judaism, they would be at the mercy of the demands from the Roman authorities to demonstrate political loyalty by practicing the official religion. Even if the non-Jewish part of the Jesus movement could accept certain compromises, they generally seem to have considered it impossible to combine faith in the God of Israel with active participation in the cult of Greco-Roman gods and the imperial family. A new, equally impossible dilemma was apparently a fact.

In order to succeed, the non-Jewish Jesus believers had to stress their dissociation from the very same ethnic group that was responsible for the Jewish War—the Jews. In this case, they could even take advantage of the anti-Semitism prevalent in society, especially in the period after the war. But things were more complicated. Judaism had something the non-Jewish Jesus movement lacked, something that was extremely important when it came to convince the authorities of its raison d'être—ancient traditions stretching very far back in time.

It was possible to introduce new cults in the Roman Empire. This was often the consequence of incorporating new territories in the empire, or of immigration—new inhabitants in Roman cities brought their local cults with them. This usually caused no problems, but the Roman authorities were somewhat suspicious regarding new cults, fearing that they could be used as a guise, masking groups with subversive intentions. Of course, Judaism had ancient traditions, for which Greek and Roman authors had especially expressed admiration, but due to the war, the Jewish people had also become associated with rebellion against Rome. In order to have a chance to persuade the Roman authorities of its legitimacy, the non-Jewish Jesus movement had to succeed with the achievement *of both distancing themselves from the rebellious Jews and at the same time laying claim to the traditions of Judaism.*

If the basic presuppositions behind the process of separation were as I have described them here, we should find among representatives of the non-Jewish Jesus movement violent polemics aimed at the Jews, attempts to take over the religious traditions of the Jews, and efforts to convince the authorities of the excellent qualities of the new movement. This is, in fact, also the case.

In the beginning of the second century CE, roughly around 115, Ignatius, bishop of Antioch, was arrested and taken to Rome. Here he was bound to suffer martyrdom, something he, by the way, anticipated very much. In course of his journey to Rome, he wrote seven letters to different Christian communities in Asia Minor. In several passages in these letters, he touches upon the relations to Judaism, and it is evident that he represents a perspective from *outside* Judaism. A good example can be found in his letter *To the Magnesians* (8:1-2):

> Be not be deceived by false opinions or old fables that are of no use. For if we have lived according to Judaism until now, we admit that we have not received God's gracious gift. For the most divine prophets lived according to Jesus Christ. For this reason also they were persecuted. But they were inspired by his gracious gift, so that the disobedient became fully convinced that there is one God, who manifested himself through Jesus Christ his son, who is his Word that came forth from silence, who was pleasing in every way to the one who sent him.

Ignatius here established a clear-cut breach between Judaism and the religion he himself represents—which is clearly not Judaism. Previously, but no longer, he and his adherents lived according to "Judaism." The passage makes most sense if by "Judaism" we understand the Jewish part of the Jesus movement. If so, Ignatius refers to a period when his community was closely associated with the Jewish Jesus movement, whose teaching they now consider as "false opinions" and "old fables." The movement Ignatius now represents is in no way compatible with the Judaism he had previously adhered to, and "Judaism" is in fact contrasted against "God's gracious gift" in a way that foretells the subsequent development.

But Ignatius was unable to dissociate himself from everything Jewish—he still had to link up with the old traditions of Judaism in order to create a legal foundation for the continued existence of his non-Jewish movement. The strategy employed by Ignatius, and which subsequent Christian theologians also adapted, involved an extensive redefinition of the Jewish biblical tradition. This development is hinted at in *Magn.* 8:2, cited above, where Ignatius claims that "the most divine prophets lived according to Jesus Christ," which is the reason as to why they were persecuted. In *Magn.* 9:2, Ignatius goes even further, stating that the prophets in reality were disciples of

Jesus "in the spirit" and "awaited him as their teacher." Thus the Magnesians are admonished to "lay aside the bad yeast, which has grown old and sour, and turn to the new yeast, which is Jesus Christ" (Ign. *Magn.* 10:2), and they should be aware that it is "outlandish to proclaim Jesus Christ and practice Judaism" (Ign. *Magn.* 10:3). Thus, as early as the beginning of the second century, the process of the non-Jewish overtaking of the whole Jewish religious tradition is fully operative, resulting in the creation of a new kind of "Judaism"—one completely without Jews.[18]

During the following centuries the themes we have seen elaborated by Ignatius can be found among other Christian authors. For example, some time during the later half of the second century, bishop Melito of Sardis invented the term "deicide"—the idea that the Jewish people collectively were guilty of the death of Jesus, and accordingly, of God. The basic theme of Melito's Easter sermon, *Peri Pascha,* is the presentation of the sufferings of Christ as a series of accusations against the people of Israel, written with God's faithfulness to the Jewish people as a background. Melito summarizes the theme thus (72):

> It is he that has been murdered.
> And where has he been murdered? In the middle of Jerusalem.
> By whom? By Israel.
> Why? Because he healed their lame
> and cleansed their lepers
>   and brought light to their blind
>   and raised their dead,
>   that is why he died.

From this it seems clear that Melito blames the Jewish people for the death of Jesus, but further on in the text (96), he gives this accusation a new dimension—*the Jews have killed God himself.*

> He who hung the earth is hanging;
> He who fixed the heavens has been fixed;
> He who fastened the universe has been fastened to a tree;
> The Sovereign has been insulted;
> The God has been murdered;
> The King of Israel has been put to death by an Israelite right hand.

As a result of being responsible for the death of Jesus, the Jewish people are damned, an idea Melito already had prepared his audience for. Previously (43), he asserted that Judaism and the Jewish people really had merit—prior to the establishment of the church. In his day, he claims, "things once precious have become worthless, since the really precious things have been revealed." As early as in the middle of the second century, the non-Jewish part of the Jesus movement had successfully launched the idea that the church had superseded the Jews as the elected people.

Melito's *Peri Pascha* has exerted a tremendous influence on Christian anti-Semitism as it very likely has served as a model for the so-called *Improperia*. These laments about Israel's disobedience were included in the Latin liturgy for Good Friday in the early Middle Ages. In spite of the fact that their aim was not specifically to point out accusations against the Jewish people but to incite *Christians* to self-examination, their actions had anti-Jewish consequences. In modern times, the Jewish population in Eastern Europe lived in terror of the Christian Easter, as the Good Friday liturgy generally incited members of local Christian congregations to commit violent acts against the Jews.

Christian anti-Semitism may have originated in a specific historical situation and constituted originally a kind of ideological resource in the struggle of the early church to develop a legally recognized religious identity. Quite soon, however, it became wrenched from its historical context and started to live a life on its own. The non-Jewish Jesus movement's plan to create a new religion and a legal basis for its activity had a protracted lifetime. It was only in the fourth century that real progress was made: in 311 the Emperor Galerius issued an edict of tolerance for all religions, including Christianity; in 313, the Emperor Constantine issued an edict at Milan stating that the empire should be neutral with regard to all religions, and in 380 Christianity became the only permitted religion in the Roman Empire.

However, in course of the development of Christianity from being a forbidden religion to becoming a state religion, the contempt of Jews and Judaism became a well-integrated part of the theology of the church. The main opponent of Christianity was not, as one might imagine, Greco-Roman religion, but Judaism. Thus what started as a Jewish messianic movement evolved within a comparatively short period—roughly a hundred years—into a religious movement that in all essentials contradicted its origin.[19]

Law versus Grace—Luther and Protestantism

The Early Church and the Problem of Sin and Grace

First-century Judaism seems to have been occupied with eschatological issues to a much higher degree than later rabbinic Judaism, and according to the Gospels, Jesus repeated the message of John the Baptist: "Repent, for the kingdom of heaven has come near" (Matt 3:2). The firm conviction within the early Jesus movement that non-Jews also could be saved led to extensive discussions, as we have seen above, about how this could come about, and several ideas seem to have coexisted within the Jesus movement.

When the Christian church emerged as a non-Jewish religion in the beginning of the second century, the theological reflection of the church underwent a radical transformation. While Paul mainly was interested in how the respective collective groups of Israel and the non-Jewish peoples were to be saved, the issue of the individual's redemption increasingly became a point of focus. As early as Tertullian (ca. 160–ca. 220), we encounter the complex of problems that much later would culminate in the breach with the majority church in the West caused by the Reformation: the relation between grace and merit and the respective divine and human elements in redemption. Already here it is clear that the issues differ from the ones that occupied Paul's mind.

It was Augustine, however, (354–430) who laid the foundation to the doctrine of grace that Luther later formulated. Augustine mainly developed the theology regarding sin and grace in his controversy with the monk Pelagius, who appeared in Rome shortly before 400. Pelagius argued that it was possible to live a sinless life, as humanity is endowed with free will. In contrast to Augustine, he rejected all notions that humanity, through the fall of Adam, was marred by a defect—original sin—passed on from generation to generation. Sin, according to Pelagius, was only the result of single acts

of volition, and the individual will at last be judged on the basis of
whether evil or good deeds have predominated in his or her life.
"Grace" for Pelagius was both a kind of divine inspiration, helping
people to make the right choices, and the new law, revealed in the
New Testament.[20]

Against this notion, Augustine asserted the opposite. A person is
totally unable to do anything that can affect his or her prospect of
redemption. According to Augustine, humans lack not only the ability,
but also the will to perform good deeds, and are hopelessly lost without divine intervention. No human effort to please God is possible,
which in the long run means that God decides who is to be saved and
who is predestined to perdition. This doctrine of double predestina-
tion caused extensive discussions and strife and resulted in what later
came to be called Semipelagianism. The Semipelagians accepted
Augustine's doctrine of original sin, but at the same time argued that
humans carry the seed to do good deeds, which can be aroused by
divine grace. In the redemption of a person, the grace of God thus acts
together with the free will, and a person is capable of either accepting
or rejecting the grace of God. Rejection, of course, leads to perdition,
but this is against the will of God, who wants to include the whole of
humanity in his salvation.

Semipelagianism at first prospered, and was confirmed at the
Synod of Arles in 473. But this was not the last word on the subject. At
the Synod of Orange in 529, the Semipelagian viewpoint was rejected
in favor of a modified Augustinianism. In a formal sense, the dispute
about sin and grace was settled, although discussions about the salvation of humanity continued for a long time and, of course, became one
of the main issues during the Reformation. In practice, however,
Semipelagianism became the official position of the medieval church,
and the Occamist doctrine of grace, which Luther turned against, was
largely characterized by Semipelagian ideas. The English theologian
and philosopher William of Occam (ca. 1285–ca. 1349) reasoned in the
same manner as Pelagius that a person was capable of loving God
above all, as original sin had not destroyed his or her nature; only the
sin of Adam was ascribed to the individual. Sin consists only of single
volitional acts, and when a person, by his or her own effort draws near

to God and performs good deeds, God infuses the grace that leads to salvation as a reward.

Martin Luther, Grace, and the Jews

It was precisely this theological element that led to the spiritual crisis causing Luther's radical reinterpretation of Paul. Martin Luther (1483–1546) had encountered the theology of Occam during his studies in the beginning of the sixteenth century. After his ordination as a priest in 1507, he studied Occamist dogmatics in the Augustinian monastery in Erfurt. The notion of merit and reward that became more and more prominent in the late medieval doctrine of grace gave rise to a seemingly unsolvable conflict for Luther. Occamist theology implied that God would infuse his grace as a reward, provided that a person first did what was in his or her power. But what happens if a person is unable to meet the demands of God? With Luther the experience of not being able to offer God enough repentance and love led to the logical conclusion that he was predestined to condemnation. It was during this inner conflict he found the solution in Romans 1:17: "The one who is righteous will live by faith."

While previous theologians, influenced by a juridical theology that strongly emphasized the importance of the sacraments, had almost equated God's righteousness with his judgment, Luther interpreted Paul in an entirely different manner. According to Luther, the Christian gains access to the righteousness God possesses by faith *and faith alone*. This was, Luther claimed, what should be understood by the term "grace." As a consequence of this ascribed righteousness, good deeds follow, which in the long run means that the distance between the ascribed and the real righteousness diminishes and is completely wiped out in eternity. Luther thus puts the Occamistic notion of sin and grace on its head. Good deeds follow as a result of grace and are not requirements for it. Additionally, in spite of the fact that all humans are sinners, the Christian is declared righteous in the eyes of God and is consequently simultaneously a sinner and righteous (in Latin *simul justus et peccator*).

In Luther's theological system, the law has a very special function. The external fulfillment of the commandments is entirely abrogated in Christ. In this respect, the law was valid only for a certain people — the

Jews — and for a limited period of time — until the gospel was revealed in Christ. But according to Luther, the law also has a higher purpose and is completely in the service of the gospel. The law lays down what a person must do, but as it is impossible for anyone to fulfill the demands of the law, the contrition Luther himself experienced, and which Occam's theology could not relieve him of, sets in. The law defines sin, but in the individual's contrition and knowledge of his or her own wretchedness and inadequacy, God in Christ comes to meet him or her with unconditional forgiveness, being dependent on nothing but the grace of God.

With Luther, the law thus represents something good, in fact, the will of God, but its fulfillment is at the same time something unattainable. Anyone who imagines that he or she by means of the law can attain a relation to God is guilty of the most fundamental sin of all — self-righteousness — based on the false assumption that God can be pleased through human effort. For such a person, the law does not lead to grace and forgiveness, but to punishment and damnation.

It is important to realize that Luther's reading of Paul is by no means a historical reconstruction of the Pauline situation. The problems Paul wrestled with are different from those of Luther, and the historical situation in which Paul wrote his letters was quite different from Luther's. Even though Protestant biblical scholarship has been rather evasive regarding these matters, it is important to clearly state that Luther created theology — not a historical reconstruction — when he read Paul.

It is easy to see how this theology affected the view of Judaism. As even the mere thought of relating to God by means of the law by definition represents a hopeless endeavor, Luther's doctrine of grace and atonement implied the complete rejection of Judaism. The law is unable to bring forth any good deeds and can only provide knowledge of the sin that finally will result in damnation. As will be evident, this is exactly the conclusion Luther himself arrived at regarding Judaism.

In 1543, Luther published the pamphlet *Von den Jüden und iren Lügen* ("The Jews and Their Lies"), one of the most savage anti-Jewish documents ever written. It may be that Luther had expected the German Jews to convert to Protestant Christianity and that the rage that he expressed in this pamphlet in part was caused by the fact that they showed no eagerness to do so. Twenty years earlier, Luther had published another pamphlet, a missionary tract addressed to a Jewish public. It resulted, however, in no conversions. Instead, Christians started to adapt Jewish customs in a way that bears resemblance to the situation in antiquity. *Von den Jüden und iren Lügen* presents a veritable sample card of all the stereotypes passed on down through the centuries in European culture, primarily by the Christian church. In this respect, Luther's views on Judaism were by no means unique. He transmitted the standard medieval myths stating that Jews had kidnapped and maimed children, poisoned wells, and that they were mendacious, greedy, and striving for world domination. What was new with Luther was the motivation of the eternal damnation of the Jews.

A problem for Luther was that the law incontestably was given to the Jewish people. He solved the problem by arguing that there in fact were *two* kinds of Jews. The Jews Moses brought out of Egypt, to whom the Torah was entrusted, were the kind of Jews Luther seems to have viewed positively. The law given at Sinai was supposed to be kept by Israel until the day the Messiah revealed himself. But according to Luther, contemporary Jews were not descendents of these Jews, but of the ones who shouted "Crucify him!" in response to Pontius Pilate's question about what was to be done to Jesus.

Luther could not even accept that Jews in the land of Israel lived according to the Torah. Because everything Moses had established had fallen into decay, the law of Moses could hence no longer be in force. For this reason the Jews should nowhere be allowed to live according to the law. Instead, Luther recommended that their synagogues and houses be burned, all Jewish literature and property confiscated, and the rabbis forbidden to teach. It is perhaps no wonder that Adolf Hitler in *Mein Kampf* included Luther among the great heroes of history and that excerpts from *Von den Jüden und iren Lügen* was distributed by the Nazis in Germany. What Luther proposed in *Von den Jüden und iren Lügen* Hitler later carried out to the letter, while giving a new and ghastly meaning to Luther's exhortation *to get rid of the Jews forever.*

Because of the role the law was given in the religion Luther created, there simply was no room left for Judaism. The normal way for Jews to relate to God—through the Torah—represents the inevitable road to perdition. Luther, of course, linked up with the anti-Semitic tradition the church had harbored for centuries, but at the same time he created a new theological foundation for annihilating Judaism. Of course,

Luther cannot be held responsible for the atrocities during the Nazi regime, and his view of Jews and Judaism must surely be seen against the cultural climate of his own time and be related to his struggle with the Roman Catholic Church. Yet, it is certainly no exaggeration to characterize the religion Luther represented as anti-Semitic in principle.

Nineteenth-Century Effects

Returning to the nineteenth century, then, it is no wonder that F. C. Baur found a fundamental and absolute contradiction between Judaism and Christianity in a cultural environment permeated with Lutheranism. The incompatibility of Judaism and Christianity, as well as the demonizing of the Jewish people, had been drummed into people in the course of history of the Christian church. The negative image of Jews and Judaism has simply become an integrated part of Western culture. During the nineteenth century, the specific Christian anti-Semitism merged together with a secular, putatively scientific anti-Semitism that was based on racial-biological ideas. In connection with nationalistic ambitions that surfaced at the time of the unification of the German states in the 1870s, this led to an increased marginalization of European Jewry, which was perceived as an alien body.

At the end of the nineteenth century, then, one might claim that the cultural climate as regards Judaism in Germany was characterized by the fact that Martin Luther had proved Judaism to be predestined to extinction. F. C. Baur had, with the help of Hegelian philosophy, scientifically proved the absolute superiority of Christianity in relation to Judaism, and the racial-biological research had substantiated that the Jewish race was inferior to the Aryan. It is quite self-evident that these circumstances influenced the research on Judaism that was carried out in Germany at the end of the nineteenth century. How the concrete results of this were manifested we are now going to scrutinize more closely.

The Myth of Jewish Legalism: Ferdinand Weber and the Scales of Balance

In 1880 Ferdinand Weber published *System der altsynagogalen palästinischen Theologie aus Targum, Midrasch und Talmud* ("The Theological System of the Ancient Palestinian Synagogue Based on the Targum, Midrash, and Talmud"). The depiction of ancient Judaism that Weber presents in this book would exert an extraordinarily strong influence on New Testament research during almost a century. The intention of Weber, who grew up in pietistic circles, was to start a missionary work aimed at bringing the gospel to the Jewish people, and for that purpose he began studying Judaism. Even though he never became a missionary, the results of his studies would for a long time constitute the standard view scholars used as a background for their work on the New Testament. Weber's basic view of Judaism was thus passed on in several other works, and because of this, a specific picture of Judaism that fit Protestant New Testament research like a glove was sanctioned.

The title of Weber's book already hints at a fundamental problem. Weber tried to create a systematic theology out of Jewish sources that in no way were suitable for the purpose. The Mishnah, finally edited around the year 200 CE, is a thematic collection of traditions dealing with how to apply the commandments of the Torah with regard to, for instance, purity regulations, the Sabbath, and the temple cult. In the Talmud, finally redacted in the sixth or seventh century CE, the Mishnah is commented on alongside various anecdotes and legends covering the most diverse fields. Midrashim are creative, sometimes playful interpretations of the biblical text, verse by verse, often aimed at discovering the deeper meaning of the divine revelation.[21] To try to describe a systematic "Jewish theology" using rabbinic literature is patently absurd. What Weber did was to graft the nineteenth-century Protestant theological system and its current theological issues onto the Jewish sources, and it is evident that prescientific points of departure governed his account. *Weber knew in advance that Judaism was the antithesis of Christianity*, and his studies also led him to this conclusion.

According to Weber, Judaism is characterized by legalism and the idea that God is distant from humanity. He found the basis of this conception in a rather bizarre interpretation of the fall of humanity. When the Jewish people entered into the covenant with God at Sinai, Weber argued, the consequences of the fall of Adam were obliterated, and the relations between God and the Jewish people were restored. This condition, however, was short-lived, because the incident of the golden calf (Exod 32:1-14) resulted in a specific "Jewish fall" with ill-fated consequences. Weber claimed that the Jewish people, due to the incident of the golden calf, were again separated from God, who henceforth became unapproachable and distant. The only option remaining for the Jew was now to try to return to the absent God by means of the Torah. Thus when the Torah is observed and the individual performs good deeds, the acquired merits are placed in one scale of balance, and each transgression is placed in the other one. The scale carrying the most weight when the individual enters eternity determines the final fate of that person.

This system, according to Weber, of course leads to a righteousness based on deeds, or at its worst, to self-righteousness and an emphasis on the ritual aspects of religion. Judaism is thus, Weber asserted, characterized by empty law observance with no inner commitment. In Judaism, the individual strives for redemption but can never really know how his or her relation to God is—one final transgression and the scale tips over. In Lutheran Christianity matters are of course different— salvation is freely offered by grace, and God in Christ is accessible to everyone. In contrast to this depiction of Judaism, created by means of a selection of texts, which in many cases were misread, Christianity appears as a superior religion in all respects. This was exactly the purpose of Weber's presentation of ancient Judaism and its success was guaranteed—at the end of the nineteenth century, Weber's distorted picture of Jewish legalism was the standard interpretation among New Testament scholars. Christianity had acquired a perfect dark background against which it could shine all the more brilliantly.

The Influence of Weber

Thus Weber's basic ideas of Judaism lived on and influenced several influential works. Between 1866 and 1890, the New Testament professor Emil Schürer (1844–1910) published a three-volume set on Judaism in the times of Jesus, *Geschichte des jüdischen Volkes im Zeitalter Jesu Christi* (*The History of the Jewish People in the Age of Christ*, 1897; 1973–1987), a work that in many aspects is a most useful handbook of geography, archaeology, religious groups, and literature of first-century Judea. When Schürer dealt with the relation of Judaism to the Torah, however, his dependence on Weber became evident. Judaism was seen as synonymous with legalism, according to Schürer, and

characterized by retributive, penal, and recompensive thought patterns, resulting in an emphasis on external behavior, not inner life. In
order to demonstrate the absurdity of such a religious system, Schürer
selected detailed descriptions from the Mishnah dealing with various
Jewish customs, such as the Sabbath celebration and the purity laws.
Against this backdrop, of course, the criticism of the Torah by Jesus and
Paul appears as an excellent example of the superiority of Christianity.

At the end of the nineteenth century, New Testament scholarship
was further advanced by the emergence of the so-called "history of religions school" (*religionsgeschichtliche Schule*) centered on a group of scholars at the University of Göttingen. Its purpose was to examine the
biblical texts against the background of the near-Eastern environment
by employing a historical-critical method. In this respect, the school
portended a modern approach for analyzing the biblical texts, and some
of the early findings have also had a durable value. But at the same time,
one must keep in mind that this research was not carried out without a
confessional bias. As pointed out by William Baird, the "s" in *Religions-
geschichte* does not indicate a plural, but a genitive singular.[22] The history
of religions school was not concerned with "religions" but with
"Christianity." Even though the school was basically a reaction against
the criticism leveled at Christianity by the Enlightenment and an
attempt to adapt the theological discourse to new epistemological conditions, apologetic traits were not absent.

In 1903, one of the members of the history of religions school,
Wilhelm Bousset (1865–1903), a New Testament professor as well,
published a work called *Die Religion des Judentums im neutestamentlichen
Zeitalter* ("The Judaic Religion in the New Testament Era"), with the
overall purpose of depicting the background of Christianity. Bousset's
picture of the Judaism contemporary with Jesus was unequivocally
negative. Like Weber earlier, Bousset stressed that Judaism was characterized by a boundless chasm between God and humanity, a view for
which he found support in the apocryphal and pseudepigraphal Jewish
literature. In Jesus, Bousset found the absolute opposite of Judaism, as
Jesus bridges the chasm to God and calls him his heavenly Father.
According to Bousset, a sense of alienation and inadequacy permeated
Jewish piety. Moreover, the fundamental problem of Judaism was that
it did not provide a system permitting the individual to reestablish a

broken relationship to God, as Judaism had neither sacraments through which the individual could reach God nor any means by which the grace of God could be channeled. In short: Judaism represented a perverted form of religion and its cardinal sin was that it was not Christianity.

The influence of Weber is also apparent among other scholars not only at this time, but also well into the twentieth century, as we will see later on. Jesus and Paul were generally seen against the background of a Judaism characterized by legalism and belief in an absent God. It was viewed as a religion that was simply unable to create a relationship between God and the individual. In stark contrast to the somber picture of the religion of both Jesus and Paul, Christianity was presented as the contradiction of all this. But it is important to notice that the picture of Judaism to which Christianity was compared *was a Christian theological construction*, the outcome of two thousand years of contempt for and persecution of the Jews, in combination with specific theological issues within the Christian church.

Before we look more closely at the reasons why this theological construction started to be called in question seriously within the field of New Testament scholarship, we will first see how the picture of a legalistic Judaism contributed to the creation of the traditional picture of Paul. In this process, Bousset played an important role, partially because it was through his works that the picture of Judaism became more generally available to New Testament scholars, and partially because one of the most influential scholars during the twentieth century happened to be one of his students — Rudolf Bultmann.

3

THE FORMATION OF
THE STANDARD VIEW OF PAUL

Rudolf Bultmann

Theologian and Biblical Scholar

Rudolf Bultmann (1884–1976) was indeed one of the most influential biblical scholars during the twentieth century.[1] Due to his importance both as a scholar and theologian, Bultmann is central in the development of the traditional view of Paul that was firmly established in the middle of the twentieth century.

As were many young theologians at the turn of the century, Bultmann was originally heavily influenced by the theological liberalism that swept through Europe. The scientific optimism that had resulted from the Enlightenment, of which F. C. Baur and the Tübingen School had been part, quickly developed into an overarching new approach among leading theologians. Prominent representatives were, among others, Albrecht Ritschl, Wilhelm Herrmann, and Adolf von Harnack. Herrmann and Harnack were, by the way, two of Bultmann's teachers. The liberal scholars, while emphatically opposing Lutheran orthodoxy, dogmatism, and metaphysics, were, however, still deeply involved in the Protestant project of establishing the idea of "righteousness by faith," and the distinction between Judaism and Christianity still constitutes a vital assumption in their works.

Equipped with rationalism, skepticism, and historical criticism, the liberal theologians strove to adapt the gospel to the post-Enlightenment world by concentrating on the timeless tidings of Christianity. By down-playing the supernatural dimension of the Gospels while focusing on the ethical teachings of Jesus, they sorted out what they regarded as the "simple teachings" of Jesus, which, as Albert Schweitzer pointed out in 1906 in his famous *Von Reimarus zu Wrede* (*The Quest of the Historical Jesus*), to a large extent seemed to agree with the prevalent values of the late-nineteenth-century bourgeoisie.[2]

As a scholar, Bultmann was trained in the history of religions school, and his contributions to the understanding of the evolution of the gospel tradition truly belong to the most important trailblazing efforts in the field of New Testament scholarship during the twentieth century. In his groundbreaking form-historical work from 1921, *Geschichte der synoptischen Tradition* (*The History of the Synoptic Tradition*), Bultmann took an interest in the oral traditions that are assumed to constitute the basis of the written Gospels. By identifying the literary form of a certain passage and trying to figure out its setting in life (*Sitz im Leben*), form-historians believed they could determine the historicity of the text. Bultmann reached the conclusion that even though the Gospels provide some reliable information of what Jesus did and said, they do not present us with a biography of Jesus' life or an unswerving description of his personality. In Bultmann's view, the church created most of this material, and it is impossible to arrive at any substantial knowledge of the historical Jesus. The chasm Bultmann opened between the historical Jesus and the Jesus of the Gospels signified the deathblow to theological liberalism.

If Bultmann as a historian believed it was virtually impossible to reach the historical background of the Gospels, as a theologian he completely ignored the importance of the historical dimension for the Christian gospel. Instead, he carried on one aspect of the liberal theological project: the attempt to find a place for the Christian message in a world permeated with the rationalist philosophy of the Enlightenment. In 1921 Bultmann was made professor of New Testament exegesis at the University of Marburg and became acquainted with the existentialist philosopher Martin Heidegger, then working on his early work *Sein und Zeit*, published in 1927 (*Being and Time*). Heidegger exerted an enormous influence on Bultmann, who found a direct parallel to his own understanding of the Christian faith in Heidegger's ideas of the conditions of human existence. While liberal theology by means of historical analysis tried to arrive at an understanding of the universal applicability of Christianity, Bultmann denied the importance of the historical background of Christianity. On the contrary, he argued that the message of Christianity was in no way dependent on its historical context. The focal point of the Christian faith was not the *historical* Jesus, but the *kerygma*—the message of the death of Jesus and his victory over death. From this viewpoint, matters of historicity would, according to Bultmann, conceal the actual purpose of the texts, which was to challenge humanity to recognize its true existence and liberate people from the anguish their occupation with transient matters leads to.

According to Bultmann, the supernatural features of the biblical texts constitute an impediment to take in the true message of the gospel, as the advances of science make it impossible for modern people to accept the biblical worldview. But whereas liberal theology simply eliminated all supernatural matters from the Christian message, Bultmann meant that what he regarded as myths should be interpreted against the background of the basic message of Christianity. Hence, what Bultmann termed "demythologizing" implies that the aspects of Christianity that do not agree with the modern worldview when understood literally—the belief in miracles and even in the resurrection—should be given an "existential interpretation."

Ultimately, Bultmann's theology is of course the consequence of his understanding of Luther's theology of justification. Bultmann argued that the demands for believing such things as the miraculous that are contrary to reason *represent an achievement, and accordingly, requiring such belief is something that does not agree with the notion of a faith without works.* The fact that Bultmann was a Protestant theologian for whom Luther's distinction between faith and works was central, even though a new dimension was added to it, led Bultmann to transmit the negative nineteenth-century image of Judaism into the twentieth century. Even Bultmann's picture of Judaism, which he very likely had inherited from his teacher Wilhelm Bousset, is clearly influenced by the standard nineteenth-century view.

Bultmann on Judaism

In his 1949 book, *Das Urchristentum im Rahmen der antiken Religionen* (*Primitive Christianity in Its Historical Setting*), Bultmann clearly states his view of ancient Judaism. In the introduction, Bultmann claims to have no apologetic ambitions. He neither wants to prove the veracity of Christianity nor present it as superior to other religions. He even dissociates himself from the Hegelian view that Christianity represents the culmination of the evolution of religions. Instead, Bultmann considers himself to be a historian, and he only wants to clarify the conditions pertaining to the origins of Christianity so that the individual can form an opinion of its veracity. Bultmann maintains that the claims of truth of Christianity, as well as those of other religions, are dependent on the standpoint of the individual, and that no historian has the right to deprive any person of the responsibility of taking up a definite position. In this case, it is in all probability the existentialist theologian speaking.

Bultmann's description of Judaism in the times of Jesus opens with a short historical survey ending with the fall of the temple in 70 CE. With the cessation of the temple cult, the focus of religion changes from sacrifice to the study of the Bible, and the synagogue, not the temple, assumes the central position. This leads to something entirely unique in the ancient world—a religion not revolving around the sacrifice of animals. Bultmann argues, however, that the fact that the focus of Judaism is transferred from the sacrificial cult to the study of the sacred text leads to an interior contradiction: by increasingly identifying itself with history, Judaism loses contact with the present and thus ceases to shoulder any responsibility for the contemporary social and cultural situation. This basically existential-philosophic criticism leads, according to Bultmann, to a situation where God is also relegated to history. The actions of God are seen in the past—and expected in the eschatological future—but not in the present. Here again we meet the notion of the absent God we recognize from the works of Weber, Schürer, and Bousset, albeit from a new philosophical point of departure.

The emphasis on God's action in the past—and in the eschatological perfection of the future—leads to the existence of Israel itself outside of history, according to Bultmann. Due to this, the notion of God's transcendence underwent a change, and as the Jewish people became detached from history, God also came to be seen as active outside history. Hence, the bonds between the God of Israel and the Jewish people were broken. Instead of being the God of Israel, God became the God of the whole world, the judge of the world, and the almighty creator of the universe. The God of Israel, traditionally perceived as deeply united with the Jewish people, came to be viewed as a cosmic highest being, enthroned in heaven, surrounded by the heavenly host, separated from the world of humanity.

According to Bultmann, the change of outlook regarding the relationship between Israel and God, caused by the loss of the Jerusalem temple, led to the divine law taking its place at the center of attention. The temple cult was substituted for the sermons in the synagogue and resulted in the emergence of a legalistic system controlling the entire life of the individual down to the minutest details. The ethical dimension of the law was rendered totally subordinated to the ritual, and henceforth Jewish piety became dominated by strict formalism, with an emphasis on the performance of obsolete commandments, incomprehensible to the individual. As the law was assumed to be of divine origin, Bultmann argues, it became virtually impossible to change. In spite of the fact that many of the commandments no longer were possible to apply, and for this reason were considered to be devoid of meaning, the law in its entirety still had to be kept. The commandments could not be adapted to new conditions, but the religious leadership, the rabbis, strove to expound the text as close to the original meaning as possible.

Bultmann, of course, was familiar with the Jewish interpretive tradition developed during the centuries after the fall of the temple, but regarded it as primitive and stereotyped. It could in no way stand against a comparison with the Greek search for true knowledge in a scientific sense, Bultmann stated, and one central problem he identified was that the Jewish scribes only strove to collect as many interpretations as possible without attempting to indicate which one was the true one.

The result of living with an unchangeable sacred text and a hermeneutic tradition that endeavored to uphold the original meaning of the text was, according to Bultmann, that observance of the law became an intolerable burden for the individual, especially since new amendments were added to the original ones. This legalistic system forced the individual to embrace the notion that it was possible to fulfill the demands of the law. What was demanded of the individual was simply to perform empty rituals and abstain from doing what was forbidden without any pronounced commitment. This, Bultmann claimed, led to the conclusion that a person in reality was free to do as he or she pleased. The law could not possibly cover every conceivable situation and was therefore full of loopholes, providing the individual with an outlet for every egoistical impulse and all kinds of passions. But because the *lex talionis* principle — "an eye for an eye and a tooth for a tooth" (Exod 21:24; Lev 24:20; Deut 19:21; Matt 5:38) — determined whether a person would have a share in the world to come, there were of course weighty reasons for him or her not to stray from the narrow path. Bultmann's conception of the relation of the Jew to the punishing God and the function of the law in this legalistic system is directly derived from Weber, and he minutely repeats the idea of justification earned by one's own efforts as the fundamental Jewish soteriological system.

Judaism was thus characterized by a strict system of weighing good and bad actions. Observance or transgression of the law determined the relation of the Jew to the absent God. No one could in advance be sure of his or her salvation either, but the prayer "we have sinned before you" was, according to Bultmann, constantly on the lips of the pious Jew.

In the middle of the twentieth century, Bultmann's view of ancient Judaism completely agrees with the picture that emerged at the end of the nineteenth century. Judaism was characterized by a far-reaching legalism, belief in a God that no longer acted in history, and a soteriological system based on merits, which leaves room for both religious hypocrisy and a feeling of uncertainty about one's relationship to God. According to Bultmann, this was exactly what Jesus reacted against and is ultimately the religious system criticized in the Gospels. We will now see what consequences Bultmann's notion of Judaism had for his understanding of Paul's relationship to the Jewish law and the term "justification."

Bultmann on Paul

In the first part of *Theologie des Neuen Testaments* (*Theology of the New Testament*), originally published in 1948, Bultmann deals with his understanding of Pauline theology. Regarding the approach to the Jewish law and the justification of the individual, it is evident that in Bultmann's opinion, Paul makes no distinction between Jews and non-Jews. The theology of Paul concerns humanity in general, and his message is directed toward all people. Of principal importance here is Paul's discourse on the function of the law, with the aim of contrasting the Jewish conception of justification through works against the Christian view of justification by faith. Before God all distinctions between humans are dissolved, according to Bultman's reading of Paul.

Like Luther, Bultmann is of the opinion that the Torah was given to the Jewish people and reveals the will of God. But as the revelation of the will of God, it also applies to all of humanity, even though God's will is not concretized in the specific form of the Torah for non-Jews, and the purpose of the law was originally to lead humanity to life. Had humanity been able to keep the entire law, this would have led to justification and thus to salvation. The problem, of course, is that no one can fulfill what God demands, which is why the law cannot lead anyone to life — only to death. As a consequence of the law being impossible to keep, Bultmann claims that no one should even attempt to achieve salvation by means of the law, which is the reason why Judaism embodies the most basic sin of all — the striving for self-justification. This, according to Bultmann, is Paul's main criticism of the Judaism he abandoned.

But how does Bultmann understand Paul's view of why the law was given in the first place, as it evidently cannot lead humanity to righteousness? In order to clarify this matter he takes Romans 3:20 as his point of departure, where Paul, in his view, claims that the law can only give a person "the knowledge of sin." Bultmann's interpretation is that Paul here not only claims that the law defines sin, but that it actually leads humans into sin. This happens, according to Bultmann, for two reasons: first because the natural desire of humanity compels people to transgress the commandments, and secondly because the mere thought of fulfilling them in itself constitutes a grave sin. Hence the original purpose of the law — to lead to life — is nullified by the desires of humanity, and the actual purpose of the law becomes clearly revealed, namely *to lead humanity to death in order to make God manifest as God.*

Entirely in accordance with the Lutheran understanding of justification, Bultmann argues that Paul contrasts the law with grace. It is only when confronted by the law and the inability to fulfill what God demands that a person realizes his or her complete dependence on God and thus attains salvation. Anyone who trusts in his or her own works is predestined to failure, whereas the person who puts his or her trust in God without good works is declared justified, and in addition to this is vouchsafed a more perfect way of acquiring the knowledge of the will of God. A Christian does not need the law to ascertain the will of God, because the one who believes in Christ can experience what the Jew only knows through the law, namely the perfect will of God through the Christian message of love. Compared to this, the law only represents a limited and, of course, inferior form of revelation.

Thus the principal difference between Judaism and Christianity is that Judaism represents a religious system that has never worked. The way Jews traditionally relate to God — through the Torah — is doomed to failure, according to Bultmann's understanding of Paul. In all aspects, the religion Bultmann claims that Paul represents — Christianity — is a better and higher form of religion. Judaism, in short, leads to death, whereas Christianity, faith without works, leads to righteousness and eternal life. Judaism's hope of justification is understood in an entirely eschatological manner. Only when God in the future intervenes and brings the present age to an end will the individual Jew know his or her relationship to God. The Christian, on the other hand, is justified in the present and can accordingly be sure of his or her salvation.

Evidently, Bultmann reads Paul through Lutheran ideologically-colored eyeglasses, against the background of the negative image of Judaism handed down throughout the entire history of the church, and explicitly expressed by the scholarly tradition of which Bultmann was a part. Ultimately, Paul is the one who lends his voice to all this, as Bultmann imagines that he is describing the theology of Paul, not a Christian reassessment of the apostle's thoughts.

We will now see how two of Bultmann's most influential adepts dealt with Paul and Judaism: Ernst Käsemann and Günther Bornkamm.

The Bultmann School

Ernst Käsemann

In 1963, Krister Stendahl published the article, "The Apostle Paul and the Introspective Conscience of the West" (originally published 1960 in Swedish), in which he questioned the importance of the individual's conscience and consciousness of sin in Lutheran tradition. Stendahl calls attention to the fact that Paul hardly seems to have been bothered by a conscience tormented by the law. On the contrary, Paul alleges that "as to righteousness under the law" he has been "blameless" (Phil 3:6). This, Stendahl asserts, strikes a discordant note when compared with the notion of the Protestant Reformers that the law induces a contrition from which a person can only be released through the forgiveness and justification of Christ. But Paul does not seem to have been bothered by any remorse and bears no witness to having any difficulty in keeping the Torah.

According to Stendahl, Luther's interpretation of Paul must be seen against the background of the medieval complex of problems that focused on the forgiveness of sins. Paul, however, rarely uses the term "forgiveness," and his discussion of the law, Stendahl argues, appears in a context *where the salvation of the non-Jews is at stake.* Thus what in the original Pauline context concerned the *possibility* of salvation for the non-Jew came instead to confirm the *assurance* of salvation for Luther. By letting the law become a general principle leading to "legalism," an extraordinary twist occurs, which Stendahl describes in the following manner:

> Paul's argument that the Gentiles must not, and should not come to Christ *via* the Law, i.e., *via* circumcision etc., has turned into a statement according to which all men must come to Christ with consciences properly convicted by the Law and its insatiable requirements for righteousness. So drastic is the reinterpretation once the original framework of "Jews and Gentiles" is lost, and the Western problems of conscience become its unchallenged and self-evident substitute.[3]

In a way that in many respects anticipates the later development of Pauline scholarship, Stendahl claims that there is a considerable difference between what Paul originally had in mind when discussing the law and the interpretation it was given later in Lutheran tradition. Through this claim he breaks up the alliance between historical exegesis and theological reflection that traditionally has characterized the Lutheran view of Paul and relates the problem to a salvation-historical context, allowing for a theological development of Pauline themes. In addition to this, Stendahl clearly demonstrates that Christian theology does not have to give rise to a conflict between Paul and Judaism. It is worth

noticing that even though more recent scholars have proceeded even
further in placing Paul within Jewish tradition, Stendahl offered a plausible alternative to the traditional view of Paul and Judaism already in
the beginning of the 1960s.

What Stendahl ultimately calls in question is the function of the law,
and by this he attacks a cardinal point in traditional Lutheran theology.
Stendahl's article serves as a most appropriate point of departure for
presenting Ernst Käsemann's approach to the relation between Paul
and Judaism. In 1969, Käsemann published the book *Paulinische
Perspektiven* (*Perspectives on Paul*), in which he devoted an entire chapter
to criticizing Stendahl's interpretation of Paul.

Ernst Käsemann (1906–1998) wrote his doctoral thesis in Marburg
under the supervision of Rudolf Bultmann and defended it in 1931.
Käsemann was perhaps the Bultmann disciple who most explicitly
broke with his teacher. The breach, however, was confined to theological and scholarly matters, and in this he was even spurred by Bultmann,
who readily encouraged his disciples to develop their own standpoints.
Bultmann was, as we noted above, programmatically uninterested in
the historical Jesus. For Käsemann, who believed that Paul's doctrine
of justification was based on the teachings of Jesus, it was crucial to
build a bridge between the historical Jesus and the gospel of the early
church. Thus Käsemann was one of the scholars responsible for the
fresh impetus to carry out research on the historical Jesus enjoyed in
postwar Germany. After holding teaching posts in Mainz and Göttingen,
he became a New Testament professor in Tübingen in 1959, a post he
retained until his retirement in 1971.

In several ways, Käsemann was a radical scholar, driven both by
the ambition to combine theology with exegetical scholarship and by a
social commitment. Prior to his academic career, he argued for the right
of women to preach, and later on he partially supported the growing
student movement of the 1960s. Even when it comes to Paul, Käsemann
broke with Bultmann by emphasizing that God's justification is not
only given as a gift, but that it should also be seen as a transforming
power that overcomes the present evil age and places the entire creation under the supremacy of God. Although this may be seen as a
reaction against the traditional, individualistically oriented Lutheran
understanding of justification, Käsemann, as we will see, was deeply

rooted in the prevalent tradition of the Reformation regarding the approach to Judaism.

Käsemann's critique of Stendahl shows above all that his interest was not restricted to the historical question of whether or not the center of Paul's theology was "justification by faith." He opens his treatment of Stendahl with a description of the mainly negative theological consequences he sees resulting from viewing the New Testament texts from a salvation-historical perspective. Käsemann fears that Stendahl's ideas might have negative consequences for the Protestant church. Thus when Käsemann defends what he views as the focal point of Pauline theology — justification by faith — it is important to note that he does not solely, or even mainly, deal with the matter from a purely historical perspective. Käsemann, like Bultmann, personifies the synthesis between a New Testament exegete and a Protestant theologian, and the conclusions he arrives at are essentially subordinated to theological considerations.

Käsemann does not deny that Paul adopted a salvation-historical perspective. On the contrary, he argues that it is impossible to understand Paul without taking salvation-historical aspects into account. But in Käsemann's opinion, Paul does not view history as an ongoing evolution, but considers it to be determined by the contrast between Adam and Christ. According to Käsemann, Paul expresses this contrast by means of the opposing terms "death" and "life," "sin" and "salvation," "law" and "gospel." In this way, there is no direct contradiction between a salvation-historical perspective and Paul's teaching of justification by faith. In Käsemann's view, it is simply a consequence of Paul's apocalyptic view of history.

Paul's doctrine of justification by faith, however, emanates from his conflict with Judaism, Käsemann argues. But the fact that this is a "fighting doctrine, directed against Judaism" (*antijudaistische Kampfeslehre*) does not mean that it should be given a subordinate place in Pauline theology. If this were the case, Käsemann continues, a chasm would open between modern Protestantism and the Reformers' interpretation of Paul, thus between modern Protestantism and the Reformation itself. The fact that justification by faith traces its origins from a specific historical situation does not render it devoid of meaning.

On the other hand, the doctrine of justification by faith stands and falls with the struggle against Judaism, and one must ask what this represents today. According to Käsemann, Jewish nomism ultimately reflects the community of "good" people who turn the promises of God to their own benefit, using his commandments as a means for self-sanctification. This attitude characterizes the Pharisees, the Zealots, and the Qumran community. But Käsemann claims that God, on the contrary, turns to the "ungodly," the tax collectors and sinners, but not the pious, those who were mainly his adversaries and finally crucified him. Against Stendahl, Käsemann contends that Paul's ultimate theological focal point is justification by faith, which is also the interpretive key with which all Pauline texts should be read. This is further emphasized in Käsemann's 1969 commentary on Romans, *An die Römer* (*Commentary on Romans*), in which he again and again maintains that the basis for understanding Paul is the latter's unique understanding of Habakkuk 2:4 in Romans 1:17, which, according to Käsemann, is without parallel in Jewish sources.

The principal problem of Israel is not sin, Käsemann claims, but "pious works." By trusting in legal deeds, the Jews have placed themselves outside the possibility of salvation and are at the mercy of the cosmic powers that keep those who do not surrender to grace imprisoned. The inability of the Jewish people to comprehend God's plan even has a demonic aspect, according to Käsemann, for it leads to an active resistance to the spirit of God manifested through the Christian message. According to the doctrine of justification by faith, salvation is only possible for the lost and the damned — the ungodly — while the "good" and the "pious" imagine that they can escape the impending judgment by means of their deeds. But in Käsemann's opinion there is also hope for Israel, because Paul in Romans 9–11 most explicitly expects Israel to be saved in the last days after they have abandoned the way of deeds and turned to the way of grace.

Käsemann's interpretation of Paul's relationship to Judaism is completely determined by classical Reformation theology, which rests on the contrast between the law and the gospel, between Judaism and Christianity, and which presupposes the image of Judaism that we have already seen represented by Weber, Bousset, and Bultmann. Käsemann repeats most of the stereotypes: Judaism represents legalism and the striving for self-justification, and Paul's theology is distinguished by a radical criticism of the basis for Jewish piety — the Torah. Judaism is characterized by insecurity regarding the salvation of the individual, while Christianity is distinguished by enjoying peace with God. While the original aim of the law was to give evidence of God's salvation, the Jewish attitude to the law is a complete misconception of this end. Paul, and consequently Christianity, represent grace and mercy through "the justification of the ungodly," and Paul's doctrine of justification by faith ultimately constitutes the proclamation of the kingdom of God, as proclaimed by Jesus.

Günther Bornkamm

Günther Bornkamm (1905–1990) wrote his doctoral thesis under the supervision of Bultmann in the beginning of the 1930s and occupied the New Testament professorial chair in Heidelberg between 1949 and 1971. In this capacity, he, like Bultmann and Käsemann, came to exert a great influence on the generation of theologians that emerged in the postwar era, and stands with both feet squarely planted in German Protestant soil. Bornkamm also was deeply engaged in the research on the historical Jesus and was one of the forerunners in the redaction-historical work with the Gospel texts. But he was also an expert on Paul and, as was the case with Bultmann and Käsemann, he personified the synthesis between scholar and theologian. The hermeneutic framework guiding his scholarship is basically the same dialectic relation between the law and the gospel that we see in Luther's writings.

In 1969, Bornkamm published the book *Paulus* (*Paul*), consisting of a historical survey of the life of the apostle and an exposition of his principal theological ideas. It is evident here that even though Bornkamm distanced himself from Bultmann in many areas, he follows in the footsteps of his teacher when it comes to the relationship between Paul and Judaism. This appears, for instance, in his interpretation of Paul's letter to the Romans. A fundamental question that has occupied many scholars is whether Romans constitutes a summary of Paul's theology, or if Paul was dealing with some specific issue in the Roman community. Based on Romans 11:11-24, Käsemann, for instance, maintains that the purpose of the letter was to cope with a schism within the community, caused by the Jesus-believing non-Jews who considered themselves superior to the Jesus-believing Jews and accordingly treated them with arrogance. Bornkamm argues, however,

that the letter rather represents Paul's spiritual testament, at least historically. It was not a specific situation in the Roman community that
caused Paul to write Romans, but his own past experience with his
churches. This is how one can understand the thoroughgoing polemic
character of the letter: it is the struggle against Judaism that is the
focal point. Paul's adversaries in Romans do not belong to any special
group in the community: they are the Jews and the Jewish understanding of salvation. The Jew, Bornkamm continues, represents the
"religious man," who through the law gains insight into what God
demands, and because of this claims a special place in the divine plan
of salvation, but refuses to admit his or her failure to comply with
God's demands, and hence is abandoned to sin and death.

The center of Pauline theology is, of course, the doctrine of justification by faith, Bornkamm maintains, and he refutes the criticism
from scholars who have called this into question. In the same manner
as Käsemann, Bornkamm emphasizes the enduring importance of this
doctrine, even though it originated in a specific historical situation —
the struggle against Judaism. In spite of this, one should not attribute
less importance to it since it is precisely this unique idea that makes it
possible for Paul to break with Judaism and Jewish-oriented Christianity.
The doctrine of justification by faith made the Jews the mortal enemies of Paul, Bornkamm continues, and caused the split between
Judaism and Christianity. At the same time, it unified the church,
which was made up of Jews and non-Jews, and gave it its first real
theological foundation. In addition to this, Bornkamm argues, Paul's
theological reflection on the law, justification, and atonement shows
that Paul was a former Torah-observant Jew and that other Jews
regarded him as an apostate.

In Bornkamm's opinion, Paul entirely rejects the ability of the law
to lead anyone to salvation. All of humanity is subject to the law under
the same conditions, and all are burdened with guilt before God.
Human beings have exchanged "the truth about God for a lie" (Rom
1:25) and "natural intercourse for unnatural" (Rom 1:26), which is a
result of God's wrath. Humans know through the law what God
demands, but no one knows God. Even though Paul does not deny the
possibility that both Jews and non-Jews to a certain extent may be able
to fulfill what the law requires (Rom 2:14; Phil 3:6), such an endeavor

does not make a person righteous. In this respect the Jew represents the perfect example, according to Bornkamm: by believing to be devoted to God, attempting to obtain righteousness, the Jew hopes to gain access to God by means of the Torah. But the Jew is also lost, and the road to communion with God is closed. The original purpose of the law was to lead humans to life, but it can in reality lead no one to righteousness and salvation, according to Bornkamm's interpretation of Paul. The law can only provide knowledge of sin and is thus given a different function in the divine plan of salvation: to multiply sin and so demonstrate its devastating power in its entire fullness. Only in this way, indirectly and in a paradoxical manner, can the law function as an instrument of salvation.

It is only by means of justification by faith that a person can be saved when God ascribes his own righteousness to the sinner who is anything but righteous. This is the new covenant, which stands in direct opposition to the old Sinai covenant, which was reserved for Israel and moreover, severely flawed. Those who surrendered and were confronted with their insufficiency are justified by faith and represent the true Israel, Bornkamm asserts. This means that justification by faith becomes the deathblow to the traditional Jewish view of being a chosen people within the framework of the covenant.

Thus according to Bornkamm, Judaism represents the complete misunderstanding of God's true plan for humanity. The normal way for the Jew to relate to God by means of the law and the covenant is the best way of exemplifying the apostasy of humanity. The religious life of the pious Jew is completely rejected. Judaism is simply a perverted form of religion, characterized by a misdirected religious aspiration for righteousness. When Jews do their best to approach God, God is more remote than ever. The God of Israel is absent and inaccessible; the Jew is abandoned to God's wrath, beyond all salvation, while struggling to attain communion with him by means of the law. Paul recognized the total inadequacy of the law in making humans righteous and directing them toward salvation, according to Bornkamm. This is the reason why Paul abandoned Judaism and instead proclaimed his doctrine of justification by faith alone, which is the key to understanding the entire gospel and the absolute antithesis to the Jewish way of reasoning. With Bornkamm, the contrast between Paul and Judaism, as with Bultmann and Käsemann, is absolute.

Paul versus Judaism

The Standard View of Paul and Judaism

The view of Paul's relationship to Judaism that appears in the works of Bultmann, Käsemann, and Bornkamm in all essentials represents the standard view among the majority of New Testament scholars in the middle of the twentieth century. As such, it also constitutes an important aspect of the theological foundation for the Christian church, especially the Lutheran churches, but Roman Catholic theology also presupposes a clear distinction between Paul and Judaism. Until the 1970s, this understanding was practically unchallenged. This does not apply only to Germany: the image of Paul and Christianity as the antithesis of Judaism was shared among scholars across national and denominational boundaries. Even though the situation has considerably changed over the last decades, most New Testament scholars even today take for granted that Paul's theology resulted in his abandoning Judaism.

As we have seen with Bultmann, Käsemann, and Bornkamm, this implies that Paul criticizes Judaism *from a position outside of Judaism.* Most scholars and theologians, of course, admit that Paul once shared the Jewish faith and then adhered to Jewish practice regarding the Torah. But they usually interpret Paul's experience on the road to Damascus as a conversion from one religion to another: the Jew Saul became the Christian Paul. Hence, his statements regarding the Torah became a substantial part of the conflict between Judaism and Christianity. This also indicates how scholars usually perceive the relations between Jews and non-Jews within the Pauline communities. As Paul is assumed to have proclaimed "the Torah-free gospel" and completely rejected the relevance of the Torah for Jesus-believing Jews as well, scholars often imagine the emergence of an entirely new religious group—the Christians. This group is usually assumed to be characterized by a common religious identity expressed in terms of a common faith and a common religious behavior, which did not include Torah observance.

Paul's adversaries are primarily the Jews, but also Jesus-believing Jews who, according to Paul, misunderstood "the truth of the gospel" (Gal 2:14). This truth is usually understood as Paul's doctrine of justification by faith, sharply contrasted against the Jewish notion of justification by means of the law. As Paul is supposed to have rejected the possibility of the Torah to implement its original purpose — to lead humans to salvation — every tendency to interpret justification or salvation in Jewish categories implies a direct violation of the very foundation of the gospel.

It is important to point out that this notion of Paul is not a pure invention. In the first place, it is not unreasonable to imagine that Paul really abandoned Judaism: there are lots of examples of Jews who chose to deny their religious heritage. One of the most famous is Tiberius Julius Alexander, the nephew of the Jewish philosopher Philo, who pursued a brilliant career in the Roman army.[4] In 1 Maccabees 1:11-15, the author castigates those Jews who strove to turn Jerusalem into a Greek city and in reality aimed at becoming Greeks themselves (cf. Josephus, *A.J.* 12.241):

> In those days certain renegades came out from Israel and misled many, saying, "Let us go and make a covenant with the Gentiles around us, for since we separated from them many disasters have come upon us." This proposal pleased them, and some of the people eagerly went to the king, who authorized them to observe the ordinances of the Gentiles. So they built a gymnasium in Jerusalem, according to Gentile custom, and removed the marks of circumcision [*kai epoiēsan heautois akrobustian*], and abandoned the holy covenant. They joined with the Gentiles and sold themselves to do evil.

Circumcision constituted a special problem for Jewish men who wanted to become part of Greek society, as the Greeks considered circumcision as a vulgar mutilation and regarded it with undisguised contempt.[5] In *De medicina*, a work by the Roman author Celsus, of whom virtually nothing is known, but who probably practiced medicine during the first century CE, an operation aimed at reconstructing the foreskin is described.[6] Celsus specifically refers to circumcision (*Med.* 7.25.1):

> If the glans is bare and the man wishes for the look of the thing to have it covered, that can be done; but more easily in a boy than in a man; in one in whom the defect is natural, than in one who after the custom of certain races has been circumcised.

It is quite likely that this is what Paul refers to in 1 Corinthians 7:18 when he admonishes Jesus-believing Jews not to "remove the marks of circumcision [*mē epispasthō*]."[7] This implies that at least some Jews were prepared to suffer considerable pains in order to achieve a new religious and social identity.

Josephus mentions another example of a Jew who became a Greek. In Antioch, during the Jewish War, Josephus states, a certain Antiochus, the son of the "chief magistrate of the Jews," "entered the theatre during an assembly of the people and denounced his own father and the other Jews, accusing them of a design to burn down the whole city in one night" (*B.J.* 7.47). Evidently, this Antiochus had gone so far in his renunciation of Judaism that he actually had adopted Greek cultic customs. Josephus continues (*B.J.* 7.50) by stating that Antiochus "further inflamed their fury; for, thinking to furnish proofs of his conversion and of his detestation of Jewish customs by sacrificing after the manner of the Greek, he recommended that the rest should be compelled to do the same." It is possible, as John Barclay has suggested, that Antiochus, like Tiberius Julius Alexander, was a Roman officer.[8] That certain Jews abandoned Judaism is rather self-evident and is also confirmed by the sources.

It is also evident that many Pauline texts may very well be used as support for the opinion that Paul abandoned Judaism. For instance, in Romans 2:17-22, Paul seems to attack the very foundation of Judaism by seemingly presenting the Jews as unable to keep the entire law:

> But if you call yourself a Jew and rely on the law and boast of your relation to God and know his will and determine what is best because you are instructed in the law, and if you are sure that you are a guide to the blind, a light to those who are in darkness, a corrector of the foolish, a teacher of children, having in the law the embodiment of knowledge and truth, you, then, that teach others, will you not teach yourself? While you preach against stealing, do you steal? You that forbid adultery, do you commit adultery? You that abhor idols, do you rob temples?

In Romans 3:21-24, Paul contrasts the justification provided by the law against justification by faith in Jesus:

But now, apart from law, the righteousness of God has been disclosed, and is attested by the law and the prophets, the righteousness of God through faith in Jesus Christ for all who believe. For there is no distinction, since all have sinned and fall short of the glory of God; they are now justified by his grace as a gift, through the redemption that is in Christ Jesus.

In Galatians 2:16, he certainly seems to state that no one can be justified through the Torah:

We know that a person is justified not by the works of the law but through faith in Jesus Christ. And we have come to believe in Christ Jesus, so that we might be justified by faith in Christ, and not by doing the works of the law, because no one will be justified by the works of the law.

In 1 Corinthians 9:20-23, he definitely seems to have abandoned the Torah and replaced it with "Christ's law":

To the Jews I became as a Jew, in order to win Jews. To those under the law I became as one under the law (though I myself am not under the law) so that I might win those under the law. To those outside the law I became as one outside the law (though I am not free from God's law but am under Christ's law) so that I might win those outside the law. To the weak I became weak, so that I might win the weak. I have become all things to all people, that I might by all means save some. I do it all for the sake of the gospel, so that I may share in its blessings.

There is nothing incongruous in principle in the idea that Paul abandoned Judaism or rejected the salvation system of the Torah. Some Jews evidently did so. Moreover, there are undoubtedly passages in Paul's letters that lend support to this idea.

However, it is important to realize that the interpretations hinted at above are not the only possible ones, and that they are dependent on the overarching assumption that Paul abandoned Judaism. Thus the idea that Paul abandoned Judaism does not unequivocally follow from an absolute interpretation of certain passages in his letters. In fact, to a considerable degree, it is quite the opposite: the specific interpretations

of certain Pauline texts that result in the conclusion that Paul opposed
Judaism are often the result of the assumption that he actually abandoned Judaism. As we will see in the next chapters, it is fully possible
to create a coherent picture of Paul from the assumption that he did not
break with Judaism but remained a Torah-observant Jew even after his
experience on the way to Damascus.

There is a good deal of truth in Stanley Fish's observation:

> Sentences emerge only in situations, and within those situations, the
> normative meaning of an utterance will always be obvious or at least
> accessible, although within another situation that same utterance, no
> longer the same, will have another normative meaning that will be no
> less obvious and accessible.[9]

Fish's point is that the same utterance can be given several, equally
intelligible interpretations depending on the assumption of the interpreter.
However, the fact that a text can be understood in a certain way is no guarantee that it is understood in the way the author intended. As in every
semiotic system, that is, a system that uses signs and symbols, texts need
to be decoded in order to produce meaning, and since the interpretive key
is linked to a certain context, or "situation" to use Fish's terminology, familiarity with the original situation is crucial if we aim at decoding the original meaning of a certain text. Thus to some extent it is true that a given
text means only what the interpreter claims it means, and the reader can
only understand it against the background of his or her own experience.

When we read texts from our own time, in our own language, it is
likely that we "understand" them correctly, that is, as the author
intended them to be understood. But even contemporary texts may be
difficult to interpret. To perceive irony or allusions to other texts or cultural idiosyncrasies is not always an uncomplicated matter. With regard
to some literary genres, such as poetry, it is not entirely certain that the
author intended to convey one specific meaning only.

When trying to understand texts from another culture, separated
from our own by an ocean of time and written in a language no longer
spoken, and dealing with cultural or religious phenomena that are not
entirely known, the probability that our interpretation agrees with the
author's intention diminishes considerably. An obvious danger, for

example, is that our experience of modern phenomena similar to the ones we read about in ancient texts influences our understanding. When someone with a Christian background reads about "the cup of blessing," "the bread that we break," and "the body of Christ" in 1 Corinthians 10:14-16, it is likely that knowledge about the modern Christian Eucharist influences the interpretation of the text. A Jewish reader would perhaps rather see a parallel to the Sabbath celebration, which is probably closer to the truth. Either way, the danger of anachronism is looming when approaching texts from antiquity.

The meaning of a word and its syntactic function certainly limits the number of possible interpretations of a certain text. But even if we know the meaning of a specific word and its syntactic function in a sentence, this does not mean that we understand the word reference. What does Paul *mean* with the term "works of the law" in Galatians 2:16? The Greek words *nomos* and *ergon* can be looked up in a dictionary, and by means of a grammar one may find out that "law" is a genitive attribute to the word "work" and that the construction may be translated verbatim as "works of the law." *But what does it actually mean?* In order to understand this, we have to leave the specific text world and search for the same, or a similar expression, in other literary works, in order to understand Paul's reference. Regarding this specific expression, central to our understanding of Paul's view of the Torah, things are somewhat complicated since the only known parallels are found in the Qumran texts, and the meaning of the phrase in these texts is disputed.[10]

Hence no texts can be understood without an interpretive framework, and no texts are in fact read without a certain interpretive framework that determines the outcome of the reading. It is important to realize that the traditional picture of the antithetical relation between Paul and Judaism rests on two cornerstones that are partly intertwined: a long anti-Jewish tradition within the Christian church, and Luther's emphasis of an absolute contradiction between the law and the gospel. This means that the traditional view of the relationship between Paul and Judaism is primarily a theological construction that has constituted the normal interpretive framework for generations of Pauline scholars. The image of Judaism that evolved at the end of the nineteenth century was not intended to present Judaism on its own terms. What was

presented was the Christian conception of Judaism, and the sole purpose was to create a background for understanding the New Testament.

Ironically, this basically Protestant paradigm seems to have been
adapted also by Roman Catholic exegetes. The emphasis within Protestantism on the biblical text—*sola scriptura*—was an important early
impetus to biblical scholarship and was, of course, also a reaction
against the Roman Catholic stress on the importance of tradition. Moreover, the struggle against modernism in the Roman Catholic Church
around the turn of the last century also meant that severe restrictions
were imposed on Roman Catholic scholars when it came to employing
the heritage from the Enlightenment. It was only after the papal encycli-
cal *Divino afflante spiritu* of Pius XII was promulgated in 1943 that
Roman Catholic exegetes were encouraged to use modern methods,
something that was also emphasized by the Second Vatican Council
(1962–1965). However, in the case of the view of Judaism, Protestant
biblical scholarship had already worked out a framework of interpretation about which there was a near consensus.

Early Protests

In spite of the scholarly consensus established in the late nineteenth
century concerning the nature of Judaism, there were some who raised
objections. In 1914, the British scholar Claude Joseph Goldsmid
Montefiore (1858–1938) published the book *Judaism and St. Paul*. In the
first essay, "The Genesis of the Religion of St. Paul," he posed the question whether rabbinic Judaism, which Christian scholars had mainly
used as a model for reconstructing the Judaism contemporary with
Paul, really was the religion Paul had turned against. Montefiore was
one of the few Jewish scholars who at this time took an interest in
Christianity, and against the background of his insights into rabbinic
Judaism, the consensus opinion that Paul came from a tradition similar
to rabbinic Judaism seemed peculiar.

Against Bultmann's reconstruction of ancient Judaism, for
instance, Paul's rejection of it appears intelligible. If the Judaism Paul
knew really was characterized by legalism, belief in a distant God, and
was unable to lead anyone to righteousness and salvation, it is no wonder Paul had raised objections against it. But Montefiore's picture of

rabbinic Judaism is an entirely different one. He begins his essay by criticizing Christian scholars for not having taken pains to check whether their ideas of Judaism were substantiated by Jewish texts. Quite sardonically he writes:

> Rabbinic Judaism seems to be the one department of learning about which many great scholars have been willing to make assertions without being able to read the original authorities, or to test the references and statements of the writers whom they quote.[11]

Montefiore asserts that in fact rabbinic Judaism presents God as personal and exalted, but at the same time present and utterly involved in the history of the Jewish people. The God of the rabbis is above all characterized by love and mercy and can be accessed without any mediator. The relationship between the Jewish people and the God of Israel is like the one between parents and children. God has endowed his people with his most precious gift, the Torah, with the purpose of giving them joy and helping them fulfill their calling to be a holy people.

The Torah, according to Montefiore, is solely a manifestation of God's concern for his people, and the rabbis considered it a privilege and an honor to be chosen to live according to the Torah. Measures were, of course, taken against violations, and faithfulness toward the Torah was rewarded, but no one really believed they could earn their salvation by observing the Torah. Montefiore emphasizes that the Torah was intended to be kept in its entirety, and that failure to do so incurred God's wrath. But God's mercy and grace are greater than his wrath, which is the reason why the Torah includes an opportunity for Jews to atone for their sins and restore a broken relationship to God. Thus the Jews' inability to keep the Torah is already envisioned by the Torah itself and possible to deal with.

Against the background of Montefiore's view of rabbinic Judaism, it appears highly unlikely that Paul would have found reasons to abandon Judaism. Montefiore poses the question whether Paul in fact, held views characteristic of rabbinic Judaism prior to his "conversion" and reaches the conclusion that Paul must have been familiar with some other form of Judaism and was influenced by other non-Jewish intellectual systems. According to Montefiore, Paul cannot be understood against the background of rabbinic Judaism.

Montefiore was not alone in lodging these kinds of objections. Already in 1909, the Jewish theologian Salomon Schechter (1847–1915) had given a similar presentation of rabbinic Judaism and posed the same question regarding Paul.[12] Toward the end of the 1920s, George Foot Moore (1851–1931), the professor of Hebrew language and literature at Harvard, in his work *Judaism in the First Centuries of the Christian Era,* was astonished by the fact that Paul so completely seemed to have ignored the Jewish atonement system clearly evidenced in rabbinic literature.[13] In 1921, Moore published a remarkably sharp critical article about Christian research on Judaism entitled "Christian Writers on Judaism," which ends with a complete rejection of the scholarship of, for instance, Weber, Schürer, and Bousset. With regard to the characterization of ancient Judaism as "legalistic," Moore notes that this is a new feature that never occupied scholars during the seventeenth and eighteenth centuries "who knew the literature immeasurably better than their modern successors."[14] The reason why Weber had now brought it to the fore is, according to Moore,

> not a fresh and more thorough study of Judaism at the beginning of our era, but a new apologetic motive, consequent on a different apprehension on Christianity on the part of the New Testament theologians who now took up the task. The "essence" of Christianity, and therefore its specific difference from Judaism, was for the first time sought in the religion of Jesus—his teaching and his personal piety. . . . Jesus' conflict with the Scribes and Pharisees prescribed for this apologetic the issue of legalism; the "Father in heaven," the piety assumed to be distinctive of Jesus and his teaching, demanded an antithesis in Judaism, an inaccessible God, which Weber from his starting point was supposed to have demonstrated.[15]

The critique of Montefiore, Schechter, and Moore, among others, had no real impact. Their criticism was drowned out by the emerging Protestant biblical scholarship and the distorted picture of Paul as the definite opposite of Judaism continued to dominate both within theology and at the universities. These early protests demonstrated, however, something quite essential: those who knew rabbinic Judaism did not feel at home with the traditional view of the religion Paul was supposed to have abandoned. For the traditional image of Paul, the Christian construction of Judaism was indispensable, and the critique thus pinpointed the very important question, *how to understand Paul if the traditional assumptions were incorrect*. This will be the focus of our next chapter.

4

TOWARD A NEW
PERSPECTIVE ON PAUL

A Changed World

The Post-War Era

World War II fundamentally changed the conditions for research on
Judaism and early Christianity. When the atrocities of the death
camps became widely known, time was ripe for a serious reassessment
of the synthesis between theology and biblical scholarship. It became
increasingly evident that there was a direct relationship between the
anti-Jewish Christian theology and the industrialized mass murder of
six million Jews. The Christian church that almost twenty centuries
had defined itself in contrast to a distorted picture of Judaism no
doubt shared the responsibility for the worst crime against humanity
in history.

A tangible step on the way toward increased understanding
between Christians and Jews was the establishment of various organizations like The Council of Christians and Jews in the United Kingdom,
founded in 1942, and L'Amitiés Judéo-Chrétienne de France, founded
in 1947. The same year, more than sixty Roman Catholic, Protestant,
and Jewish theologians met in Seelisberg at the International Confer-
ence of Christians and Jews with the purpose of promoting "brotherly
love toward the sorely-tried people of the old covenant."[1] When the
World Council of Churches met for its constituent general assembly in
Amsterdam in 1948, the relationship between the church and the

Jewish people was also on the agenda. In one document, it was clearly stated that the churches "in the past have helped to foster an image of the Jews as the sole enemies of Christ, which has contributed to anti-Semitism in the secular world" and that anti-Semitism "is a sin against God and man,"[2] revealing that an awareness of the liability of the church had begun to take shape. Within the Protestant churches, official commissions started to form with the aim of dealing with matters pertaining to the relations of the church with the Jewish people.

Prior to the Second Vatican Council (1962–1965), the relations between the Roman Catholic Church and Judaism were not that formalized, but dependent on certain individuals and organizations within the church. In spite of this, several concrete results could be noticed, not the least of which were changes in certain liturgical texts. In 1955, Pope Pius XII introduced a genuflection at the prayer for the Jews in the Good Friday liturgy, and in 1960 Pope John XXIII removed the adjective *perfidis*, "faithless," so that the prayer was now simply "for the Jews." In September 1960, Pope John XXIII instructed the Secretariat for Promoting Christian Unity to prepare a declaration for the forthcoming council regarding the relations of the church with the Jews. Five years later the declaration *Nostra Aetate,* concerning the relations of the church with the non-Christian religions, and including a specific passage on the Jews, was voted through by a large majority. The declaration states that "the Jews should not be presented as rejected or accursed by God,"[3] but also mentions that many Jews interfered with the spreading of the gospel. "Jerusalem did not recognize the time of her visitation," it is stated, "nor did the Jews in large number accept the Gospel; indeed not a few opposed its spreading."[4] The church is presented as the new people of God, and no explicit comments touch upon the old accusation that the Jews should be considered guilty of deicide.

Earlier drafts of the document had been much more far-reaching, but had to be rejected for political reasons. One version from 1964 even expressed the gratitude of the church toward the Jewish people and clearly repudiated the charge of deicide.[5] The final official declaration is no doubt a watered-down version compared to previous drafts, but still probably represents the most radical attempt to clarify the relationship of the Christian church to Judaism. It is, furthermore, clear that there were strong forces striving to work for an even more radical wording.

Even though this incipient change, both in the Protestant churches and the Roman Catholic Church, meant a certain improvement of the official relations between Christianity and Judaism and led to some practical alterations, one must also point out that among the absolute majority of scholars and theologians, the attitude was "business as usual." It is worthwhile to notice that Bultmann in his works at the end of the 1940s not only passed on the classic view of Judaism without reflection, but also, only a few years after the war, formulated his thesis that the purpose of Jewish law was to lead to death. Did he, in the unspeakable sufferings of the Jewish people under the Nazi regime, see the fulfillment of the "curse of the law" (Gal 3:13), or was he simply unable to discern the connection between a specific theology and its practical consequences? As we have seen above, Käsemann and Bornkamm also reproduced a traditionally Lutheran and basically anti-Jewish view of Judaism. The connection between anti-Jewish theology and anti-Jewish political ideology is, however, not entirely uncomplicated. Although the works of Bultmann, Bornkamm, and Käsemann are based on a very negative image of Judaism, Bornkamm and Käsemann were active in the German Confessing Church (*die bekennende Kirche*), which openly opposed the Nazi ideology, and Bultmann at least supported it.[6]

But even though most scholars and theologians continued to repeat the traditional stereotypes about Paul and his relationship to Judaism, others seriously started to ponder other alternatives, often inspired by the evolving Jewish-Christian dialogue. An excellent example of this is Krister Stendahl, with whose work we have already become acquainted.

Exegetical Reorientation—Krister Stendahl

Krister Stendahl (1921–2008) earned his Ph.D. from Uppsala University and was New Testament professor at Harvard Divinity School between 1958 and 1984. He went on to serve as the Bishop of Stockholm until 1988, then returned to the United States where he was for many years a prominent figure in the Jewish-Christian dialogue. As early as the beginning of the 1960s, he held a series of lectures bearing witness to a rare ability to assume a critical stance toward his own tradition and a far-reaching desire to understand the New Testament against the background of its proper context. Stendahl's works contain many of the basic perspectives later to be found in more recent research on Paul, which means that he must be regarded as an extraordinarily farsighted scholar.

In contrast to many other Lutheran scholars, Stendahl makes a clear distinction between the original meaning of the text, its impact on society during the course of history (*Wirkungsgeschichte*), and the meaning it may have for the present-day church. Such a hermeneutically flexible attitude does not make it necessary to strive for a complete unity between the historical meaning of the text and the theology of the church. It is rather natural, Stendahl claims, that the church emphasizes other aspects than the author originally stressed. In the article discussed above in the section on Käsemann, "Paul and the Introspective Conscience of the West," Stendahl points out that there is a considerable difference between Paul's original intention and the interpretation ascribed to him by the Reformation, and just this is what Käsemann criticizes.

In a famous essay, "Paul among Jews and Gentiles," published only in 1976, but also based on lectures held in the beginning of the 1960s, Stendahl argues that the relationship between Jews and non-Jews wholly determined Paul's theology, not least his emphasis on "justification by faith alone," which Stendahl claims has been fundamentally misunderstood. The problem Luther wrestled with—how to find a merciful God—was not Paul's quandary. Paul's main interest was instead precisely the relationship between Jews and non-Jews. His reasoning on justification must also be seen as a special and unique argument in this complex of problems, Stendahl argues, and does not create a contrast between "Christianity" and "Judaism" or between "the law" and "the gospel."

The same misunderstanding concerns Paul's so-called conversion. It was not a question of Paul converting from one religion, Judaism, to another, Christianity, as most people have understood the texts in Acts, Stendahl asserts. Paul's own narrative of his changed outlook in Galatians 1:13-16 should rather be seen as one similar to the vocation of prophets we know from Isaiah and Jeremiah, where we also find allusions to the non-Jewish peoples. Isaiah 49:6 states that God will make his servant "a light to the nations" so that the salvation of God "may reach to the end of the earth." Similarly, Jeremiah is given the mission to be "a prophet to the nations" (Jer 1:5). According to Stendahl, Paul serves the same God as before, admittedly in a different way, but still directly linked to what was already part of Jewish tradition. Here again Stendahl maintains that we can see what determines Paul's theology: the conviction that he has been called to be an apostle to the non-Jews and not the conception that humans must be delivered from Jewish legalism or a guilt-ridden conscience.

Paul's reasoning on justification in Romans and Galatians must also be understood in connection with the relationship between Jews and non-Jews, which Stendahl argues does not have any bearing on the all-embracing question of whether humanity in general can be saved, or how a person's deeds will be judged some day. The question of justification should instead be related to those matters that constitute the actual center of the letter, namely Romans 9–11, according to Stendahl, where Paul deals with God's plan for the final salvation all of humanity and how the mission to the Jews fits into this plan. After emphasizing God's promises to Israel in the beginning of Romans 9, Paul continues by noting that the refusal of the Jewish people to accept Jesus as the Messiah of Israel has led to the situation where salvation now has been offered to the non-Jews. Stendahl argues that, according to Paul, God's plan seems to have anticipated the "no" of the Jews so that non-Jews also could be included in God's "yes." And in the end, Israel also will be saved (Rom 11:26-27), and there is evidently no contradiction between God's promise to Israel and the fact that non-Jews have been offered the same opportunity for salvation. Ultimately, Stendahl argues, this is exactly what the term usually translated "justification" means, namely "victory" and "salvation," and that God's righteousness in the end will set everything right.[7]

Stendahl's work has been extremely important for the development of the new view on Paul and has served as an inspiration for many scholars. What has already been pointed out, but deserves highlighting again, is the fact that much of what has come to characterize the latest research on Paul was already present in Stendahl's works in the 1960s. But those who questioned the traditional view of Paul in the 1960s and '70s had a common problem: the total dominance of the prevailing paradigm regarding Judaism in antiquity. Even those who did not share the view that Paul rose in rebellion against a dead, legalistic, self-righteous, and fundamentally perverted Judaism were confronted by a wall of Protestant lack of understanding—and not infrequently by a theologically motivated disinclination to understand. What was needed was a radical calling-in-question of the foundations of the predominant paradigm—a sweeping criticism of the negative Christian image of Judaism—so convincing that it simply had to be taken seriously.

The Prerequisite—A New View of Judaism

E. P. Sanders and Covenantal Nomism

In 1977, the American scholar Ed P. Sanders published the book *Paul and Palestinian Judaism*. This study, his first larger work, has probably contributed to the change in the view on ancient Judaism more than any other scholarly work of the twentieth century. Sanders was professor at McMaster University in Canada between 1966 and 1984, then at Oxford University in Great Britain until 1990, when he moved to Duke University in the United States.

   Although many of Sanders's conclusions had been hinted at in the works of other scholars, it was not until the emergence of Sanders's study that a true breakthrough was noticeable among New Testament scholars with regard to Paul's relationship to Judaism. However, Sanders's settlement with earlier research on Judaism has probably been more important than his suggestion about how Paul should be related to it. As we shall see, the conclusion concerning Paul that Sanders arrives at is in fact rather traditional, and the works of many later scholars stand out as far more radical.

The Pattern of Religion

Sanders notes that both Montefiore and Moore had made important contributions to the view of Paul's relationship to Judaism. As we saw in the previous chapter, they found it incomprehensible that Paul should have ignored the atonement institution found in rabbinic literature and reached the conclusion that he must have been familiar with some other kind of Judaism. When using the idea of how the individual attains salvation in rabbinic Judaism as a starting point, Paul's criticism of Judaism seems to rest on a fundamental misunderstanding. The flaw of previous scholarship, according to Sanders, was that it mainly focused on how certain individual Pauline motives also could be found in Jewish thinking. But what is really required, Sanders asserts, indicating his basic method, "is to answer the question of the basic relationship between Paul's religion and the religion reflected in Palestinian Jewish literature."[8]

Accordingly Sanders wants to broaden the issue to include a more basic comparison between the religion of Paul and Palestinian Judaism, especially with respect to the *function* of religion. This Sanders calls the "pattern of religion," which focuses on how "getting in" and "staying in" are perceived by the adherents of a certain religion. Sanders pays attention to individual motives only if they can be related to this overarching pattern, that is, their significance in the pattern of admitting and retaining members. By analyzing texts composed in the land of Israel between 200 BCE and 200 CE, Sanders thus aims at understanding the principles for the starting point of the religious life, its end, and what takes place in between.

Sanders starts his survey with a blistering criticism of how the notion of legalism and work-righteousness in rabbinic Judaism had been passed on from generation to generation. The main problem, Sanders states, is that New Testament scholars uncritically had taken over Weber's view of rabbinic Judaism without checking whether the sources supported this notion. This brings to the fore an important problem in all scholarship, namely, that most scholars are reduced to relying on other scholars when it comes to matters lying outside their own special field. A New Testament scholar must have a competence in a wide range of areas—philology (Greek, Latin, Hebrew, Aramaic), Greco-Roman religion, cultural and social history, Jewish studies, theology, and textual criticism. But few scholars are experts in more than one of these fields. In fact, most scholars have a good command only of parts of a larger field of scholarship. When it comes to matters outside the primary competence of the individual scholar, he or she is reduced to the standard views available in secondary literature.

These conditions are especially pertinent in the field of rabbinic literature. In order to master rabbinics, the scholar certainly must have a profound knowledge of Hebrew and Aramaic but also has to be intimately familiar with the literary genre as such. Rabbinic literature does not present a well-laid systematic theology, but is made up of extensive halakic discussions and creative, sometimes very imaginative, interpretations of the biblical text. The topic under discussion is often only hinted at since the rabbis assumed the reader to be conversant with the argument. To pan out "rabbinic theology" from this literature is an extremely difficult task, and requires a broad range of experience and a careful mode of procedure. There are indeed many pitfalls, and conclusions too hastily drawn may have far-reaching consequences, as the case of Weber and Jewish legalism clearly demonstrates.

Covenantal Nomism

Sanders continues his survey by scrutinizing the rabbinic Tannaitic literature, that is, the literature evolving during the period between the destruction of the Jerusalem temple in 70 CE and the completion of the Mishnah roughly around 200 CE, focusing on how the rabbis regarded the role of the covenant, the salvation of the individual, and the restoration of a broken relationship with God.

Sanders's reading of the Tannaitic literature completely contradicts the picture forwarded from Weber onwards. In fact, the entire interpretive framework upon which the traditional description of ancient Judaism was based is faulty, according to Sanders: the starting points were wrong, the texts were consistently misunderstood, and they were interpreted by means of a specific theological preunderstanding. This, Sanders states, is why the traditional picture of Judaism, from which the absolute majority of New Testament scholars started, in no way should be relied on.

The fundamental error, Sanders claims, is that scholars such as Weber and Bousset completely overlooked the importance of covenantal theology in rabbinic Judaism. The covenant is nothing less than the very key for correctly understanding the statements concerning punishment and reward in rabbinic Judaism. The foundation is the election—the idea that God has chosen Israel and entered into a covenant with the Jewish people. Israel in its turn has accepted the status as God's chosen people and, accordingly, the special conditions the covenant implies.

Within the framework of the covenant, God has given Israel the Torah, the commandments, which every individual is expected to keep to the best of his or her ability. God certainly punishes transgressions and rewards obedience, but Sanders, in contrast to Weber and in line with

Montefiore and Moore, points out that the Torah itself offers a system for expiating transgressions. The pattern, Sanders states, is as follows:

> God has chosen Israel and Israel has accepted the election. In his role as King, God gave Israel commandments which they are to obey as best they can. Obedience is rewarded and disobedience punished. In case of failure to obey, however, man has recourse to divinely ordained means of atonement, in all of which repentance is required. As long as he maintains his desire to stay in the covenant, he has a share in God's covenantal promises, including life in the world to come. The intention and effort to be obedient constitute the *condition for remaining in the covenant,* but they do not *earn* it.[9]

Thus whoever violates the commandments of the Torah can become reconciled with God, and the relationship between God and the individual can be restored. Keeping the Torah is not a means by which the individual can earn his or her place in the world to come, but a manifestation of a desire to remain in the covenant God has entered into with the Jewish people. This means that the rabbis were perfectly aware of the fact that the commandments were going to be violated, and precisely because of this there were far-ranging discussions on how various sins should be expiated. The individual striving to live according to the Torah fails now and then, but uses the opportunities the Torah offers to maintain a relationship with God. Such an individual is considered "righteous," and all the promises of the covenant are valid—even the one concerning a place in the world to come. The discussions about punishment and reward in Tannaitic literature, Sanders emphasizes, must be seen against this background—the basic pattern of rabbinic Judaism, which Sanders summarizes in the phrase *covenantal nomism:*

> Briefly put, covenantal nomism is the view that one's place in God's plan is established on the basis of the covenant and that the covenant requires as the proper response of man his obedience to its commandments, while providing means of atonement for transgression.[10]

Sanders then proceeds to examine the apocryphal and pseudepigraphal Jewish literature and the literature from Qumran. Even though he finds some deviations from the Tannaitic pattern of covenantal

nomism regarding specific details and how various aspects are emphasized, Sanders still arrives at the conclusion that in principle all literature
he has examined bears witness to the same basic pattern—covenantal
nomism. The Qumran sectarians indeed defined the covenant in a much
narrower way than other groups, believing that they alone were included
in the "true" covenant, while all other Jews and non-Jews were outside
it, and consequently in the end would face a terrible fate. But essentially
the religious system of the Qumran community also presupposed that
remaining within the covenant was ultimately dependent on the grace of
God: "the means of atonement are not precisely identical, but there is
agreement on the place of atonement within the total framework,"
Sanders states.[11]

In only one text, Sanders found that covenantal nomism had col-
lapsed and been replaced by legalistic perfectionism. The author of the
apocryphal book *4 Ezra* advocates an extreme degree of law-observance
in order to enable the individual to remain in the covenant, and seems to
have excluded the option of contrition and restoration. In *4 Ezra*, there
are no signs of divine grace, and only the one who can live a perfect life
can hope to be saved. Hence, according to the author, those who finally,
and after severe suffering, are saved will be a very small number.
Sanders believes that *4 Ezra* represents the opinion of an extreme minority and that its deep, dark pessimism must be seen against the background of the time when it was written—as a result of the destruction of
Jerusalem and the temple in 70 CE. These views, Sanders claims, were
not widely held prior to the fall of the temple, and the survey of Jewish
literature proves that they cannot be judged as representative for the
period after the destruction of the temple either.

Thus Judaism during the period in question, 200 BCE to 200 CE,
was, according to Sanders, characterized by covenantal nomism, a type
of religion where Torah observance was related to the idea that the
Jewish people had entered into a covenantal relationship with God.
God ultimately guarantees everyone who remains in the covenant a
place in the world to come, not as a result of human achievements, but
because of God's mercy.

Sanders's showdown with the traditional view of ancient Judaism
undoubtedly implied a serious challenge to New Testament scholarship.
Jewish "legalism" and "works-righteousness" had constituted such a

perfect background for explaining both Jesus and Paul. The idea of covenantal nomism as the characteristic pattern of Judaism thus called in question virtually all previous scholarship on Jesus, Paul, and the early Jesus movement. If the Pharisees did not represent legalism and hypocritical works-righteousness, why did Jesus criticize them? If it was possible to be reconciled with God within the framework of Judaism, what was the point of the redeeming death of Jesus? And why did Paul criticize the Torah if it was only a token for the will to live in communion with God?

These and similar questions were the direct consequences of Sanders's study. His presentation of Judaism would eventually result in a completely new direction with regard to the study of Paul. While previous scholarship mainly had taken for granted that Paul opposed Judaism, some scholars now started to ponder if it was possible to make Paul fit in with the Judaism of the first century CE. This new direction would eventually lead to a new opposition: between the traditional view of Paul and a new perspective in which the conflict between Paul and Judaism is significantly downplayed. However, as will be evident in chapter 6, Sanders's revision of first-century Judaism has not convinced all scholars, and there are indeed reasons to question whether Sanders was correct in all his conclusions. Before we engage in studying the development of the so-called new perspective on Paul, however, we will first see how Sanders viewed Paul's relation to a Judaism characterized by covenantal nomism.

New Perspectives on Paul

From Solution to Plight—Sanders on Paul

In *Paul and Palestinian Judaism* Sanders begins his description of Paul's religious system by questioning an important point of departure for Bultmann and Bornkamm, among others. They assumed that Paul first presented the reasons as to why humans were in need of salvation and then presented the solution to the problem—Christ. Thus according to the traditional perspective, Paul's argument runs *from plight to solution.* According to Sanders, however, Paul's reasoning was rather the opposite: Paul, in fact, started with the solution—God's redemption in

Christ—and then went on by explaining why humanity was in need of being saved in this specific way.

As Stendahl had done before, Sanders notes that Paul, prior to his experience on the road to Damascus, hardly expressed any need for salvation. Nor did Paul seem to have found it impossible or even difficult to live according to the Torah. Paul's conviction that both Jews and non-Jews were in need of salvation, Sanders argues, seems rather to have its basis in the idea that God actually had sent Jesus with the purpose of saving the world. Thus if God really had sent Christ as a savior, such a savior, of course, must have had been needed. With Paul the train of thought thus runs directly counter to the Protestant scheme from law to gospel, Sanders claims. Paul, in short, argued "backwards" from solution to plight.

Paul represents another type of religion than the one found in the Jewish literature, Sanders argues. There are certainly many points in common: for example, Paul seems to share the view that salvation comes about by grace, while deeds constitute a necessary condition for remaining in contact with God. But according to Sanders, Paul's attitude to the Torah is without precedent in Jewish tradition. The main difference is that the term "justification" in Jewish thinking means that the individual who lives according to the Torah retains his or her status as a member of the covenant with God. But with Paul "justification" simply means being saved through Christ, which in turn means that the believer surrenders to the supremacy of Christ. "Justification" with Paul is what Sanders labels "a transfer term" and is only related to the issue of how to *become* a member of the religion, not how to *remain* in the system.

Paul's religion, Sanders claims, is characterized by the individual's submission to the supremacy of Christ and hence his becoming a partaker of Christ's death and resurrection. Those who have been united with Christ in this manner have also been liberated from the power and resulting impurity of sin, from immoral living, and from "idolatry."

Paul does not deny that there is a righteousness coming from the law (Phil 3:9), but that is another kind of righteousness than the one that comes from faith in Jesus, which is the only one that leads to salvation. For this very reason, all other attempts to attain salvation are wrong. Paul's main objection to the Torah, according to Sanders, is that it does not constitute the way to salvation staked out by God. This is why it is wrong to follow the Torah. Not that the Torah per se is something evil, and certainly not because it represents a striving for self-righteousness. Instead, Sanders states that Paul's problem with Judaism is simply *that it is not Christianity*. Thus in Sanders's view Paul denies three vital aspects of Judaism: the election, the Torah, and the covenant.

In a later book, *Paul, the Law, and the Jewish People* (1983), Sanders repeats his basic understanding of Paul's view of the Jewish law, but more extensively develops how he conceives that Paul related to the Jewish people and to Judaism in general. Sanders argues that Paul actually created a "third race," that is, a new ethnic group in addition to Jews and non-Jews—the "Christians" (although Paul does not use this term). What speaks in favor of this, Sanders claims, is that Paul considers both Jews and non-Jews to unite with Christ in the same way—by faith. Even though a Jew who wants to become a member of the Jesus movement does not have to abjure anything and in theory can continue observing the Torah, it is no longer merely enough to be a member of the Jewish people to be included in God's salvation. The condition for entry is now faith in Jesus, and that goes for both Jews and non-Jews.

At the same time, there are certain doubts whether to identify this new group as "Israel." Sanders is of the opinion that Paul actually considers Jews and non-Jews to be the "true Israel," but notes at the same time that Paul does not employ this term. Only in one instance does Sanders believe that Paul applies the label "Israel" to both Jesus-believing Jews and non-Jews. The interpretation of this verse is, however, not entirely clear. In Galatians 6:16 Paul writes: "As for those who will follow this rule—peace be upon them, and mercy, and upon the Israel of God." Before the phrase "upon the Israel of God," the Greek text has the conjunction *kai,* usually translated as "and" or "as well." This is how the NRSV, quoted above, has understood the phrase. Sometimes, however, *kai* can have an epexegetical function, and then mean "that is," in this case serving as a description of "those who will follow this rule." The difference in meaning is, of course, considerable. In the latter case, the non-Jews to whom the letter is addressed are included in "God's Israel" while in the former case "Israel" represents a separate group to which Paul also wishes peace and mercy. Sanders argues that the second interpretation is the most likely one, but also notes that Paul refrains from using the term "Israel" for Jesus-believing Jews and non-Jews, probably because he knows that "Israel" also exists in the sense "Jews who do not believe in Jesus," and that this Israel will also eventually be included in the salvation of God (Rom 11:26-27).

According to Sanders, Paul's critique of Judaism includes two main points: first, the inability of the Torah to lead any individual to righteousness in the sense of "salvation," and second, the idea that the Jewish people, through the covenant, enjoy a special standing in relation to God. The opposition between Judaism and Christianity thus still remains also in Sanders's interpretation. At the same time, one should observe that even if Sanders in fact arrives at roughly the same conclusion as the upholders of the traditional paradigm regarding the relationship between Judaism and Christianity, he does it in a new manner, which to a certain extent takes the sting out of the anti-Jewish theology that characterized the absolute majority of previous scholarship. Paul's problem with the Torah is not that it is impossible to keep or that it leads to self-righteousness. The fundamental problem with the Torah and Judaism is simply that God has chosen to save humanity by other means, that is, by faith in Jesus.

Sanders's controversy with the earlier view of Judaism and his understanding of the Torah and Paul's relation to the Jewish people led to a number of new studies on Paul. Some scholars, as we shall see later in this chapter and in chapter 6, also assumed a critical attitude to Sanders's interpretation of Paul, while others seriously tried to consider the consequences of Sanders's revision of ancient Judaism. Among the first was the British Professor of Divinity, James D. G. Dunn, who coined the term "the new perspective on Paul." However, before we deal with the emergence of this new perspective on Paul, we shall take a brief look at a rather different approach taken by the Finnish New Testament scholar Heikki Räisänen, who already in 1983 had incorporated some of Sanders's fundamental conclusions on ancient Judaism in his work. Thus while being based primarily on assumptions from the traditional perspective on Paul, Räisänen's approach could nevertheless be said to form a kind of a bridge between the old and the new perspective on Paul.

The Inconsistent Paul—Heikki Räisänen

In a rather controversial book, *Paul and the Law* (1983), Heikki Räisänen, for many years Professor of New Testament Exegesis at the University of Helsinki, seriously questioned the fairly common assumption in the beginning of the '80s that "all the problems of the early Christians concerning the Torah were solved by Paul's clear, cogent and penetrating thinking."[12] Räisänen's picture of Paul's view of the Torah is not exactly covered by words like "clear" or "cogent," rather it is aptly framed by his conclusion: "Paul's thought on the law is full of difficulties and inconsistencies."[13] As an inventory of Pauline contradictions (from certain points of view, of course), this book is a masterpiece.

In the introduction, Räisänen makes the important observation that even though scholars, with few exceptions (he specifically mentions Percy Gardner, James Parkes, Paul Wernle, and Alfred Loisy), regard Paul as a logical thinker and the theologian *par excellence* of Christianity, there seems to be little consensus about what he really meant. As we also have noted, scholars often reach diametrically opposed views with regard to Paul's intention. Räisänen concludes:

> We thus face a curious dilemma. On the one hand, the clarity, profoundity and cogency of Paul's theological thinking is universally praised. On the other hand, it does not seem possible to reach any unanimity whatsoever as to what his message really was.[14]

The problem is, Räisänen states, that scholars who have perceived inconsistencies in Paul's writings have downplayed them in various ways, and tensions have been resolved by, for example, theological dialectics, theories of interpolation, or theories of development. Räisänen, however, has no intention of trying to explain away Paul's inconsistencies in a similar way. Instead, his aim is to test Paul's reasoning with regard to the law and pay attention to both the internal consistency and the validity of the premises.

Now Räisänen is quite aware of the limitations of his approach and is readily willing to admit that analyzing Paul from the point of view of common sense logic runs the risk of being somewhat anachronistic. Thus Räisänen does not mean to suggest that his approach is the one and only approach for understanding Paul, nor that it is the most important one. But the fact that Paul has become a theological authority calls for an investigation of his way of reasoning, not least because Paul's argumentation is often referred to as the role model for interreligious dialogue. Räisänen believes that his work will primarily affect "the theological cult of the apostle who may indeed have been at his best in areas other than speculative theology."[15]

The influence from Sanders is clearly visible in Räisänen's acceptance of the idea of "covenantal nomism" as a dominant theme within ancient Judaism. Räisänen states that when "the Jewish religion of Paul's day is allowed to speak for itself, the notion of it as perverted anthropocentric legalism turns out to be a vicious caricature."[16] First-century Judaism was not characterized by legalism, Räisänen continues in full agreement with Sanders, and Torah observance never functioned as a means to enter the covenant, only as an expression for wanting to stay within it. In sum: with regard to first century Judaism, Räisänen has in all essentials taken over Sanders's view, which seems to have been quite natural: in the preface of the book he reveals that he had been thinking along the same lines even before reading Sanders.

Concerning Paul's view of the Torah, however, Räisänen differs significantly from Sanders. For example, contrary to Sanders, Räisänen maintains that Paul *affirms* the election, the covenant, and the giving of the law:

> God has *not* revoked the election of Israel (Rom 9.4f.). Perhaps contrary to the inner logic of his position, Paul explicitly *acknowledges* (in Romans, at least) the *covenant* as a gracious act of God in his conscious reasoning. He pays, we might say, lip service to covenantal nomism.[17]

Nevertheless, characteristic of Paul is that his thinking often develops in several directions simultaneously, Räisänen states. Thus when it comes to election, covenant, and Torah, Paul may pay "lip service" to covenantal nomism, but he certainly also effectively abrogates the very fundamentals of Judaism: "He points in one (covenantal) direction and goes in another."[18] According to Räisänen, many of the problems Paul gets involved in stem precisely from the discrepancy between what Paul really says and the logical conclusion of his way of arguing, of which Paul may not have been really aware.

Räisänen examines the inconsistent Paul in five main chapters, and we will briefly summarize some of his most important conclusions. One fundamental problem is that Paul never really explains what he means by the term "law" (*nomos*), which, according to Räisänen, leads to much confusion. For example, in contexts where the word *nomos* clearly denotes the Torah, Paul seems to be simultaneously arguing that the non-Jews are subject to the Torah and that they have been liberated from it. Moreover, Paul seems to imply that no one can fulfill the law and Jews and non-Jews are thus under sin on the same terms, but at the same time it is equally clear that Paul believes that some non-Jews actually do what the law requires. But despite Paul's negative view on the possibility of fulfilling what God requires in the Torah, "the Christians" are both able to fulfill the Torah and do fulfill the Torah, while it is not obvious what they fulfill since Paul often reduces the Torah to a moral law, ignoring its ritual side (except when among Jews for missionary reasons). In general, however, Paul did not live among non-Jews as a Torah observant Jew, Räisänen claims. Furthermore, Paul generally states that the purpose of the law was a negative one: to increase sin and even bring about sin. But in some instances he argues the opposite — that the purpose of the law was positive — to lead humanity to life. "These problems," Räisänen states,

> indicate that Paul vacillates in his theological attitude to the law. All his "main" letters, Romans included, witness to a process of thought that has not come to an end. Paul is still looking for arguments for a radical stance toward the law, while at the same time trying to maintain a more conservative outlook.[19]

The fundamental reason why Paul ends up with this peculiar view of the law (which he predominantly developed during the conflict with the "Judaizers," especially during the Antioch incident) is the inner struggle with an issue that cannot be solved: the problem that a divine institution, the Torah, has been abolished through Christ, Räisänen states. The fundamental problem Paul faces, and which he is unable to solve, is the question of why God gave this weak and imperfect law in the first place. According to Räisänen, Paul gives two incompatible answers:

> Either he must attribute to God an unsuccessful first attempt to carry through his will (as if it took God a long time to devise an adequate means for this), or else he gets involved in the cynicism that God explicitly provides men with a law "unto life" while knowing from the start that this instrument will not work.[20]

None of these, however, are really satisfactory. Thus the insolvable psychological conflict caused by Paul's unconscious attempt to live, on the one hand, totally oriented to the new Christ experience, while on the other hand trying to relate this new experience to the authoritative tradition (which, among other things, claimed a divine origin of the Torah) is the main reason for his failure to formulate a consistent theology on the Torah, according to Räisänen.

To some extent, it could be argued that Räisänen's carefully outlined study displays a tendency similar to the one he finds with Paul. Not even Räisänen seems to be able to completely break away from the old. Having deconstructed the Christian myth of ancient Judaism as characterized by legalism and works-righteousness, Räisänen's main problem (as it is Sanders's) is to explain Paul against a new view of Judaism. However, Räisänen clearly accedes to the traditional assumption that Paul broke with Judaism, an assumption he never questions, and even though he aims at studying the logic of Paul's way of arguing, it is evident that the traditional paradigm still constitutes the fundamental background that determines the internal consistency and the validity of the premises. In this regard, Räisänen's study could be regarded as a parallel to Sanders's interpretation of Paul. Both scholars have come to realize that there is something fundamentally wrong with the traditional view of first-century Judaism, and both scholars find new ways of legitimizing the traditional view—that Paul ultimately abandoned Judaism. For the subsequent development of Pauline studies, it should, however, be noted that Räisänen's analysis clearly acknowledges that abandoning Judaism was no easy task even for Paul, the advocate of the law-free gospel. As such, *Paul and the Law* thus opens the door to a road seldom traveled until then — a Paul fully rooted within Judaism. In this process, the so-called new perspective on Paul has been of vital importance.

The New Perspective on Paul—James D. G. Dunn

In 1982, James D. G. Dunn, for many years the Lightfoot Professor of Divinity at Durham University, delivered a lecture at the University of Manchester, published the following year as "The New Perspective on Paul." In the introduction he notes that previous research on Paul certainly has resulted in some important conclusions, for instance in the field of rhetoric and sociology. Yet in none of these recent studies has Dunn found "what amounts to a new perspective on Paul."[21] The only work Dunn considers to have really broken the mold is Sanders's *Paul and Palestinian Judaism.*

Dunn fully accepts Sanders's critique of the Protestant scholarly tradition, which has created and maintained the idea of a fundamental antithesis between Paul and Judaism. With the idea of covenantal nomism, Dunn states, Sanders has now given New Testament scholars

> an unrivalled opportunity to look at Paul afresh, to shift our perspective back from the sixteenth century to the first century, to do what all true exegetes want to do—to see Paul properly within his own context, to hear Paul in terms of his own time, to let Paul be himself.[22]

At the same time, Dunn notes that Sanders himself has failed to consider the consequences of his own work. Instead of exploring how Paul's theology might be explained against the background of Jewish covenantal nomism, Dunn states, Sanders was still too busy ferreting out the differences between Paul and first-century Judaism. Dunn's observation is correct, for it really seems as Sanders already presupposes in his basic assumptions a distinction between Paul and Judaism. Thus in reality, Sanders starts from the very picture of the relationship between Paul and Judaism he aims at criticizing. Sanders's intention, we recall, was to compare Paul's religion with Palestinian Judaism, but since he takes for granted that Paul represents a different religious system, it is precisely the differences that come to the fore. According to Dunn, Sanders's reconstruction for this reason is only a little better than the traditional view. "The Lutheran Paul," Dunn states, "has been replaced by an idiosyncratic Paul who in arbitrary and irrational manner turns his face against the glory and greatness of Judaism's covenant theology and abandons Judaism simply because it is not Christianity."[23]

Dunn's critique is well founded, but could also be leveled against his own suggestion concerning how Paul should be understood, which clearly demonstrates how difficult it is to exchange one interpretive paradigm for another one. In spite of the best intentions and a considerable hermeneutic consciousness, Dunn too finally slips back into the traditional opposition between Paul and Judaism, as we shall see.

The fundamental problem with the Torah and Judaism, according to Sanders, was that God after all had opened another way to salvation by faith in Jesus. But with the opposition Sanders creates between the Torah and faith in Jesus, it becomes difficult to understand how Paul on the whole could give a positive verdict on Jews and Judaism and even claim the superiority of the Jewish people as, for example, in Romans 9:4-5:

> They are Israelites, and to them belong the adoption, the glory, the covenants, the giving of the law, the worship, and the promises; to them belong the patriarchs, and from them, according to the flesh, comes the Messiah, who is over all, God blessed forever.

The same can be said of Romans 11:1-2, where Paul poses the question, "has God rejected his people?" but immediately answers: "By no means! I myself am an Israelite, a descendant of Abraham, a member of the tribe of Benjamin. God has not rejected his people whom he foreknew." This means, Dunn argues, that Sanders's black-and-white opposition between Paul and Judaism is not credible. Instead, Dunn believes that the new perspective on first-century Palestinian Judaism, opened up by Sanders, really can be used for understanding Paul's theology. As his point of departure, he uses Galatians 2:16, a passage which at first seems to create precisely a clear-cut opposition between faith and works:

> We know that a person is justified not by the works of the law but through faith in Jesus Christ. And we have come to believe in Christ

Jesus, so that we might be justified by faith in Christ, and not by doing the works of the law, because no one will be justified by the works of the law.

This, Dunn states, is probably the first time Paul formulates the idea of righteousness through faith in Jesus, and he asserts that it is important to see that Paul pronounces this statement when giving his version of what happened when he and Peter were at loggerheads in Antioch (Gal 2:11-14). According to Dunn, the Jesus-believing Jews in Antioch had accepted non-Jews in their community and had also come to an agreement that they did not have to become Jews to be part of the Jesus movement. At the common meals, the Jesus-believing Jews had abandoned the Jewish dietary precepts and other distinctive Jewish cultural features, such as the rules regarding ritual purity, tithing, and idol food. What the delegation from James reacted against was precisely that the Jesus-believing Jews had abandoned the traditional Jewish lifestyle, and it was in order to demonstrate their fidelity to Jewish faith that Peter, Barnabas, and "the other Jews" began avoiding the communal meals. This behavior aroused Paul's anger and resulted in a sharp admonition against Peter, who was accused of being a hypocrite.

Dunn argues that Galatians 2:16 must be understood as a part of what Paul said to Peter, and it is evident that Paul is speaking from a Jewish perspective and is using the Jewish covenantal terminology. In the previous verse (2:15), Paul writes: "We ourselves are Jews by birth and not Gentile sinners." This indicates, Dunn continues, that Paul in 2:16 refers to something *all Jews* in the Jesus movement were in agreement on. Thus from this assumption, Paul's understanding of justification does not at all differ from how Jews in general understood the term. Paul's reasoning, Dunn argues, *presupposes* the covenant and the election and alludes to the view on "righteousness" presented in the Psalms and Isaiah. *Thus the righteousness of God is the same thing as God's recognition of Israel on the basis of the covenant.*

When it comes to the idea that justification is by faith, Paul is also in agreement with mainstream Judaism, according to Dunn. The very idea of the covenant in Jewish tradition rests on the foundation that God is the initiator of the covenant with the Jewish people and the belief that God, by grace, upholds it. Hence, the central question is regarding which point Paul and the Jews outside the Jesus movement were at variance. Is it faith in *Jesus* that is the problem, or the idea of justification by *faith?* Dunn argues that the dividing line was between those who believed that Jesus was the Messiah and those who did not. Thus all Jews agreed that Jews within the covenant were righteous, and that this righteousness, given by grace, comes from faith, not from works of the law. The law, Dunn sums up, only functioned as an identity marker of covenantal status, and Jews in general did not believe they were made righteous by observing the Torah.

But if it only was the faith in Jesus that separated Jesus-believing Jews from the Jews outside the Jesus movement, and both groups agreed that righteousness comes from faith within the limits of the covenant, what is it then Paul objects to? The mistake Sanders made, Dunn claims, is that he believed that Paul's statement in Galatians 2:16—"no one will be justified by the *works of the law*"—means the same as "no one will be justified by the *law.*" But Paul had no objections against the law as such, but *the works of the law* understood as Jewish marks of identity. What Paul ultimately reacted against, Dunn argues, was *Jewish particularism,* the tendency of defining the covenant in ethnic terms, where works of the law, primarily the food laws, circumcision, and the Sabbath celebration, create a distinction between the Jew and the non-Jew, and where the covenant is reserved for Jews. Of course, Paul did not object to statements like "you shall love your neighbor as yourself" (Lev 19:18) in the Torah. It is not covenantal nomism Paul criticizes, but he objected to an overly narrow interpretation of the covenant in Jewish tradition that excluded everyone else but Jews. To assert that God's actions toward a person should depend on works of the law (in the sense of Jewish identity markers) contradicts that righteousness depends on faith in Jesus, Dunn states. By this, the meaning of the covenant is not invalidated, but expanded to include all believers, regardless of ethnic identity.

Peter's mistake in Antioch, Dunn continues, was that he thought that Jewish identity was compatible with faith in Jesus, and that the works of the law were still relevant, and for that reason were a natural response to God's grace in a covenantal context. But in reality, Dunn says, there is only one identity marker that unites all believers—faith in Jesus—and that makes all other markers superfluous. Thus to summarize, the decisive corollary which Paul saw and which he did not hesitate to draw, was that the covenant is no longer to be identified or characterized by such distinctively Jewish observances as circumcision, food laws and sabbath. *Covenant* works had been too closely identified as *Jewish* observances, *covenant* righteousness as *national* righteousness.[24]

Undoubtedly, Dunn makes important observations. It is correct that Sanders focused too much on the difference between Paul and Judaism without seriously studying how Paul could be understood within the framework of covenantal nomism, and that he opened an unnecessarily wide chasm between two separate religious systems. The reminder that Jews in general probably shared the view that righteousness is connected to the covenantal context and is the result of faith, not works, also constitutes an important component in the understanding of Paul's relationship to Judaism.

In general, Dunn has rather convincingly shown that Sanders's idea of covenantal nomism can very well be used also for understanding Paul. However, one cannot help wondering if Dunn also failed to draw the right conclusions from his observations. Dunn rightly criticizes Sanders for having focused too much on the dissimilarities between the religion of Paul and Palestinian Judaism. As we noted above, Sanders presupposes a distinction between two ideological systems. Yet one might argue that Dunn is working from a similar assumption. For instance, Dunn's reading of the Antioch incident is vital for his argument. Dunn claims that the problem in Antioch was that important aspects of the Torah, especially the food regulations, had been set aside. But as indicated in chapter 1, this is far from certain, and in this respect, Dunn too seems to operate with the basic assumption of a sharp opposition between Judaism and Christianity. Thus regarding Paul's relationship to Judaism, the traditional distinction between Judaism and Christian remains also in Dunn's interpretation, although it focuses on other aspects and is expressed in another manner. In Dunn's reconstruction, the Protestant opposition between the law and the gospel is certainly done away with, but only replaced by a new one—between Jewish particularism and Christian universalism, which, in effect, is between Jewish and Christian identity. In fact, Dunn clears away the foundation for Judaism just as efficiently as Luther did. In a world where traditional Jewish identity markers no longer are valid, clinging to them becomes a manifestation of particularism, which in Dunn's reconstruction is what Paul regarded as the cardinal error of Judaism.

However, in "A New Perspective on Paul," Dunn clearly demonstrates what Sanders failed to do in both *Paul and Palestinian Judaism* and in *Paul, the Law, and the Jewish People* that a new view on first-century Judaism is of immense relevance for reinterpreting Paul, and that there are serious alternatives to the traditional, absolute contradiction between the Torah and the gospel of Jesus Christ. As such, Dunn's article belongs to the rather few scholarly contributions that have had a radical impact on the whole field of research, even though one may not agree with his conclusions. As the starting point for a scholarly alignment that aims at understanding Paul from within Judaism, not outside, in contrast to, or apart from Judaism, Dunn's interpretation certainly can be regarded as a significant breakthrough in Pauline scholarship. With the publication of Dunn's article, the "new perspective on Paul" was born.[25]

The Consistent Paul—N. T. Wright

Even though Dunn coined the term "the new perspective" in 1983, some of its major components can be found a few years earlier in an article by Nicholas Thomas (N. T.) Wright. Wright has held several important academic positions at, for instance, McGill University and Oxford University, but now serves as the Anglican Bishop of Durham. He has published extensively in various areas within the field of New Testament studies, and is presently, together with Dunn, probably the most well-known proponent of the new perspective on Paul.

In his article from 1978, "The Paul of History and the Apostle of Faith," Wright takes his point of departure in the discussion between Käsemann and Stendahl that we dealt with above in this chapter and finds reason to criticize aspects of both Käsemann's and Stendahl's position. He is right in pointing out, for example, that both scholars represent a normative theological position. While Käsemann does so more openly, it is also clear that Stendahl is dependent on twentieth-century theological presuppositions, for instance, in his tendency to view the Jewish people as having their own way of salvation apart from Christ and the Christian church.[26]

The most important issue the debate has raised, Wright states, concerns the relation between "theologies of history" and evils in Germany as well as "a theology which has seen 'the Jew' as the symbol of all that is false and dangerous in religion."[27] In the article, Wright questions "whether the traditional understanding of Judaism and of Paul's attack on it is not fundamentally mistaken."[28] His fundamental assumptions reveal that only a year after Sanders's publication of *Paul and Palestinian Judaism*, the revised view on ancient Judaism, prepared by Moore, Montefiore, and Stendahl, among others, had become a natural point of departure for some scholars. Wright thus refutes the traditional idea that Paul found Israel guilty of "legalism" or "works-righteousness." Instead, he believes the problem is centered around "national righteousness," the idea that "fleshly Jewish descent guarantees membership of God's true covenant people."[29] This is basically what Dunn also proposes, and the idea of a Jewish "national righteousness" is a recurrent element within the dominant strand of the new perspective of Paul.

In order to gain a fuller understanding of Wright's view of Paul, we will, however, turn to a more recent presentation: the monograph *Paul: In Fresh Perspective* from 2005. This book is based on the Hulsean lecture series given in Cambridge University 2004, and is an excellent summary of many important aspects of Wright's previous scholarship as presented, for instance, in *What Saint Paul Really Said* (1997) and *The Climax of the Covenant* (1992). In this present monograph, Wright not only summarizes his previous scholarship but he also develops it further, which makes this book especially apt for our purposes.

In the first chapter, Wright sketches a picture of Paul's religious-political context. His first "world" was, of course, Judaism, in which he remained, Wright states, even though he said shocking, even destructive, things no one within that world had ever said before. Hellenistic culture, which had permeated most of the Mediterranean world by Paul's days, constituted Paul's second world, and the Roman Empire his third. Paul also belonged to the "family of the Messiah"—his fourth world. According to Wright, this meant "embracing an identity rooted in Judaism, lived out in the Hellenistic world, and placing a counter-claim against Caesar's aspiration to world dominion, while being both more and less than a simple combination of elements from within those three."[30]

Wright states that this multifaceted and complex world of Paul could be described

> in terms of its multiple overlapping and sometimes competing *narratives:* the story of God and Israel from the Jewish side; the pagan stories about their gods and the world, and the implicit narratives around which individual pagans constructed their identities.[31]

The underlying narrative structure in Paul plays an important role in Wright's scholarship and constitutes, in his view, the most significant development within the "new perspective," and is vital for understanding Paul's message. Building on the work of Richard B. Hays,[32] Wright suggests that certain "controlling stories" governed Paul's way of arguing. In antiquity, Wright states, small allusions to stories and myths shared by a speaker and the audience could evoke entire implicit narratives. In the case of Paul, the entire narrative of Abraham constitutes, for instance, the controlling story behind Galatians 3 and Romans 4. According to Wright, Paul believed that the coming, the death, and the resurrection of Jesus had opened a new chapter within the story in which he believed himself to be living.

In the first main part of the book, Wright explores three themes aimed at presenting fundamental structures of thought with Paul. The first theme Wright labels "creation and covenant." These twin themes were always central for Paul, Wright claims, as they always have been in Judaism. The fundamental assumption is the belief that God, in his double role as covenant and creator God, will rescue and deliver his people from the enemy. Originally, the covenant was established in order to come to terms with problems within creation. God's covenant with Abraham was intended to solve the problem of evil, and Israel was supposed to have a prominent role in the salvation of the world. However, in a corresponding way, creation is invoked to solve problems within the covenant. Wright continues:

> In both cases, we should note carefully, it is assumed that something has gone badly wrong. Something is deeply amiss with creation, and within that with humankind itself, something to which the covenant with Israel is the answer. Something is deeply amiss with the

covenant, whether Israel's sins on the one hand or Gentile oppression on the other, or perhaps both—and to this the answer is a re-invoking of creation, or rather of God as creator.[33]

This idea, common within Second Temple Judaism and frequently alluded to by Paul through references or allusions to Genesis, Deuteronomy, the Psalms, and Isaiah, constituted an important controlling narrative and remained basic "within the very Jewish thought of Paul," according to Wright.[34] This, Wright suggests, is the proper background for understanding Paul's view of human plight and the solution to that problem.

The dilemma, Wright continues, is that the Jewish people, who through the covenant were supposed to bear the solution, in fact were found to be part of the problem. The narrative background—God's calling of Abraham, the creation of a family, and the promise of a land—implies that the fracturing of human relationships constitutes the basic human predicament. This was what God's covenant with Israel was intended to correct. The Torah, the covenant charter of Israel, defines what a genuinely human life looks like, but those who were entrusted with the task of being a light of the world acted precisely in opposition to God's original intention with the covenant. Instead of fulfilling God's intention of uniting the world, the Jewish people treated the Torah as an exclusive privilege, making it into an idol. When God fulfills his covenant through Christ, he reveals his faithful covenant justice and deals both with the problem of sin and enabling the family of Abraham "to be the worldwide Jew-plus-Gentile people it was always intended to be."[35]

This is the reason, Wright claims, why Paul seems to be dealing simultaneously with the inclusion of non-Jews and the issue of justification, which proponents of the "new perspective" have frequently pointed out. Wright's interpretation of Paul, however, makes it possible to integrate this aspect with the traditional view—that Paul deals with the question of how sinners are put right with God. According to Wright, there is no contradiction: both aspects are in fact part of the same thing, since God originally intended to deal with the problem of sin within humanity by the creation of a worldwide family.

The next twin themes Wright explores are "Messiah and apocalyptic." These are closely interconnected with the previous themes "creation and covenant." Contrary to what is often assumed, Wright suggests that the concept of the Messiah played an important role with Paul. Scholars have usually argued that the word *christos*, which is the Greek translation of the Hebrew word *mašîaḥ*, meaning "anointed one," has almost entirely lost its messianic overtones and become a proper name. Wright, however, shows convincingly that Paul also in this case built on ideas prevalent within Second Temple Judaism, for instance, belief in a royal Messiah who would conquer evil as God's representative, bringing the history of Israel to its climax.

Paul's conviction that Jesus is the Messiah of Israel, God's instrument in restoring humanity into one family (contrary to Jewish national righteousness), also suggests an apocalyptic element with Paul. Wright integrates the themes dealt with so far:

> God's full and final revelation of his restorative justice, his plan to put the whole world to rights, is what will occur at the end, with the royal presence of Jesus as judge and saviour. But this restorative justice, this covenant faithfulness through which creation itself will be redeemed, has been unveiled already, in advance, in the apocalyptic events of Jesus' messianic death and resurrection.[36]

The identification of Jesus with the Messiah of Israel would inevitably have political implications in the Roman Empire, Wright continues, suggesting a final set of themes: "Gospel and Empire." Recognizing Jesus-the-Messiah as the true ruler of the world, as Paul did, means directly confronting the imperial ideology according to which epithets like *kyrios* (lord) or *sōtēr* (savior) could only apply to Caesar. Even in this respect, Paul drew from Jewish tradition, Wright claims, showing that the Hebrew Bible is full of Jewish critique of pagan rulers; from the Exodus narrative, via the prophets, to Daniel, whose work was later used by the authors of *4 Ezra* and *2 Baruch*.

In the second part of the book, Wright outlines the shape of Paul's theology in a new way, being deeply dissatisfied with the traditional systems. Again, the Jewish character of Paul is brought to attention. In contrast to scholars advocating the traditional paradigm, Wright claims that Paul should not be seen as *abandoning* a Jewish framework, but *redefining* it. Wright even states that Paul's primary target is not Judaism, but paganism.

The first aspect Wright deals with is monotheism. The Jewish form of monotheism, which differed substantially from the two main contemporary rivals: pantheism (especially in the form of Stoicism) and Epicureanism, Wright labels *creational and covenantal monotheism*.[37] This kind of monotheism was characterized by the idea that the one God had created the world and remained in a dynamic relationship to it, especially through the covenant with Israel, which was aimed at dealing with the problem of sin in the world. The most important expression of human sin within a Jewish theological framework was idolatry, which explains why Jewish monotheism so often was related to the pagan world. As such, paganism embodied the human failure to live according to the intention of the creator. According to Wright, Paul shared this basic view of monotheism, but he also redefined it in several important directions, anticipating later developments within the church such as the doctrine of the Trinity. According to Wright, Paul comes very close to creating a complete identification between the Messiah of Israel (and of the world) and God.

Paul also redefined, or rather reworked election, Wright continues. This was not only an aspect about which Paul theorized, but he also carried out in real life. Hence, Paul *reworked* election. While previous Jewish ideas on election emphasized the connection between the importance of a Jewish ethnic identity and membership in the people of God, Paul reshapes election around Jesus. According to Paul, to have a share in the new life is not defined in terms of fleshly identity, Wright states, but in terms of "the Messiah's own new life, a life in which all nations can share equally."[38] This process, Wright claims, means that the later idea of the church as a "third race" *can* be traced back to Paul, and in this sense, Wright seems to suggest that Paul embraced a kind of replacement theology. Those who respond to the gospel are "the people of God," "the Jews," "the Israel of God," regardless of ethnic identity; they are given the status of *dikaios*, "righteous," which should be understood in terms of "being within the covenant." This does not mean, Wright underlines, that Paul left Judaism. In fact, election redefined in this way creates a single people from all nations, which, after all, was God's original intention with Israel.

Obviously, this also calls for a redefinition of eschatology. Again Paul remains deeply Jewish, Wright points out, but his eschatology is "reimagined around the Messiah."[39] According to Wright, one of the most important features of Paul's theology can be described as *inaugurated eschatology*, that is, the idea that God's ultimate future has broken into the present evil age through Jesus while the church is in a sense living simultaneously within God's future world and the present one. Grounded in the belief in the resurrection, Wright finds another vital aspect of Paul's redefinition of Jewish eschatology: the idea that God already has done for the Messiah what Israel expected him to do for all his people at the end of time. In sum: Paul reshapes all the main elements of Jewish eschatology around Jesus.

In the final chapter, Wright brings up the issue of the relationship between Jesus and Paul. This question, Wright states, has normally been posed in the wrong way, leading to different ways of polarizing Jesus and Paul. The problem is that scholars often have assumed that Jesus and Paul were trying to do the same thing. According to Wright, however, both Jesus and Paul lived in the synthesis Wright has presented—creation and covenant, messiahship and apocalyptic, and gospel and empire—but they hardly understood themselves as being called to carry out same task. Jesus was addressing a Jewish world and by his death and resurrection Israel's history had been brought to its climax. Paul, on the other hand, believed himself to have a very specific role in this cosmic drama, namely, to call the nations and establish the worldwide community where ethnic boundaries were eliminated. Thus the apparent differences between the message and work of Jesus and Paul is really a matter of context and task, Wright states. In reality, Jesus and Paul "were at one in the basic vision which generated their very different vocations."[40]

This is in many respects a remarkable book, first and foremost because of Wright's fascinating presentation of Paul as completely coherent. It is quite interesting to compare Wright's view of Paul with Räisänen's. Whereas Räisänen found Paul to be utterly inconsistent and incoherent, Wright finds an all-embracing, wonderful harmony. Every aspect of Paul's theology is fully rooted within Judaism *in which Paul is said to have remained*. The traditional opposition between "Judaism" and "Christianity," between "law" and "grace" is significantly toned down. In Wright's systematic presentation, Paul finds nothing wrong with Judaism—only with unbelieving Jews who advocate "national righteousness." They too, however, are part of the divine plan and can be grafted back in.

Wright's fundamental method of reading Paul against a carefully determined context (Jewish theology, controlling stories, imperial ideology, and so forth) is justified. As has been pointed out previously, no text can be read unless the reader constructs or assumes some kind of background that makes the text intelligible. The decisive point, which Wright is very well aware of, is of course the nature of that background. All too often Paul has been read against the Judaism–Christianity dichotomy. In this respect, and especially in relation to the traditional paradigm, Wright undeniably offers a fresh exegetical perspective (and indeed also a fresh theological perspective for the contemporary church) taking Sanders's revised view of Judaism seriously. In *Paul: In Fresh Perspective*, he has also eloquently incorporated important aspects from one of the most recent developments within Pauline scholarship: Paul and politics (to which we will return in chapter 7).

Both Dunn's "new" and Wright's "fresh" perspective of Paul offer challenging theological alternatives to the traditional Lutheran interpretations without entirely undermining many of the major aspects of Lutheran theology. As we noted above, Wright even aims at resolving the tension between the old and the new perspectives on Paul by emphasizing that Paul dealt both with the general inclusion of non-Jews and the issue of how individual sinners are put right with God. The same tendency is discernible also with Dunn.[41] Thus even from the position of the new perspectives, a fairly traditional Christian theology seems possible, even though some of its critics sometimes tend to view things differently (as we will see in chapter 6).

While the new perspective most likely still represents a radical challenge to normative Christian theology, it is today probably justified to speak of it as representing an exegetical middle position. From the traditional standpoint, the new perspective indeed offers an alternative reading of Paul against a more nuanced view of ancient Judaism. Yet, some scholars have gone even further with regard to locating Paul within a Jewish context. Even though proponents of the new perspective emphasize Paul's Jewishness, it is important to note that Dunn's Paul has abandoned important aspects of the Torah. Wright's Paul remains within a Judaism stripped of most of its hallmarks, so redefined that ethnicity no longer matters, and "Israel" becomes a designation for Jews and non-Jews fused together into a third entity, indeed no longer pagan, but not really Jewish either, at least not from the standpoint of most Jews in antiquity.

The new perspective on Paul should at least partly be regarded as a Christian theological attempt to come to terms with the new view of Judaism while still establishing a well-defined distinction between Judaism and Christianity. In conspicuous contrast, we will in the next chapter look at some scholars who argue that Paul remained significantly more Jewish than the proponents of the so-called new perspective assume. Some of them question the proposition that Paul really ceased observing the Torah or maintained that ethnic identities no longer matter in Christ.

5

BEYOND THE NEW PERSPECTIVE

Paul and the Parallel Covenants—Lloyd Gaston

Lloyd Gaston was New Testament professor at Vancouver School of Theology in Canada from 1972 until he retired in 1995. In 1987, he published the book *Paul and the Torah*, a collection of ten articles some of which had been previously published in other books and journals. The overall theme is Paul's relationship to the Torah and to Judaism, with Sanders's new view on Judaism as an obvious point of departure. But the conclusions Gaston arrives at differ radically from Sanders's and Dunn's.

What motivates Gaston is the insight that the Holocaust must result in a complete reversal of Christian theology, but not in a revision of the biblical texts: "Recognition of the consequences of the church's centuries-long 'teaching of contempt' should indeed lead to repentance and a resolve to do theology better in the future, but it should not inspire an apologetic revision of texts written in the past."[1] If anything, Gaston argues, New Testament scholarship must reveal and bring out underlying anti-Semitic currents, and it is against this background that his own work should be seen. Another important circumstance behind his work is the resurrection of the state of Israel in 1948. The very existence of a Jewish state makes it difficult to disregard the fact that Judaism exists as a living religion. Through contact with modern Judaism, Christian theology can acquire new perspectives, and scholars can more easily understand the historical situation in which Paul lived and acted, Gaston argues.

In spite of the ambition to create a better theology than the one that has portrayed Judaism as a dark background to the Christian church,

127

Gaston is basically a historical-critical scholar with a strong hermeneutic consciousness and a considerable ability to differentiate between theological issues and scholarly considerations. He thus especially emphasizes what he calls a "radical criticism" of scholarly assumptions, and in addition to this, he recommends the use of what he labels "a hermeneutic of experimentation" when approaching a certain problem.[2] What happens if a specific issue is dealt with from an entirely different angle than the usual one? Such an approach, Gaston claims, invites the reader to assume a skeptical attitude to the problem, and it is in this spirit he has written this book.

By way of introduction, Gaston notes that Paul, according to the traditional view, was considered to have assailed the very foundations of Judaism. In most Christian circles, the opinion that "the ultimate goal of the church is the complete elimination of an Israel faithful to Torah" prevails,[3] but Gaston ventures the question of whether the church in this traditional understanding *must* become anti-Semitic. Since every attempt to deny Jews the right to exist on their own terms is a form of anti-Semitism, Gaston argues, and if Paul repudiated any of the foundations of Judaism, God, the Torah, or Israel, he would be guilty of this.

But was Paul really guilty of this? According to the majority opinion, Paul is supposed to have held the view that the Torah had ceased to be a valid way to salvation even for Jews, and the Christian church has replaced Israel as God's chosen people. But Paul himself, Gaston emphasizes, seems to have defended himself against such accusations: "Do we then overthrow the law by this faith? By no means! On the contrary, we uphold the law" (Rom 3:31); "I ask, then, has God rejected his people? By no means!" (Rom 11:1).

What determines the matter, Gaston argues, is the question of to whom Paul addressed his letters. Galatians 2:1-10 is crucial for understanding the addressee issue, Gaston continues, for there Paul clarifies that his special mission was to the non-Jews: "We," Paul writes in Galatians 2:9, "should go to the Gentiles and they," the other apostles, "to the circumcised." At the apostolic council in Jerusalem (Acts 15), the participants agreed to divide the mission—Peter was instructed to carry the gospel to the Jewish people, and Paul became "the apostle to the Gentiles." Consequently, Gaston argues, it is reasonable to assume that Paul wrote to non-Jews dealing with problems relevant for them and that he did not discuss any matter pertaining to the situation of Jews and Judaism. Thus the conflicts arising between Paul and other Jews within as well as outside the Jesus movement exclusively concerned the question of the situation of the non-Jews.

When Paul discusses the Torah and even comments on it in a negative manner, it concerns the Torah in relation to the non-Jews, not the role of the Torah in a Jewish context. When it comes to the matter of the function of the Torah within the framework of the covenant, Gaston claims that Paul and the rest of the Jews were in agreement: the Torah leads to righteousness within the covenant. The problem is that non-Jews have no part in the covenant, as it was made between God and the Jewish people, and for non-Jews, the Torah thus acquires an entirely different meaning. For those outside the covenant, the Torah exclusively becomes a verdict on those who do not keep it. This is based on Jewish notions about the nature of the Torah, Gaston states, and refers to a midrash (Jewish biblical interpretation), *Exodus Rabbah* 5:9, describing how the word of God issued from Sinai when Israel was given the Torah: "'How did the Voice [of God] go forth?' R. Tanḥuma said: 'The word of the Lord went forth in two aspects, slaying the heathen who would not accept it, but giving life to Israel who accepted the Torah.'"

The notion that the Torah functions in two different ways for those within and those outside the covenant is bound up with the notion that God offered the Torah to all humanity, but that it was only Israel who accepted it. In Jewish thinking, the conception of the Torah evolved in two manners, Gaston argues. On the one hand, it was conceived as the revelation of God precisely within the covenant with the Jewish people, and accordingly includes the atonement system that makes it possible to restore the relation between God and the individual. On the other hand, the Torah also came to be identified as "Wisdom," conceived in the first nine chapters of Proverbs as an independent being, present when God created the world. The Torah, conceived in this way, permeates the entire creation, and is not specifically revealed to the Jewish people. In the apocryphal text Sirach, various consequences for the non-Jews are described:

The Lord created human beings out of earth,
and makes them return to it again. (17:1)

[...]
He filled them with knowledge and understanding,
and showed them good and evil. (17:7)
[...]
He bestowed knowledge upon them,
and allotted to them the law of life.
He established with them an eternal covenant,
and revealed to them his decrees.
Their eyes saw his glorious majesty,
and their ears heard the glory of his voice.
He said to them, "Beware of all evil."
And he gave commandment to each of them concerning the neighbor.
(17:11-14)
[...]
He appointed a ruler for every nation,
but Israel is the Lord's own portion. (17:17)

When the Torah is identified with Wisdom, the result is that all the nations have also been given knowledge of God's will and that they also are subject to the Torah. God also ordained "rulers" over the non-Jewish peoples, angelic beings, assigned to take care that God's law was kept. Over Israel, of course, God himself rules. These beliefs in divine beings ruling over nature and national gods were, according to Gaston, self-evident elements in the worldview of the first century CE and in principle were shared by both Jews and non-Jews. Paul alludes to these beliefs and develops them from a Jewish perspective when he describes the conditions under which non-Jews live and the circumstances from which they must be delivered, Gaston states. The non-Jewish peoples who had now abandoned God's law are still subject to it, but they are outside the context of the covenant, which is why the law brings death to them, while the same law conveys life to the Jews who live within the context of the covenant. Outside of the covenantal context, the Torah becomes a curse, and the cosmic powers form a negative sphere of influence ruling over the non-Jewish peoples. Hence it is from this situation they have to be delivered.

Gaston claims that the term "works of the law" that Paul uses in Romans 3:20 and 28 and Galatians 2:16, 3:2, 5, and 10 refers to the situation of the non-Jews. Furthermore, he insists that the term should not be understood to refer to what the Torah prescribes or specific commandments carried out by someone, but rather to what the Torah *results in* for those outside the covenant. The expression "works of the law" is thus synonymous with the curse the Torah signifies for the non-Jew. The only option for non-Jews to evade the curse which the Torah implies for those outside the covenant is to be included in the covenant through Christ.

A fundamental opposition with Paul is the one between "works of the law" and "faith in Christ," as in Galatians 2:16: "we know that a person is justified not by the works of the law but through faith in Jesus Christ." Now the translation "faith in Jesus Christ" is a specific interpretation of the Greek phrase *pisteōs Iēsou Christou,* which in a strictly grammatical sense constitutes a genitive relation, and could be understood either as a subjective or an objective genitive. Taken as a subjective genitive, the phrase could thus be translated "the faith *of* Jesus Christ," and this is exactly how Gaston understands the expression. Furthermore, the Greek word *pistis* ("faith") also carries the meaning of "trust" or "faithfulness;" that is to say, Paul can be understood to mean that a person (*anthrōpos*) does not become justified by observing the law (outside the covenant), but by *the faithfulness of Jesus Christ.* The faithfulness demonstrated by Christ is the fulfillment of the promise God once gave Abraham.

Genesis 12:3 describes how God calls Abraham, who is given the promise that "all the families of the earth" will be blessed through him. God then enters into a covenant with Abraham (Genesis 15, 17), who is given the promise that he will become "the ancestor of a multitude of nations" (Gen 17:4). Only then does God introduce circumcision as a sign of the covenant between them (Gen 17:10).

Paul alludes to the story of Abraham in both Romans and Galatians (Romans 4, Galatians 3), and the point seems to be that Abraham was declared righteous by faith, that is, by trusting in God, and that he did so before he was circumcised and before the Torah was given to Moses on Sinai. This, Gaston argues, implies that the Torah also includes a plan for the salvation of the non-Jews. According to Paul, through Christ a way has been opened for the non-Jews so that they can be included in the covenant, by means of which they can be delivered from the cosmic powers and from the curse the law lays on them. The faithfulness of Jesus fulfils the promise given to Abraham concerning the non-Jewish peoples, but, according to Gaston, this does not mean that the covenant between the Jewish people and God through the Torah becomes nullified. For the non-Jewish peoples, Jesus Christ is simply what the Torah is for the Jews, the way into a covenant saving everyone who believes. Jews and non-Jews will thus be saved by two covenants running parallel to each other. Gaston concludes:

> Without at all excluding the Jews, he [Paul] is able to argue very effectively and passionately that the inclusion of Gentiles was always the goal of the Torah, which has now been realized through the right-eousness of God manifested in the faithfulness of Jesus Christ.[4]

But how did Paul relate to Judaism? He actually professes very clearly his loyalty to the Jewish people and also emphasizes his Jewish identity (Rom 9:1-5; 11:1-2; Phil 3:4-6). But at the same time, there are texts indicating that he, in certain instances, so strongly identified himself with non-Jews that one might suspect that he no longer considered himself bound by the Torah. What does he mean, for example, in Galatians 2:19 where he writes that he "through the law" has "died to the law," or in Galatians 4:12, where he exhorts the Galatians to "become as I am, for I also have become as you are." How is one to understand the strange passage in 1 Corinthians 9:19-23?

> For though I am free with respect to all, I have made myself a slave to all, so that I might win more of them. To the Jews I became as a Jew, in order to win Jews. To those under the law I became as one under the law (though I myself am not under the law) so that I might win those under the law. To those outside the law I became as one outside the law (though I am not free from God's law but am under Christ's law) so that I might win those outside the law. To the weak I became weak, so that I might win the weak. I have become all things to all people, that I might by all means save some. I do it all for the sake of the gospel, so that I may share in its blessings.

Gaston believes that Paul probably regarded himself as an apostate in relation to Israel and had deliberately placed himself outside the Jewish covenant with God. That is the reason why he claims that he also had placed his faith "in Christ Jesus" in order to become justified "by faith in Christ, and not by doing the works of the law" (Gal 2:16). At the same time, it is precisely in his role as the "apostle to the Gentiles" that he fulfils Israel's vocation to be a light for all peoples. By denying the importance of the benefits of the Sinai covenant, Paul appears as a "true Israelite." In reality, this means that Paul tried to combine two roles that are incompatible. Gaston claims that this attitude was limited to Paul himself. He did not exhort any other Jews to abandon the Torah, and in no way did he deny God's righteousness for Israel through the Torah:

> Paul affirms the new expression of the righteousness of God in Christ for the Gentiles and for himself as Apostle to the Gentiles without in any sense denying the righteousness of God expressed in Torah for Israel.[5]

Gaston's interpretation of Paul represents a far-reaching attempt to challenge the traditional picture of the relationship between Paul and Judaism. According to Gaston, there never was any opposition between Paul and Judaism, and the only criticism Paul voices toward his Jewish compatriots is that they do not accept God's plan of salvation for the nations. Even though Paul himself had voluntarily assumed the status of the non-Jews, this does not mean that Judaism as such was invalidated or that it represented an inferior form of religion. Paul is occupied with the problem of how the non-Jews also could be embraced by God's salvation. Gaston's reconstruction of Paul represents a plausible alternative to the traditional image and most distinctly demonstrates the shortcomings of the earlier, confessionally oriented research.

One of the problems of the scholarly tradition represented by Bultmann, Käsemann, and Bornkamm is the confusion of Christian theology with historical scholarship. From a scientific viewpoint it is, of course, self-evident that ecclesiastical considerations should not be allowed to play any part when it comes to historical studies on the early Jesus movement and the early church, but traditionally the bonds between exegesis and normative theology have been strong—and still are. That is why it is important to notice that Gaston, just like Stendahl, is an example of a Christian scholar who, unlike Käsemann, for example, does not believe the church would suffer serious damage if indeed Paul held the conviction that God's promises to Israel had not ceased to be valid with the coming of Christ.

Paul and Halakah—Peter J. Tomson

The Jewishness of Paul is a salient feature also in the work of Peter J. Thomson. In the monograph *Paul and the Jewish Law* (1990), Tomson, who is professor of New Testament Studies at the Faculty of Protestant Theology in Brussels, focuses on "the roots of Paul's teaching in the halakah, the legal tradition of Judaism."[6] Tomson's very broad competence in Jewish studies, New Testament studies, and patristics makes him particularly apt to connect Paul to contemporary Judaism. This is evidently also his intention: the book "represents an approach on the Pauline letters as if they were another area of the study of ancient Judaism."[7]

Tomson challenges three traditional assumptions on which previous scholarship has been based: "(1) the centre of [Paul's] thought is a polemic against the Law; (2) the Law for him no longer had a practical meaning; and (3) ancient Jewish literature is no source for explaining his letters."[8] It is, in fact, a "re-arranged inversion"[9] of these traditional assumptions that Tomson himself takes as his point of departure, assuming that Paul's historical background was in Judaism: polemics against the Torah was not his constant concern, and the Torah still retained a practical function.

Tomson's overview of previous scholarship focuses on the dialectic between studies that represent decisive steps taken toward a new approach to Paul and those who have defended a traditional standpoint. The review of literature is most illuminating with regard to the fact that the new approach on Paul really is quite old. Tomson shows that rudimentary aspects of "a new perspective on Paul" can be found, for instance, with Adolf von Harnack (a reluctant recognition of Jewish elements in Paul's thinking) and especially with Albert Schweitzer, who suggested that Jewish apocalypticism comprised the historical background of Paul and believed that Paul himself observed the Torah and expected other Jewish Jesus-believers to do the same. With Schweitzer, the three traditional assumptions are questioned for the first time, Tomson states.

While being highly appreciative of Sanders's reinterpretation of ancient Judaism, Tomson is rather critical of his way of studying Paul as apart from Judaism, which Tomson considers a "serious drawback."[10] The same is true with regard to Sanders's introduction of the patristic idea of a "third race," which is the result of influences from the classical idea of a uniform church.

Having defined Paul as a Hellenistic Pharisee, with close affinity to Palestinian Jewry and "a natural familiarity with the language and imagery of apocalyptic,"[11] Tomson proceeds by stating that Paul's letters hardly can be seen as systematic, theological treatises, centered around the theme of justification (which is the dominant view), but rather as ad hoc letters written to different communities in various situations. These situations, Tomson argues, not only involved theological issues but also practical questions related to everyday life, and while Paul's Pharisaic background has been recognized with regard to his exegesis, it has not been sufficiently considered in connection with his general thinking. But, according to Tomson, Paul's theological and practical instructions involve both continuous reference to Scripture and a concern for the situation of the addressees in a way that bears a striking resemblance to rabbinic midrash.

With regard to the general communication situation, Tomson argues that all of Paul's letters were exclusively directed to non-Jewish Jesus believers and concerned problems pertaining to their specific situation. This is true also for Romans, even though Paul here addresses a community where Jews also had a prominent place.

Another basic question that Tomson deals with concerns the relationship between halakic discourses in the letters of Paul and his theology of justification. Is it possible, Tomson asks, that elements of Jewish traditional law could exist side by side with the theology of justification in Paul's mind? After having analyzed two important parenetic passages, 1 Corinthians 8–10 and Romans 14:1–15:13, Tomson reaches the conclusion that the typical aspects of justification theology do not occur in these passages. In the section from Romans, for instance, the word *nomos* ("law"), which occurs seventy-four times in Romans, is not used once. The word *ergon* ("work") occurs only once. The same is true for *dikaiosynē* ("righteousness"), but the usage here (Rom 14:17) is not connected to Paul's justification theology: "For the kingdom of God is not food and drink but righteousness and peace and joy in the Holy Spirit." Another keyword, *pistis*, occurs only four times, which should be compared to forty times in Romans as a whole.

Turning to passages where Paul certainly presents a theology of justification (predominantly Romans 1–4 and Galatians 3), Tomson finds that the concept of justification, rather than being the center of Paul's theological system, functions within a midrash "in which Paul brilliantly combined his gospel for Jew and Greek, the spiritual descendants of Abraham and the share in the world to come inherent in it, and the central concept of faith."[12] Furthermore, Tomson argues that Paul's theology of justification does not preclude observance of the Torah. As in other strands of ancient Jewish literature, the concepts of "faith," "salvation," or "righteousness" could very well function in connection with other important themes. From Galatians 5:3, where Paul states that "every man who lets himself be circumcised . . . is obliged to obey the entire law," Tomson concludes that Paul refers to a rule that actually was in force. Thus justification theology and halakah exist independently in Paul's writings, according to Tomson, which implies that it is theoretically legitimate to treat halakic discourses in Paul's parenesis independently from his theology of justification.

In the main part of the book, Tomson offers detailed analyses of a large number of Pauline texts. Passages from 1 Corinthians dominate because of the "halakic character" of the letter,[13] but in a chapter on table fellowship between Jews and non-Jews, Tomson also deals with texts from Galatians and Romans. A highly informative chapter on laws concerning idolatry in early Judaism and Christianity forms the background of an analysis of 1 Corinthians 8–10, which illustrates Tomson's presentation of Paul's thinking as firmly rooted in Jewish halakic tradition. The prohibition of idolatry is, of course, vital in Jewish tradition and serves, for instance, as an introduction to the Decalogue in Exodus 20. As is often the case, however, the biblical commandment requires a halakic clarification. The biblical text only states that it is forbidden to *make* idols and to *bow down* to them and to *worship* them (Exod 20:4-5). To some extent, this interpretive process takes place already within the Hebrew Bible, and when these commandments are repeated in, for instance, Exodus 21–22 and 34, further commandments and definitions are added. But not even these commandments were explicit enough and did not cover every situation later generations encountered.

The halakah of the Tannaim reveals that social interaction between Jews and non-Jews had become an increasing problem that had to be regulated in specific halakoth. Accordingly, we find in the Mishnah (especially in the tractate *'Abodah Zarah*) regulations, for instance, on how to relate to non-Jews on their way to pagan religious festivals; during which circumstances pagan foodstuffs may be handled or even consumed; and when it may be considered appropriate to sell goods that could possibly be used in pagan cults. The dominant principle, Tomson states, seems to have been the idea that the power of idolatry had no real connection to the nature of things themselves *but in the way people treated them.* That is to say, when objects or provisions were associated with idolatry they were forbidden, but if no such connection was at hand, it was appropriate for a Jewish person even to enjoy non-Jewish wine in the company of non-Jews. Wine constituted a particularly complicated problem due to its frequent use in libation offerings to pagan gods.

Traditionally, 1 Corinthians 8–10 has been taken as evidence for the idea that Paul considered the Torah invalid and obsolete. From his previous analyses of 1 Corinthians, Tomson, however, has reached the conclusion that halakah was of vital importance for Paul. Thus when analyzing Paul's teaching on idol offerings in 1 Corinthians 8–10, the continuing significance of the Torah and the relevance of halakic literature constitute Tomson's fundamental hypotheses. Against the background of rabbinic halakah on idolatry, Tomson argues convincingly that, contrary to what is commonly assumed, Paul's aim is to prevent the Corinthians from getting involved in idolatry. The issue at stake in 1 Corinthians 8–10 is not whether a non-Jewish Jesus-believer is permitted to eat idol food—according to Tomson, Paul is crystal clear on this; eating idol food is always prohibited—but how to *define* idol food in doubtful cases. Decisive for his interpretation is how to understand the word *syneidēsis*, which usually is translated "conscience." Emphasizing the idea in rabbinic literature that it is the *intention* toward an object that defines whether it should be considered associated with idolatry, Tomson argues that is better translated as "consciousness." Such a translation has far-reaching consequences for understanding Paul's teaching on idolatry and for determining his relation to the Torah.

According to Tomson, Paul introduces the problem with idol food in 1 Corinthians 8. In 10:1-22, he clearly states that idolatry is strictly forbidden: "flee from the worship of idols" (1 Cor 10:14). In 1 Corinthians 10:25-29, Paul continues by defining idol food in doubtful cases using the principle that the reality of idolatry is not in the object—the idol itself or food involved in sacrificial rites—but in the human conscious-ness. Thus eating food a non-Jew considered an offering to a pagan deity would in effect constitute an act of idolatry for a non-Jewish Jesus-believer, while eating food not explicitly defined as "idol food" would be permitted. The same principle is operative in 1 Corinthians 8. The problem addressed, Tomson states, is not that the "weak in faith" have not yet reached the insight that "no idol in the world really exists" (1 Cor 8:4), a view Paul probably shared with the "knowledgeable" in Corinth, but that the indifference of the knowledgeable with regard to pagan food could influence the new non-Jewish members of the com-munity to continue eating pagan food as if it really was food offered to pagan deities. This would make them guilty of idolatry.

Thus according to Tomson, the Torah certainly had practical signif-icance for Paul, and Jewish halakah "is invaluable for studying his practical instructions."[14] The source that Paul seems to have given priority is what Tomson labels "Apostolic tradition," that is, halakah taught by Jesus. In some cases, as with regard to regulations about divorce and the Eucharist, the "Apostolic tradition" resembles Essene halakah. But Paul also uses general Jewish tradition as a source, especially Hillelite tradition, which displays a certain openness toward non-Jews.

In general, Tomson's study shows that it is quite possible to make Paul intelligible from rather different assumptions than the tradi-tional ones. The Tomsonian Paul is fully rooted within Jewish tradi-tion, which he obviously did not oppose. His law polemic is not the center of his theological thinking but is directed toward Jesus-believing non-Jews. Paul's theology of law and justification only aims at supporting "equal rights 'in Christ' of gentile believers and in fact it serves Paul's pluriform ecclesiology which is rooted in actual prac-tice."[15] Both Jews and non-Jews are liable to observe certain commandments: Jesus-believing Jews are still supposed to adhere to the Torah and Jesus-believing non-Jews the Noachian code, which in reality means a basic version of the Western text of the apostolic decree (Acts 15).

With Tomson (and Gaston) we find the basic assumptions used by scholars who aim at interpreting Paul "beyond the new perspective." According to these scholars, Paul was still part of Judaism, and there is no contradiction between believing in Jesus as the Messiah of Israel and observing the Torah. For Jesus-believing Jews, this is the normal way of living a Jewish life. The polemics against the Torah are not the center of Paul's theology but directed toward Paul's addressees—non-Jews. Thus the problems within the early Jesus movement are primarily connected to the relationship between non-Jews and Jews, and only in this context is the Torah a vital aspect. We will now turn specifically to the issue why Paul dismissed the Torah as a way to salvation for non-Jews.

Paul and Self-Control—Stanley Stowers

A considerable number of points made by Gaston can also be found in Stanley K. Stowers's 1994 study of Romans: *A Rereading of Romans*. While Gaston mainly gave prominence to the Jewish cultural environment, Stowers, Professor of Religious Studies at Brown University, points out that the background of the Pauline worldview must be sought in both the Jewish and the Hellenistic milieu. If one underlines the fact that Paul was, at least partly, a product of the Hellenistic cultural environment, this leads to some very important conclusions regarding how to understand his letters. Is it, for instance, conceivable that Paul's modern interpreters are prevented from fully understanding his message due to the fact that he used ancient rhetoric, easily decoded by his contemporary readers, but not immediately accessible to the modern reader? What cultural codes did Paul have in common with his contemporary readers?

By way of introduction, Stowers points out that human communication through language works because it is rooted in social conventions and contexts shared by everyone in a certain society: "a person must understand both the wider language and a specific practical context."[16]

This means that the reader of a text, besides knowing the actual language, also must be familiar with the cultural codes to which the text alludes. However, when cultural codes and social contexts change, this also affects the understanding of the text. This is exactly what has happened in the case of Romans, Stowers argues, and his basic methodological approach is to read the text against the background of the cultural environment of the original addressees. This, of course, leads to the question of who the recipients of Romans were: Jewish or non-Jewish followers of Jesus, or perhaps a combination of both groups? Stowers states that one has to distinguish between the *real audience,* that is, those who actually read the letter, and the *implied audience* — "the reader explicitly inscribed in the text."[17] It is hardly possible to know anything about the former group, Stowers argues, but the latter group is defined, for instance, in the preamble of the letter: "we have received grace and apostleship to bring about the obedience of faith among all the Gentiles for the sake of his name, including yourselves who are called to belong to Jesus Christ" (Rom 1:5-6).

Regardless of who actually read Romans, Paul intended to write to non-Jews, Stowers claims, and this is crucial for understanding the text. Moreover, trying to read Romans as the first readers did makes it necessary to consider the cultural features assumed to have been common for both Paul and the addressees. Two such important characteristics are the ideal of "self-control" (*enkrateia*) and classical rhetoric. These aspects, in combination with Paul's Jewish background and the fact that he wrote to non-Jews, lead Stowers to read Romans in a manner quite different from the traditional one.

Stowers means that the ideal of self-control is conclusive for understanding Paul's letter to the Romans. Practicing self-control was a basic ethical principle that everyone, especially men, should strive for. It was a feature characterizing a true man, and masculinity was a quality that had to be won against the background of the pronounced warrior model. The ability to lead others, suffer hardship, abstain from luxury and sex, and strive for hardness and physical strength were characteristics young boys were encouraged to acquire and for which they were systematically trained. Women, of course, represented the opposite of all this and were associated with frailty, softness, and an exaggerated interest in such things as food and sex. Because of this, women were seen as a serious threat as they tempted men to abandon their masculinity. The only disadvantage a man suffered by not marrying was the loss of an heir—a son.

Stowers points out that Jews in the Greco-Roman cities had rather limited opportunities to demonstrate their loyalty to the state, as they could not take part in the official cult or the cult of the emperor. At the same time, it was for their own good if they could be regarded capable of showing leadership, in order to keep their right to limited self-determination and continue practicing their religion. For this reason, Jews readily called attention to the fact that they were a people characterized by an extraordinary degree of self-restraint, and they even had a special law, the Torah, as a means of attaining this goal. According to Stowers, Jews emphasized exactly those ideals that society as a whole valued. The Jewish philosopher Philo, for example, presents the Jewish law as a model when it comes to acquiring self-restraint, especially the Jewish dietary rules and marriage precepts (*Spec.* 4.92-100).

Stowers claims this explains why non-Jews seem to such an extent to have been interested in Judaism, a fact that for a long time has puzzled many scholars. As the ability to practice self-control was connected to social status, it is very likely, Stowers argues, that the emphasis on the ability of the Torah to help people acquire self-control appealed to individuals bent on advancing in society. Philo, Josephus, and other Jewish authors demonstrate that it was common for Jews to exhort non-Jews to follow the Torah in order to acquire self-control, and because of this, they could be regarded as accepted by the God of Israel, Stowers states.

The ideal of self-control in antiquity, the Jewish emphasis on the ability of the Torah to implement this ideal, and the appeal to non-Jews to observe the Torah make up the background of the problems Paul deals with in Romans. The view Paul argues against is the notion that non-Jews, by means of the Torah, can acquire righteousness before the God of Israel. In reality, the non-Jews are at the mercy of their passions and in all circumstances incapable of self-control. In Romans 1:18-21, Paul begins to deal with the situation of the non-Jews:

> For the wrath of God is revealed from heaven against all ungodliness and wickedness of those who by their wickedness suppress the truth.

For what can be known about God is plain to them, because God has shown it to them. Ever since the creation of the world his eternal power and divine nature, invisible though they are, have been understood and seen through the things he has made. So they are without excuse; for though they knew God, they did not honor him as God or give thanks to him, but they became futile in their thinking, and their senseless minds were darkened.

Traditionally this text has been understood as a description of the fall of humanity and of the universal nature of sin. But against the background of the classical model of self-control and the implied audience (non-Jews) in Romans, Stowers argues that we here have a description of the consequences for the non-Jews, who were once given knowledge of God's law, *but chose to ignore it.* For this reason God has abandoned them to all sorts of acts representing everything else but self-control. In Romans 1:24-31, Paul continues:

Therefore God gave them up in the lusts of their hearts to impurity, to the degrading of their bodies among themselves, because they exchanged the truth about God for a lie and worshiped and served the creature rather than the Creator, who is blessed forever! Amen.

For this reason God gave them up to degrading passions. Their women exchanged natural intercourse for unnatural, and in the same way also the men, giving up natural intercourse with women, were consumed with passion for one another. Men committed shameless acts with men and received in their own persons the due penalty for their error.

And since they did not see fit to acknowledge God, God gave them up to a debased mind and to things that should not be done. They were filled with every kind of wickedness, evil, covetousness, malice. Full of envy, murder, strife, deceit, craftiness, they are gossips, slanderers, God-haters, insolent, haughty, boastful, inventors of evil, rebellious toward parents, foolish, faithless, heartless, ruthless.

The entire description bears witness to a complete breakdown of the ideal of self-control. This is demonstrated, not least, in the description of what might be characterized as homosexual relations. But what Paul is referring to has little, if anything, to do with homosexuality in the modern sense of the word. According to Stowers, same-sex relations should be seen against the background of the ideology of self-control. "Natural sex" in antiquity presupposed an active and a passive part, and by definition implied the penetration of a woman, who was socially inferior. From these points of departure, same-sex relations meant that the status relations in the accepted gender constructions were upset: men playing the role of women, and vice versa.

What Paul emphasizes in Romans 1:18—2:16, according to Stowers, is that God one day will judge both Jews and non-Jews in accordance with their deeds. In Romans 2:6-11, Paul calls attention to the fact that those who do good, regardless of ethnicity, will be rewarded, whereas those who commit evil acts will be punished.

> For [God] will repay according to each one's deeds: to those who by patiently doing good seek for glory and honor and immortality, he will give eternal life; while for those who are self-seeking and who obey not the truth but wickedness, there will be wrath and fury. There will be anguish and distress for everyone who does evil, the Jew first and also the Greek, but glory and honor and peace for everyone who does good, the Jew first and also the Greek. For God shows no partiality.

In sharp contrast to the prevalent view, Stowers argues that even the non-Jew living in accordance with the law will be rewarded. "The law" should in principle be considered as the Torah, except those special precepts that are more specifically expressions of Jewish identity such as food regulations and male circumcision. The Jew who does not live according to the law enjoys no preference, as God judges impartially and takes no account of different individuals. There is, however, one problem that affects the non-Jew, but not the Jew. The Jewish people, who have the Torah placed in a covenantal context, can atone for their sins continuously. The non-Jews do not enjoy this opportunity, and their burden of guilt increases incessantly. The punishment for not having listened to God once upon a time is that they now are abandoned to act out their passions in a constant failure to acquire self-control. God, who judges all humanity according to their deeds, will one day impose a dreadful punishment on those non-Jews who do not live a righteous life.

It is important, Stowers states, to note that Paul does not place the situation of the Jews on an equal footing with that of the non-Jews. It is true that God judges everyone according to works, but Paul nowhere asserts that the Jewish people have lost their relationship with God, or that the Jews are slaves under their passions in the same way as the non-Jews. The Jew who lives within the context of the law, who sins, but is reconciled with God, will be judged on that basis. In this respect the Jewish people enjoy an advantage, and the Torah in no way has lost its role.

The non-Jews thus have a serious problem. But the solution some Jews recommend—that the non-Jews, by keeping the Jewish law, can reestablish their relationship with God—Paul strongly opposes in Romans 2:17-29. According to the traditional reading, this text is a frontal attack on Judaism. Paul certainly seems to be accusing a Jew of not being able to keep the Torah, and because of this it has been taken for granted that Paul had declared the Torah invalid, as it was impossible to keep. But Stowers argues that the purpose of the text was actually to demonstrate how incongruous it was for Jews to exhort non-Jews to try to attain righteousness by observing the Torah.

The person Paul addresses in Romans 2:17-29 is a fictitious Jewish teacher of the law, Stowers claims, representing those who exhort non-Jews to observe the Torah in order to regain control of their own lives and thus become righteous before God. Introducing an imagined dialogue partner in this manner was a very common rhetoric device in antiquity (speech-in-character), and the recipients of Romans were in all probability totally familiar with it. To anyone versed in Hellenistic literature, Paul's conversational partner was a well-known figure: "the type was made familiar not only by moralists and philosophers but also in the New Comedy."[18] This rhetorical stereotype was characterized by boastfulness, pretentiousness, pride, and a marked difference between his self-image and his real characteristics. This is consistent with Paul's imagined partner in Romans 2:17-23:

> But if you call yourself a Jew and rely on the law and boast of your relation to God and know his will and determine what is best because you are instructed in the law, and if you are sure that you are a guide to the blind, a light to those who are in darkness, a corrector of the foolish, a teacher of children, having in the law the embodiment of

knowledge and truth, you, then, that teach others, will you not teach yourself? While you preach against stealing, do you steal? You that forbid adultery, do you commit adultery? You that abhor idols, do you rob temples? You that boast in the law, do you dishonor God by breaking the law?

The Jewish teacher of the Torah, who according to Stowers should not be mistaken for a picture of "the typical Jew," represents those who certainly share Paul's notion that non-Jews do not have to become Jews in order to be accepted by the God of Israel, but think that the Torah leads to righteousness for non-Jews in the same manner as it does for the Jewish people. According to Paul, Stowers says, this is wrong for several reasons. In the first place, it is indefensible that the Jewish teacher of the law *who does not keep it himself* attempts to teach others. What Paul wants to emphasize, Stowers claims, is that the Jewish people have enough of their own problems trying to observe the Torah. Even the Jew must in the end trust in God's grace and mercy and not in his or her own deeds. Furthermore, *it is God who has abandoned the non-Jews to their desires and passions.* Offering the non-Jews a way to righteousness by means of the Torah would be to act against the will of God. God has chosen another way for non-Jews to become righteous: through Jesus Christ. According to Paul, the Torah was never intended for bringing reconciliation to those who originally had rejected God's law, and can consequently be of little use to them: "at most, the law gives them only a knowledge of their bondage to sin and their culpability."[19] It is only in the Jewish covenantal context that the Torah can function, as the Jewish people originally accepted to submit to the will of God. This perspective apparently solves many problems in Romans. One example is Romans 9:30-33:

> What then are we to say? Gentiles, who did not strive for righteousness, have attained it, that is, righteousness through faith; but Israel, who did strive for the righteousness that is based on the law, did not succeed in fulfilling that law. Why not? Because they did not strive for it on the basis of faith, but as if it were based on works. They have stumbled over the stumbling stone, as it is written, "See, I am laying in Zion a stone that will make people stumble, a rock that will make them fall, and whoever believes in him will not be put to shame."

This is one further text previously used to support the idea that Paul denied the ability of the Torah to lead an individual to righteousness, and against the background of the traditional interpretation, this seems entirely reasonable. But from Stowers's perspective, the text acquires an entirely different meaning. If Romans had been written to non-Jews in order to show them the right way to righteousness and to refute those Jews who believed that the non-Jews should observe the Torah, the text rather means that Israel strove for a law that would offer righteousness to *the non-Jews*. At the same time, the Jews did not realize that the law itself reveals God's plan for redeeming the non-Jews, that is, not through the law but by "God's gracious mercy in response to and by means of Jesus Christ's faithfulness."[20]

Stowers argues that the problem of the Jews, according to Paul, is that they do not understand that God, through Christ, has opened a way for the non-Jews to become righteous apart from the Torah. They persist in contending, like the Jewish teacher of the law in Romans 2, that their way to righteousness is the same as for the non-Jews. For this reason they have failed in their mission to be "a light to the peoples" (Isa 51:4). Paul represents that part of Israel who understands God's plan as the remnant God has saved (Rom 11:5) in order to justify the godless non-Jews through Christ. The inability of Israel to understand God's intentions in respect of the non-Jews is, however, in itself part of God's plan. For God is the one who has hardened the Jewish people (Rom 11:7). In the last days, however, "Out of Zion will come the Deliverer; he will banish ungodliness from Jacob" (Rom 11:26b).[21] Then all Israel will be saved, but also the rest of the world. God will then "reconcile to himself all things, whether on earth or in heaven," as the author of the Colossians (1:20) writes.

Stowers's interpretation of Romans is impressive. By replacing the traditional interpretive framework with one taken from the cultural environment Paul and his circle of readers moved in, Stowers creates a credible alternative to the prevailing solution of the problems within the early Jesus movement. As with Gaston and Tomson, it is the non-Jews who constitute the main problem—not the Jews—and the salvation of the non-Jews does not assume a state of opposition to the Jewish system of salvation.

Although Stowers, like Gaston, imagines that Paul "lived as a gentile in Christ" when among non-Jews,[22] he also calls attention to the fact that Paul did not doubt that faith in Jesus was wholly compatible with the Torah and actually meant that the law and the gospel about God's acting through Jesus Christ were the same thing. "I am convinced," Stowers states, "that in 10:4-8 Paul is paralleling and even at points identifying the law with the gospel of God's acts in Jesus Christ."[23] Thus in Stowers's reading of Romans, Paul appears at wholly Jewish—and Hellenistic—but harboring another idea of how Israel is to realize its mission to be "a light for the peoples."

In Stowers's book, we find several characteristics typical for scholars who have moved beyond the "new perspective on Paul." One is an emphasis on Paul as the apostle to the non-Jews. Another is the principle that Paul directed his message primarily to non-Jews, to understand Paul against his first-century Jewish context. In Stowers's case, this also means taking Paul's Hellenistic context into consideration. In conclusion then: Stowers's Paul appears firmly rooted within Judaism and found nothing wrong with Jewish followers of Jesus observing the Torah (even though Paul himself compromised on this point when among non-Jews). Paul's main problem was to make non-Jews realize why *they* could not become righteous through the Torah. This focus on Paul as the apostle among the nations is also salient in the work of Mark D. Nanos, although his Paul is even more Jewish; in fact, Nanos believes Paul was as Torah-observant as any Jew in antiquity.

Paul, the Jew Among the Nations—Mark D. Nanos

In a book that has attracted much attention, *The Mystery of Romans* (1996),[24] the Jewish scholar Mark D. Nanos, teacher at Rockhurst University, Kansas City, Missouri, offers a quite different interpretation of the relations between Jews and non-Jews in the early Jesus movement. Nanos's interpretation of the relations between Jews and non-Jews stands in stark contrast to the traditional paradigm in many respects. Not only does Nanos argue that Paul was loyal to Judaism and even observed the Torah, but also that he held that non-Jewish followers of Jesus should be compelled to respect the Torah and, in addition, adapt a Jewish lifestyle out of respect for their Jewish brothers and sisters.

By way of introduction, Nanos points out that even though many scholars now take Paul's Jewish background into consideration and even admit he was involved in intra-Jewish discussions, the view that still dominates is that Paul was an apostate, harboring the opinion that the Torah had had its day since the coming of Jesus:

> Paul is regarded implicitly, often explicitly, as an apostate: Paul no longer believed the practice of Torah or Jewish halakha were meaningful expressions of faith. He is still even portrayed by some as anti-Judaic. At the very least, Paul is painted as arbitrary and manipulative, a chameleon lacking any integrity of conviction or consitency of application where the Jewish practice of Torah as God's elect is concerned. Paul may see himself as a faithful Jew, but his contemporaries would not have, nor does the modern scholar.[25]

Even those imagining that Paul lived according to the Torah often maintain that he made concessions regarding certain points: for example, that Torah-observance was not a matter of covenant loyalty, but reflected more habit or evangelistic opportunism so that he could still relate to Jews. We have seen such viewpoints with both the advocates of the new perspective and with Gaston and Stowers. The sources reveal that this discussion is not new, Nanos states.

Both Romans and Acts bear witness to the fact that, already during his lifetime, Paul was accused of abandoning the Torah and exhorting other Jews to do likewise (Rom 3:8; Acts 21:21). Also, some of Paul's early readers complained that it was not so easy to understand what he wrote. In 2 Peter 3:16, the author claims that some things in Paul's letters are hard to understand, "which the ignorant and unstable twist to their own destruction." Thus already at an early stage, Paul's teaching gave rise to misunderstanding. But, Nanos maintains, it is important to note that Paul emphatically denied having abandoned the Torah, even making a Nazirite vow and sacrificing in the temple in order to prove this point (Acts 21:19-26).

The Paul that Nanos finds in Romans is to be understood working within Jewish communities as a Torah-observant Jew. Certainly, his activities are conditioned by the conviction that the God of Israel, through Jesus, has prepared a way to salvation for the non-Jews as well, but this did not result in Paul's breaking with the basic conceptions that characterized Judaism in the first century CE. According to Nanos, Paul thus shared the view that the Torah represents God's gift to the Jewish people and that a Jew observes the Torah as a response to God's mercy, not in order to merit justification. The compatibility with Sanders's new view of Judaism is clearly noticeable in Nanos's work.

In agreement with Dunn, Nanos believes that Paul's general problem with his Jewish brothers and sisters concerned "ethnocentrism," that is, as we have seen, when Jewish privileges are considered as valid only for the Jewish people with the result that non-Jews first must become Jewish proselytes in order to access full membership among the righteous ones. According to Paul, however, God chose Israel to bring salvation to the whole world. However, while Romans often has been regarded as dealing with "ethnocentrism" on part of the Jewish followers of Jesus in the community, Nanos argues that in Romans it is the other way round: that it is a matter of Jesus-believing non-Jews who, in relation to Jesus-believing Jews, claim to enjoy an exclusive position before God. Thus according to Nanos, the original purpose of Romans was to refute the very claims for which the letter later has come to be used.

According to the traditional view, the addressees of the letter were organized in house communities and were independent from the many synagogues in Rome. This is a conclusion that is intricately connected with the traditional presupposition that "Judaism" and "Christianity" existed in opposition to each other. Nanos, who does not share this basic assumption, argues that the Jesus movement could hardly have constituted a separate movement at the time when Romans was written. Instead, he finds many indications that the Jesus movement in Rome met as subgroups of the synagogues: "we have good reasons to believe that [the Christians] would have had no concept of their faith outside the expression of the Jewish community."[26]

There are, Nanos continues, sociopolitical reasons for doubting the notion that the Jesus movement made up a separate group. In antiquity there was undeniably a certain measure of religious tolerance: the authorities could and did permit cults that did not threaten the comprehensive religious system. Many individuals in the great ancient cities belonged to one or several so-called *collegia*, a combination of a social club and a religious society, which was often responsible for the burial rites for its deceased members. These associations, in many cases based on various occupational groups, always included a religious dimension and always existed at the discretion of the authorities. During certain periods, the authorities could simply prohibit all *collegia*, which happened in 64 BCE. The Jewish communities were regarded as a kind of *collegium* and enjoyed certain conditions that made it possible for Jews to be excused from taking part in the official cult in which other citizens were expected to participate. Against this background, Nanos argues, it is unlikely that the Jesus movement sought to exist as a separate religion outside the established religious system that was so intimately bound up with the political power. The synagogue was accordingly the most likely social location of the Jesus movement at this time. Such a conclusion means that the relationship between different Jewish groups and between Jews and non-Jews stand out in an entirely different manner, especially if one assumes, as Nanos does, that Jesus-believing Jews did not relinquish their Jewish identity.

In Acts 15:19-20, Luke describes how the participants of the apostolic council in Jerusalem ruled that Jesus-believing non-Jews should be enjoined to keep certain precepts, but not the Torah in its entirety:

> Therefore I have reached the decision that we should not trouble those Gentiles who are turning to God, but we should write to them to abstain only from things polluted by idols and from fornication and from whatever has been strangled and from blood.

Most scholars believe that these rules, the so-called apostolic decree, were not at all promulgated at this meeting around 49 CE, but represent a compromise reached at around the time when Luke wrote Acts. In Galatians 2:6, a text supposedly describing the incident Luke relates in Acts 15, Paul recounts that the other apostles did not want to impose anything more on him, which is usually taken as evidence for the idea that Paul would not have advocated anything reminding them of the Torah. Nanos, on the other hand, argues that what Luke describes represents precepts that non-Jews active in the synagogues generally observed in order to facilitate social intercourse. They are simply an early version of the so-called Noahide commandments, described in later rabbinic literature (first in *t. 'Abod. Zar.* 8:4), defining who could be considered a righteous non-Jew. As the Jesus-believing Jews did not differ from other Jews with regard to Torah observance, according to Nanos, and as the synagogue was the natural meeting-place for the Jesus movement as well as for Jews who did not follow Jesus, it was important for Jesus-believing non-Jews to respect the demands of all Jews regarding, for example, food.

But in Rome, Nanos says, a situation had arisen in which non-Jewish followers of Jesus were growing resentful toward Jews who were not accepting their claims to the rights of full members, and considering disregard for the rules regulating social intercourse between Jews and non-Jews. In addition, it is likely that at the time when Romans was written this subgroup of the Jewish community was made up of a majority of non-Jews. As we recall from chapter 2, Roman society was, to a certain extent, characterized by conflicting attitudes toward Jews: on the one hand, the Jews were feared and their special rules of conduct, especially the dietary rules and circumcision, were mocked; on the other hand, many non-Jews were attracted to the synagogues, and the ancient traditions of Judaism were viewed with respect.

In Rome, Nanos claims, there was an incipient tendency among the non-Jewish adherents of the Jesus movement to emphasize the negative aspects of Judaism. As long as the non-Jews made up only a minority, it was natural for them to submit to the Jewish majority. When the relative strength of the respective party became reversed, and even non-Jews who had not had contact with Jewish communities became members of the movement, the non-Jewish followers of Jesus were tempted to claim their right to be exempt from the rules of conduct enjoined upon them by the apostolic decree. Based on the fact that many Jews did not accept Jesus and did not recognize the status of the non-Jews as equal partners in God's salvific work, the non-Jews started to draw the conclusion that God had abandoned the Jewish people in favor of the non-Jews. Thus the triumphalism that has later characterized the Christian church started to manifest itself already in the middle of the 50s.

According to Nanos, this was the fundamental problem Paul sought to confront in Rome. Paul writes his letter to the non-Jewish adherents of the Jesus movement with the aim of reminding them of their obligations toward the Jewish people and their status: the gospel is "the power of God for salvation to everyone who has faith, to the Jew first and also to the Greek" (Rom 1:16). Above all, there are two matters Paul wants to make clear: the non-Jews must submit to the apostolic decree, and they must accept the principal precedence of the Jewish people and the role of Torah. This, Nanos states, is what Paul deals with in his discussion of the "strong" and the "weak" in Romans 14:1 — 15:3. In Romans 14:1-3, Paul writes:

> Welcome those who are weak in faith, but not for the purpose of quarreling over opinions. Some believe in eating anything, while the weak eat only vegetables. Those who eat must not despise those who abstain, and those who abstain must not pass judgment on those who eat; for God has welcomed them.

According to the traditional interpretations of this passage, Paul here criticizes Jesus-believing Jews who had not realized that the Torah was no longer in force and thus continued to follow the Jewish food laws. Contrary to this, Nanos argues that Paul refers to Jews who had not yet espoused faith in Jesus:

> Simply put, the "weak/stumbling in faith" are those Jews who do not yet believe in Jesus as the Christ of Israel or Savior of the nations: they are the non-Christian Jews in Rome. They have faith in God, but not in his "seed," Christ Jesus, or in the equal coparticipation of gentiles.[27]

Nowhere, Nanos points out, are the opinions or conduct of "the weak" criticized, and it is quite clearly stated that God has accepted those who, for example, eat nothing but vegetables. Instead, the criticism is turned toward those who assume a censuring attitude. Paul wants the Jesus-believing non-Jews to uphold practicing the precepts of the apostolic decree, in order to walk "in love" (Rom 14:15). They should not allow what they eat to "cause the ruin of one for whom

Christ died" (Rom 14:15). Those who are "strong," that is, "able to believe in Christ," "ought to put up with the failings of the weak" (Rom 15:1). By urging the non-Jew to submit to the authority of the synagogue, that is, those to whom "the adoption, the glory, the covenants, the giving of the law, the worship, and the promises" belong (Rom 9:4), Paul aims at restoring the balance of the community — and hence unity. In this way, the non-Jewish followers of Jesus are given their proper position in relation to the Jewish people — the Jew *first* and *also* to the Greek — and Paul has completed his mission "to bring about the obedience of faith among all the Gentiles" (Rom 1:5), which in effect means returning to the apostolic decree:

> The "obedience of faith" is the obligation incumbent upon gentiles who have come to faith in the One God through Christ Jesus, who as gentiles are now equally part of historical people of faith, although they are no longer pagans but "righteous gentiles" who must obey the halakhot incumbent on upon gentiles who turn to God and associate with his people.[28]

Nanos's emphasis of the Jesus movement as a fundamentally Jewish phenomenon with the synagogue as its base, in dialogue with Jews both inside and outside the movement, leads up to a considerably more complex picture of the early Jesus movement than the traditional ones. In his monograph from 2001, *The Irony of Galatians,* he further develops this perspective with regard to Paul's letter to the Galatians.[29]

In *The Mystery of Romans,* Nanos puts his finger on how sociopolitical circumstances in the Roman Empire influenced the interaction between various groups. Because of the religious system in Rome, the Jesus movement could hardly have functioned outside the synagogue institution. Hence it is almost self-evident that tensions between different groups were bound to arise. It is in this context that the theological contribution of Nanos comes into full view.

Nanos argues that Paul employs the theme of the one God embodied in the Shema to resolve these social tensions. He maintains that Paul was not against proselyte conversion in principle, but he upheld the belief that the gospel's proposition that the age to come had arrived would be compromised if Jesus-believing non-Jews became Jews, members of Israel. Rather, the non-Jew now joined the Jew in the worship of the one God, the God of Israel, and of all the other nations also. If non-Jews were to become Jews in order to become members of the family of God, then God would only be the God of Jews (Rom 3:28-31), which, although appropriate for Jewish groups that did not claim the arrival of the awaited age, was not acceptable for the Jesus-believers, who proclaimed that age to have begun with the resurrection of Jesus. Such an approach demonstrates just how Jewish is Paul's theology, as well as the Jewish orientation of his audience, for he assumed this approach would be persuasive even for the non-Jews to whom he wrote.

Paul's emphasis that Jews and non-Jews enjoyed the same status before the God of Israel and thus should commend themselves to each other as full and equal members led to intra-Jewish discussions about the position of the non-Jew within the Jewish communities of the Roman Empire, and about Israel's proper role *now* in God's plan for the salvation of humanity. The close contacts of the non-Jews with the synagogue and the obligation to abstain from "idolatry," complicated their relation to the authorities and society as a whole. New demands on social adaptation on the part of both groups arose as non-Jews and Jews within the Jesus movement became more closely affiliated.

Nanos's reconstruction of the relations between Jews and non-Jews in Rome and Paul's response to them constitutes a significant contribution to the understanding of the dynamics within the early Jesus movement. More importantly, his reading of Romans demonstrates that it is entirely possible to create a coherent historical reconstruction based on the assumption that Paul never abandoned Judaism, that he lived and died in obedience to the Torah, which he considered God's most valuable gift to his people, and that his priority was always the restoration of Israel balanced with carrying out Israel's special calling on behalf of the rest of humanity—the Jew *first*, but *also* the Greek. Thus in Nanos's reconstruction, the traditional contrast between Paul and Judaism is, in fact, completely done away with. Instead, two other opposing forces become more and more obvious: an old research paradigm and a new one. Before we study some reactions to these new views of Paul, however, we will take a brief look at a book that seriously questions another fundamental idea within traditional Pauline scholarship: that of the early Jesus movement as a "third race."

Paul and Ethnicity—Caroline Johnson Hodge

In the monograph *If Sons, Then Heirs*, which appeared in 2007, Caroline Johnson Hodge, Assistant Professor of Religious Studies at the College of the Holy Cross, questions the common idea that the earliest Jesus movement was inclusive and had rejected ethnic or racial aspects as a condition for religious identity. It is quite correct, of course, that Christianity in general is thought of as a religion that transcends ethnicity and that such markers of identity have been translated "into an ethnically neutral, all-inclusive tradition which is somehow beyond the normal human characteristics of culture, its discourses and practices."[30] Within Pauline scholarship, the notion of Christianity as an inclusive, universalistic religion has indeed been dominant. The idea that the apostle addressed a universal audience, for example, has prevailed at least as since Augustine, Johnson Hodge states, and was taken over by the Reformation theologians. What they also took over and further developed was the picture of Judaism constructed in contrast to Christianity and representing everything Christianity was not. As we have seen, faith versus works has been the dominant paradigm ever since, and Paul is usually considered to have argued that the law is insufficient for salvation, which is only possible through faith in Christ.

During the nineteenth century, Johnson Hodge states, scholars began to interpret the juxtaposition of Judaism and Christianity in terms of race and ethnicity, which was possible only because of another construction—the contrast between Judaism and Hellenism. Accordingly, Judaism was seen as representing an ethnic religion tied only to one people. Paul was often considered as the one who transcended Jewish particularism in developing the universalism of Christianity, and his gospel was commonly interpreted in bipolar terms, such as faith versus works, ethical versus legal, spiritual versus material, which is the direct result of the nineteenth century juxtaposition of ethnic Judaism and universal Christianity, Johnson Hodge states.

The anti-Jewish implications of this paradigm are usually now recognized, Johnson Hodge continues, although its legacy still remains. As we have seen, during the twentieth century there has been a tremendous reorientation with regard to the view of ancient Judaism, culminating in the work of E. P. Sanders and the development of the "new perspective on Paul." However, Johnson Hodge argues, the new perspective scholars such as Dunn and Wright, despite their contributions to Pauline scholarship, still reproduce the nineteenth century dichotomy between ethnic and universal. Within another branch of Pauline scholarship, often identified with Lloyd Gaston, there has been a more radical break with Lutheran interpretations, Johnson Hodge states, not the least of which concerns the issue of whether Paul addressed non-Jews only or humanity in general. In accordance with Gaston, among others, Johnson Hodge believes that Paul addressed non-Jews: "Paul is clear that he is the apostle to the gentiles (Rom 11:13) and that he is writing *to* gentiles, even if he writes *about* Jews at times."[31] This insight, she continues, "requires a rereading of Paul with ethnicity and kinship as a central focus."[32]

In order to be able to perform this rereading, Johnson Hodge proceeds by comparing Paul to other ancient authors, posing the questions how they define kinship and ethnicity and what interests these definitions serve. One central notion in ancient Mediterranean society is the idea that an individual is made up from his or her ancestors so that status, character, and identity are conferred by that person's forebears. This idea is one important part of the prevailing kinship structure in antiquity—patrilineal descent. Closely connected to this idea is the conception of kinship as a natural, biological process beyond human understanding. Concepts like "shared blood," "flesh," and "seed" thus become important notions in forming an authoritative logic that organizes and legitimizes various social positions and identities. At the same time, this logic of patrilineal descent, according to which certain specific qualities are conveyed, could also be used in a manipulative way—for creating a desirable identity. This, Johnson Hodge shows, was the case with Julius Caesar, who was able to transform his rather unknown heritage into one more suitable for a ruler of Rome by claiming a divine origin. Thus in this system, the creation of genealogies obviously played an important role.

The social construction of patrilineal descent was often legitimized and even created by religious rituals, such as plant and animal sacrifices.

According to Johnson Hodge, Greek sources suggest that the inclusion of a newborn child into the household was by no means an automatic process but required certain rituals and sacrifices. In a Jewish context, circumcision of males, of course, served the same purpose. Such rituals were also important in the case of adoption, a phenomenon that, as will be evident, has a direct bearing on the study of Paul. Interestingly enough and despite the fact that patrilineal descent was considered a natural process, Romans maintained a difference between the *pater*, the socially recognized father, and the *genitor*, the biological father. In such cases, the *pater* and the *genitor* were obviously not the same person, but through a ceremony of adoption, kinship ties were created comparable to those formed by birth. Here, the divine process, expressed through the ritual, replaces the natural, biological process. Thus religious rituals are involved in both sanctioning blood relations and in creating substitutes for biological kinship in the case of adoption. Essential for both is the idea that "shared blood" constitutes the basis for kinship relations and that such relations can be established or rearranged through genealogies and history writing, Johnson Hodge concludes.

Ancient peoples commonly constructed the world in terms of "we" and "them." The Greeks, for instance, made a clear distinction between themselves, the *Hellēnes*, and the *barbaroi*, the barbarians, that is, the rest of the world. The same bifurcation shaped Jewish discourses of identity—also Paul's. In his case, however, ethnic identity was indissolubly connected to a group's standing before God, Johnson Hodge states. Non-Jews were thus defined as the people who had rejected the God of Israel, and this state of affairs—the alienation of the non-Jews—constitutes Paul's central theological problem. This way of defining a certain group in contrast to another group Johnson Hodge labels "oppositional ethnic construction," which is to be distinguished from "aggregative ethnic construction," which means that one group affiliates with another group often in order to gain some advantage. Whereas traditional Pauline scholarship, and even the "new perspective," have often underlined that Paul created a new group, characterized by non-ethnic universalism, Johnson Hodge argues that oppositional and aggregative perspectives often interoperate in Paul's thinking. His argument certainly displays certain universalistic elements—Jews and non-Jews represent all people and Paul's aim is indeed the "reconciliation of the world" (Rom 11:15) — but this does not mean that ethnic labels can be abstracted or removed.

Paul's ethnic labels are mostly drawn from Scripture and reflect a Jewish perspective — the world is divided into Jews, *Ioudaioi*, and non-Jews, *ethnē*. Within the *ethnē* group, however, Paul sometimes describes a subgroup, the "Greeks" (*Hellēnes*), who probably represent Paul's target audience, that is, people who would identify themselves as participants in Hellenistic culture. Occasionally, Paul may even employ a *Greek* oppositional ethnic construction and speak of Greeks as "wise," while ascribing a negative value to "barbarians." In general, however, and when paired with *Ioudaios*, "Greek" is subordinate to *Ioudaios* and defines "the other." Paul "positions *Ioudaioi* as the norm and the center, around which others are defined and subordinated."[33] It is this contrasting conception of Jews and non-Jews that Paul is trying to redress. The problem is that non-Jews have no standing before God and have been handed over to "degrading passions" (Rom 1:26). Paul's aim is to solve this problem by creating a new identity through Christ for these people by giving them a new ancestry that will make it possible for them to achieve self-mastery, Johnson Hodge concludes.

By drawing from the social constructions of kinship and ethnicity prevalent in ancient society, Paul is able to present a solution to the problem: adoption by the Spirit. The key verse here is Galatians 3:29: "And if you belong to Christ, then you are Abraham's offspring, heirs according to the promise." Paul argues, according to Johnson Hodge, that baptism into Christ makes non-Jews descendants of Abraham, which links non-Jews to Israel and thus repairs the rift. Or put differently: an aggregative ethnic construction constitutes the solution to the problem created by an oppositional ethnic construction. Baptism thus constitutes the equivalent to other religious ceremonies whereby new kinship relations were established. This means that Paul establishes a kinship for non-Jews based, not on shared blood, but on shared spirit.

Crucial for Paul's argument is the distinction between "slaves" and "sons." In the ancient household, the father generally held the most authority. Slaves obviously held the least. Children, of course, enjoyed higher status than slaves, and in the case of sons, this was particularly true, since they were to inherit the property and the position as head over the household. Thus, Paul's way of arguing is based on the patrilineal privilege of sons. When non-Jews (most certainly including women, and slaves), through baptism, become "sons" (Gal 4:6, 7; Rom 8:14) they accordingly have the same rights and responsibilities as "true" sons, including the right to inherit the world (Rom 4:13), not in order to replace those already there, but to share the inheritance with them, Johnson Hodge states.

Equally crucial for understanding Paul's strategy for creating a new identity for non-Jews by adoption, are the phrases *hoi ek pisteōs* in Galatians 3:7, and *ek pisteōs* in Romans 4:16, Johnson Hodge argues. The NRSV translates Galatians 3:7 as "those who believe" and Romans 4:16 as "the one who shares the faith of Abraham." This, however, reflects the traditional, anachronistic understanding of *pistis* as denoting "an abstract, private disposition of the mind,"[34] and ignores the fact that the preposition *ek* typically describes the relationship between offspring and parent in contexts where kinship and descent are discussed. *Ek* can, for instance, describe how descendants come from certain lineages. So does Paul in Philippians 3:5 where he states that he is "a member of the people of Israel, of the tribe of Benjamin, a Hebrew born of Hebrews" (*ek genous Israēl, phylēs Beniamin, Hebraios ex* [= *ek*] *Hebraiōn*). Additional examples can be found in classical literature, the New Testament, and in the Septuagint.

Translating *pistis* as "faithfulness" is also to be preferred, Johnson Hodge states. The word certainly covers a wide range of meanings, but in antiquity it seldom refers to an abstract interior belief, but rather to specific character traits and resulting behavior. As we noted above, when scrutinizing the work of Lloyd Gaston, the phrase *pisteōs Iēsou Christou* could either be taken as a subjective or an objective genitive. In agreement with Gaston, Johnson Hodge argues that the former alternative "makes better sense of the grammar and challenges the 'faith versus works' interpretation of Paul."[35] Thus translating the phrase "faith of Christ" or "Christ's faith" makes "Christ," not the object of the believer's faith, but the agent of faithful and obedient action. The implications of this is important for understanding Paul's argument concerning Abraham, Johnson Hodge maintains, since Paul uses the same grammatical construction with regard to him. In Romans 4:16, the phrase *tō ek pisteōs Abraam* provides an exact parallel to *ton ek pisteōs* in Galatians 3:26. Thus Romans 4:16 reads, in Johnson Hodge's translation, "the one who comes out of the faithfulness of Abraham." Thus Paul uses the story of Abraham in Galatians 3:6-9 and Romans 4:16 to illustrate how God works in this world, that is, through patrilineal descent. God chooses a faithful person who receives his blessings, which are passed on to future generations. This principle is, of course, also applicable to Christ. Both Christ and Abraham were faithful to God and through baptism non-Jews become adopted sons through the faithfulness of Christ and are guaranteed that God's promise to Abraham will come to all his descendants, Jews and non-Jews alike.

This is possible because of another aspect of the ancient social construction of kinship—the idea, found in various texts, that something of the child is "in" the seed of the parent, meaning that the child and the ancestor of a people are identical. Through the patriarchal history, the chosen heir is identified, through whom the covenantal blessing is transmitted. The culmination of this process is Christ, and when non-Jews are baptized into Christ—the ritual of initiation into a new family—they are consequently added into the lineage of Abraham, who was blessed by God because of his faithfulness. This means that the non-Jews inherit his blessing, being "in" Abraham already at the moment he was blessed. Thus Christ does not become an ancestor of the non-Jews, Johnson Hodge argues, but a brother and a coheir (Rom 8:17, 29). Christ, being a true descendant of Abraham, hence serves as the crucial link between the non-Jews and Abraham. This, however, does not mean that ethnic identities are erased, as is commonly assumed. Johnson Hodge states that

> in any patrilineal descent group which might claim a corporate identity as descendants of a common ancestor, there are still hierarchies among the members: heads of households, sons, daughters, first-born, last-born, and so on. Unity based on kinship and social differences coexist.[36]

Ultimately, this is what Galatians 3:28 is all about: "*Ioudaioi* and Greeks, slaves and free, male and female can all be 'one in Christ' without abandoning other identities."[37] Thus in Johnson Hodge's interpretation of the relations between Jews and non-Jews within the early Jesus movement, non-Jews do not become *Ioudaioi* or "Christians," but non-Jews of a certain kind: non-Jews-in-Christ. They have rather been ethnically linked with Jews through baptism into Christ and "oppositional and aggregative strategies work in tandem to express this relationship, which includes a tension that propels both groups toward salvation."[38]

Needless to say, Johnson Hodge's interpretation challenges a cornerstone in the traditional interpretation of Paul. The idea that Paul transcended Jewish particularism and established Christian universalism has been one of the most important "truths" about Paul in almost all Pauline scholarship. This is, for instance, one of the few points where the traditional paradigm and the new perspective on Paul would agree, albeit from different points of departure. Thus Johnson Hodge's work shows that also with regard to the particularism-universalism dichotomy, a "radical new perspective" is able to present trustworthy alternatives to traditional scholarship.

Conclusion

The scholars whose works we have examined in this chapter have all moved beyond the Sanders-Dunn-Wright new perspective in several important respects. Sanders's revision of ancient Judaism, however, constitutes the natural point of departure, whereas his view of Paul has not convinced these scholars, whom for convenience I will group together as the proponents of "the radical new perspective." Thus the traditional dichotomy between Judaism and Christianity *is not* the fundamental assumption governing the outcome of these scholars' work. The common denominator is rather the opposite: these scholars work from the general assumption that Paul belonged to first-century Judaism—not that he left it.

This change of basic assumptions has led to several important shifts of focus and new results:

1. The traditional idea that Paul addressed the whole of humanity has been heavily challenged. Within the radical new perspective, it is quite clear that Paul addressed non-Jews.
2. The assumption that Paul turned to non-Jews has led scholars to the conclusion that his major theological problem concerned non-Jews, not Jews. This is true even with regard to the Torah. While traditional scholarship, often

reading Paul from a Protestant angle emphasizing a Paul-versus-Judaism perspective, has identified Paul's view of the Torah as the major dividing line between Judaism and Christianity, the radical new perspective rather points to the problem of the Torah *with regard to non-Jews*. This has led scholars to various suggestions concerning Paul's critique of the Torah. A persistent idea is that Paul himself made certain concessions when among non-Jews, while he in general found nothing wrong with Jewish followers of Jesus observing the Torah. This is, as we have seen, the view of Gaston and Stowers. Johnson Hodge also accedes to this idea.[39] In this respect, Nanos probably represents the most radical position. In his view, Paul remained fully Torah observant and meant that non-Jewish followers of Jesus should respect a Jewish lifestyle when among Jews.

3. While traditional scholarship and the new perspective often have argued that Paul created a new group, free from ethnic boundaries, these scholars maintain that the Jesus movement did not represent for Paul a "third race," but remained within Judaism, with new ideas about the appropriate ways to identify and instruct the non-Jewish members.

4. A common trait among the radical new perspective scholars is the ambition not to let contemporary Christian normative theology influence their interpretations. Quite the contrary, it is often the confusion of normative theology and scholarship that is being criticized. To some extent this is the result of the fact that not all biblical scholars are Christians anymore—an increasing number of Jewish scholars, for example, have engaged in the study of Paul during recent decades. In general, however, even Christian scholars within the radical new perspective seem less inclined to bring their scholarship in line with their respective religious affiliation. This is not to say that the radical new perspective is free from biases or represents objectivity in contrast to confessional interpretations, only that normative Christian theology plays a significantly less important role, which affects the basic assumptions from which the individual scholar argues. In this respect, the radical new perspective differs both from traditional Pauline scholarship, which aims at confirming normative theology, and from the new perspective, within which Christian theology still plays an important role, and normative issues remain part of the complex of problems.

Both the new perspective on Paul and the radical new perspective thus constitute a serious challenge to traditional interpretations of Paul, albeit for somewhat different reasons. The new perspective aims at creating a synthesis between traditional normative Protestant theology and the new view of Judaism, while the radical new perspective has thus far emphasized historical New Testament interpretive investigations, challenging the bases upon which Christian theology draws. The radical new perspective has not yet offered as much in the way of comprehensive alternative theological systems, perhaps with the exception of Jewish-Christian relations. Maybe this is the reason why the main target of recent Protestant reactions to new interpretations of Paul is not the radical interpretations of Paul but the new perspective on Paul. To such critique we are now going to turn.

6

IN DEFENSE OF PROTESTANTISM

From Plight to Solution—Frank S. Thielman

Thielman's monograph, *From Plight to Solution,* which appeared in 1989, belongs to the rather early reactions to Sanders. By the time of its publication, Sanders's revision of Judaism had become fairly well-established, and enough time had passed to give scholars a chance to reflect upon the consequences of the "new view of Judaism" for the study of Paul. Time was thus ripe for some critical evaluations of some of Sanders's main theses. As is evident from the title of Thielman's work, Sanders's suggestion that Paul argued from "solution to plight" is here under attack.

After having summarized previous research on Paul and the law, Thielman, who is Presbyterian Professor of Divinity at Beeson Divinity School, Samford University, concludes that prior to Sanders, there existed basically four explanations: (1) some scholars regarded Paul's statement of the law as a cardinal attack on Jewish "works-righteousness"; (2) others believed that rabbinic soteriology cannot explain Paul's statements, while the pessimism of Hellenistic Judaism can; (3) still others argued that Paul's view was the logical development of Jewish eschatology; (4) several scholars, finally, maintained that Paul's statements can only be explained on the basis on Paul's encounter with the risen Christ, thus outside the context of Judaism. This fourth alternative, the "Christological explanation," reached its climax with the publication of *Paul and Palestinian Judaism,* Thielman states.

While most scholars, in principle, accepted Sanders's new picture of Judaism, many remained unconvinced by his formulations of Paul's view of the law: "Räisänen felt it had not gone far enough; [Hans] Weder and Dunn felt it had gone too far."[1] Now Thielman notes that previous attempts to explain Paul's view of the law against his Jewish background, especially appeals to common Jewish eschatological notions (the third alternative in Thielman's summary above), have failed to convince the scholarly community. However, since the days of Albert Schweitzer, Hans J. Schoeps, and William D. Davies, three main proponents of an apocalyptic/eschatological perspective on Paul, the picture of Judaism has undergone substantial changes (Sanders's revision, for example) and more sources, such as the pseudepigraphal material, have become easily accessible, Thielman asserts. For this reason, he wants to "reexamine the possibility that Paul's view of the law owes its origin to an eschatological pattern common within some expressions of Judaism."[2]

As we recall, Sanders suggested that Paul argued from "solution to plight." Since Judaism was not legalistic, as had previously been assumed, but characterized by a common pattern within ancient Judaism, covenantal nomism, Paul really found nothing wrong with Judaism. The main reason Paul rejected the Torah as a way to salvation was that God had chosen another way—Jesus Christ. Paul thus started with the solution to the problem, while inventing the problem to which Jesus was the solution. Thielman, however, maintains that Paul argued the other way around: from "plight to solution." Thus by way of introduction, he starts out to show that such a common "plight-solution" pattern was prevalent within ancient Judaism.

Already in the first chapters of the Hebrew Bible, the idea that humanity "is inescapably tainted with sin" appears, Thielman states.[3] In Genesis 3, the sin of Adam and Eve is followed by the story of the first murder in chapter 4, leading up to God's decision in Genesis 6:7 to "blot out from the earth the human beings." The same theme—that of human rebellion against God—is a frequently recurrent one in the Pentateuch, in the Writings, and in the Prophets, and is often connected to the inability of God's people to keep the law. However, Thielman notes, despite this rather pessimistic outlook, the Hebrew Bible also assigns to God the future intention of relieving his people from the plight their inclination to sin constitutes. The prophets and the psalmist, for instance, clearly express this hope for the future. Thielman concludes:

> Thus Jewish scripture during Paul's day, especially in the Greek form in which Paul knew it, viewed the history of God's people largely as a history of failure to do God's will. Often this failure was expressed in terms of Israel's continual violation of God's law or covenant. Many of the same passages in which this failure was expressed, however, also extended the hope that at some future time God would intervene to destroy the vicious cycle of sin and rebellion and produce a people who would obey him from their hearts.[4]

Thielman also finds this pattern of "plight to solution" in other kinds of Jewish literature, namely in the Dead Sea Scrolls and in the Pseudepigrapha. Pointing to the fact that this pattern was not the only one, Thielman nevertheless reaches the conclusion that "both canonical and non-canonical Jewish literature from the era in which Paul lived demonstrate familiarity with a pattern of thinking about God's dealing with Israel which runs from plight to solution."[5]

Thielman now proceeds by examining the role of this pattern in Galatians and Romans. As for Galatians, which we will concentrate on, he refers to the fact that the letter has been considered Paul's most un-Jewish letter and that most scholars regard it as evidence that Paul broke with Judaism. Noticing that there are problems with this view— Paul, for instance, clearly defines himself as Jewish in Galatians 2:15— Thielman suggests that Paul's view of the law is fully in accordance with a common eschatological hope within Judaism. Thus in Thielman's view, Paul "did not simply and unambiguously disassociate himself from Judaism or even from the Torah."[6] For example, in Galatians 5:14, Paul admonishes his audience to "fulfill" the law, at least implicitly, by referring to Leviticus 19:18: "You shall love your neighbor as yourself." The whole law is summed up in this single command, Paul says. For scholars who maintain that Paul rejected every aspect of "doing" Torah, this verse constitutes an obvious problem. As Thielman states, one way of dealing with this has been to distinguish between "doing" the law in Judaism and "fulfilling" the law in Galatians 5:14.[7] Hans Hübner has suggested that Paul's statement in Galatians 5:3 ("I testify to every man who lets himself be circumcised that he is obliged to obey the entire law") certainly contradicts his assertion in 5:14, but if the latter statement is taken in an ironic sense, both statements are intelligible within the larger context of the letter.[8] Räisänen, finally, argues that the statement in 5:14 is a positive one and that it contradicts 5:3, but that is only to be expected from the unsystematic thinker Paul.[9] Thielman finds none of these explanations satisfactory, however.

The problem is, Thielman argues, that most interpreters have taken Paul's remark in Galatians 5:2-3 as an argument against "the whole law" because of his seemingly negative view of circumcision. But, Thielman continues, from other texts it is evident that Paul distinguished between "the law" and "circumcision." In 1 Corinthians 7:19, for instance, he says that circumcision "is nothing, and uncircumcision is nothing; but obeying the commandments of God is everything." Thus when Paul denies the validity of circumcision, it does not imply that the whole Torah has been superseded. Paul's aim is rather "a challenge to keep the law without the Spirit (implying it cannot be done) and 5:14, taken within its lager context, is an assertion that the challenge can be met by walking in the spirit."[10] Thus Paul indeed reserves a place for Torah observance within his eschatological scheme, Thielman concludes. This concentration on the ethical dimension of the Torah was fully in agreement with a tendency within Diaspora Judaism, Thielman states, and would have been welcomed by many Hellenistic Jews. Paul actually "argues within the conceptual world of Hellenistic Judaism that the eschatological age predicted by the scriptures has arrived."[11]

Confusion about the dawn of the eschatological age is precisely the main problem in Galatians, Thielman continues. By analyzing three texts, Galatians 2:15-16, 3:10-14, and 3:19—5:12, he reaches the conclusion that Paul's aim is to persuade the Galatians that the coming of the eschatological age has made it superfluous to accept circumcision in order to become righteous. In fact, accepting circumcision, food laws, and Sabbath observance means taking a step back into the evil age, which has ended with the coming of Christ. Paul's intention in Galatians 2:15-16 is simply to articulate the common Jewish idea that no one can do the law correctly, not to accuse Judaism of "legalism," or (contra Dunn) to criticize Jews for merely being focused on "national righteousness." In Galatians 3:10-14, Paul defines this as the plight of humanity—to be under the curse of the law brought upon humanity because of its inability to observe the law. The solution to this plight is available for those who put their faith in God's eschatological provision. One of the purposes of the law was precisely to enclose all things under sin, Paul argues in Galatians 3:19 — 5:12, which is what those who submit to circumcision will experience. However, Paul's intention was not to abrogate every aspect of the law; it still has a vital function in the eschatological age and will be observed with the help of the Spirit. Still, Thielman maintains, Paul's argument in Galatians runs, as in Judaism, *from plight to solution.*

In Romans, Thielman finds basically the same plight-solution pattern as in Galatians. In contrast to the majority of scholars who have emphasized that Paul argues not from Jewish presuppositions but on the basis of his Christology, Thielman suggests that the Jewish plight-solution pattern is the interpretive key. Thus also in Romans, the law entertains a prominent place within the eschatological situation and Paul's critique is only aimed at showing that law observance outside of Christ is impossible and brings the curse of the law upon the sinner.

Thielman's book is a massive attack on one of Sanders's main theses — "from solution to plight" — and is, at the same time, a forceful defense of Reformed theology. This latter aspect is, of course, prominent in Thielman's persistence in arguing that the law has not lost its importance in the eschatological age — with help of the Spirit, those in Christ can fulfill the law. Yet, there are some points of agreement: Thielman states that he finds the reconsideration of the Lutheran and Bultmannian interpretations to be "a healthy enterprise" and hopes to have contributed to this enterprise by questioning the idea that Paul considered that keeping the law only leads humanity into sin.[12] Paul, Thielman says, had nothing against "doing" the law — only the failure to do it. He also readily accepts Sanders's idea that Judaism was not a meritorious religion, even though he hardly agrees with Sanders regarding the function of the law — Paul, according to Sanders, does not claim that Jews cannot fulfill the law. This is one of the aspects of Sanders's picture of Paul that Thielman opposes most insistently. Only in Christ can the law be fulfilled and Christ is the solution to a real problem (a genuine human plight) a theme Thielman finds deeply imbedded in Jewish tradition. This is why Thielman, in contrast to Sanders, maintains that Paul did not "simply and unambiguously disassociate himself from Judaism or even from the Torah."[13]

In the following we will see how subsequent scholars, although in different ways, have refined the idea of interpreting Paul against a Jewish background that in decisive respects differs from Sanders's Judaism. Furthermore, the critique of Sanders and the new perspective is a recurrent theme also in more recent scholarship, as is another salient feature in Thielman's work—the legitimization of a rather well-defined normative theological standpoint.

Beyond Covenantal Nomism—A. Andrew Das

In *Paul, the Law, and the Covenant* by A. Andrew Das, Sanders's *Paul and Palestinian Judaism* constitutes the obvious point of departure. While accepting many aspects of Sanders's new view of Judaism, Das, Professor of Religious Studies at Elmhurst College, nevertheless finds reason to ask whether Sanders has not overemphasized the element of grace in Judaism, while overlooking the frequent admonitions to observe perfectly the Torah. The new approaches to Paul, Das asserts, have in common that they share Sanders's view that Jews never believed they had to observe the Torah perfectly, but could rely on divine election and the atonement system imbedded in the Torah. However, not all scholars have found, for example, Dunn's idea of national righteousness convincing, Das continues. Even if they accept Sanders's claim that Judaism was not legalistic, some still assert that Paul's problem with the Torah is precisely that it places legal demands on people that they cannot fulfill. Thus the dividing line in current Pauline scholarship concerns whether Paul believed that on Jewish terms it was necessary to obey the law perfectly or not.

Accepting Sanders's idea that Paul was no covenantal nomist leads to the crucial question of how the demands of the law are affected if the gracious framework of Judaism is denied salvific efficacy. Indeed, Das states, one would expect "the law's character as a demand to come to the fore and to emerge as problematic."[14] The problem, so Das states, is precisely that Sanders minimized the belief prevalent in Judaism that God intended the Torah to be obeyed strictly and in its entirety. In reality, Das claims, Judaism maintained a balance between strict Torah observance and the possibility of atonement, thus between a judgment according to works and a judgment according to mercy.

By rereading many of the texts that Sanders's dealt with in *Paul and Palestinian Judaism*, without downplaying those aspects that concern perfect Torah observance, Das demonstrates the interplay between the demand to perfect obedience and the possibility of atonement. In *Jubilees*, for example, it is clear that Israel, as God's elect, must live according to the precepts that distinguish them from non-Jews—the Torah. Idolatry and intermarriage are thus strictly forbidden, while the Jews must observe the Sabbath, practice circumcision, celebrate various festivals, and give tithes, among other things. Failure to fulfill some of these obligations compromises the status of the individual as among the elect. For some sins, but not all, there is atonement. Eating meat with blood or violating the Sabbath are unforgivable transgressions, while less serious sins can be atoned for through the sacrificial system, the value of which is affirmed by the author of *Jubilees*.[15]

In the Qumran literature, the emphasis on perfect observance of all the law is yet more accentuated. Even seemingly minor sins such as slandering or murmuring against the leadership resulted in automatic and irrevocable expulsion from the community with no hope for a place in the world to come. Still stricter observance was expected from those who had been members of the community for ten years or more.[16]

In the works of Philo, Das also finds evidence of an ideology focused on perfect Torah observance. Even though Philo advocates an allegorical interpretation of the Bible, he nevertheless encourages a strict observance of the Torah in all respects, especially in order to maintain a Jewish identity in relation to the surrounding non-Jewish world. Some individuals, such as Abraham, are even commended for having achieved perfect law observance, which clearly is Philo's ideal. It is, however, evident that Philo believed that faultless observance was very hard to accomplish, and sinlessness is really a characteristic reserved for God only. God is, however, thought of as merciful, and the literal meaning of the sacrificial system is never denied. Thus "God initiates and provides a resolution for the situation caused by disobedience of the law."[17]

Turning to Tannaitic literature, Das argues that several passages contradict Sanders's denial of the rabbis' demand for perfect obedience.

A more nuanced reading reveals the exact same pattern as in other Jewish literature: a tension between deserving obedience and undeserved mercy. Rabbi Akiva, for instance, while asserting that the world will be judged by mercy, nevertheless simultaneously claims that judgment is according to the majority of works (*m. 'Abot* 3:16). Rabbi Gamaliel, however, seems to have meant that God expected strict and perfect observance, leaving little room for shortcomings. Das concludes: "While most rabbis sided with Akiba that God does not judge strictly, *m. 'Abot* 3:16 shows that the rabbis *did* at times assert that God's justice requires perfect obedience."[18]

Thus the texts reviewed by Das share the underlying theological assumption that perfect Torah observance is indeed required and constitutes the obvious ideal, while this requirement is always seen in relation to the gracious framework of divine election (which is also alternately presented as an act of God's mercy or as a response to human obedience) and mercy. As such, covenant and obligation represented two sides of the same coin. However, when the covenantal aspects for various reasons were downplayed, this resulted in an increased accentuation of the demands of the law, Das states. This is what has happened in texts like *4 Ezra, 2 Enoch, 2 Baruch, 3 Baruch*, and the *Testament of Abraham*, all of which exhibit "an increase in the focus on the strict demands of the law when God's election of Israel is no longer a factor."[19] While this partly can be explained by the fact that many of these documents reflect the catastrophe of 70 CE, the increased accentuation on the demands of the law represents the natural development of the compromise constituted by the balance between grace and demands in the pre-70 setting, Das maintains.

Having thus shown the prevalence of two opposing tendencies within Judaism—perfect obedience and undeserved mercy—and that some texts reveal an increased focus on strict demands of the law when the covenantal aspects are downplayed, Das proceeds by posing the question of whether Paul would have affirmed the covenant's significance as understood by Sanders's covenantal nomisms. After having analyzed three texts, Galatians 3:15-17, 4:21-31, and 2 Corinthians 3:1-18, Das reaches the conclusion that Paul has unambiguously moved beyond covenantal nomism. In Galatians 3:15-17, Das finds no evidence that Paul considers the law to have any salvific or life-giving capacity. From Galatians 4:21-31, he deduces that Paul argues that the law no longer serves within a frame-work of grace—the Sinai covenant is a covenant of slavery connected with Hagar and Ishmael. Reading 2 Corinthians 3 with Exodus 32–34 as the main hermeneutical key leads to the conclusion that the old covenant remains a ministry of death because of the "stiff-necked" condition of the Jewish people. These aspects, among others, rule out the possibility that Paul would have affirmed the covenant as defined by Sanders's concept of covenantal nomism.

Now would Paul have affirmed covenantal nomism's emphasis on Israel's election? Das answers that Paul redefined election in terms of those who have faith in Christ. Romans 11:26 ("all Israel will be saved") offers, according to Das, the closest parallel to a Jewish understanding of Israel's national election and future salvation. But does Paul grant ethnic Israel a place in the world to come? Analyzing Romans 9–11, Das finds that Paul has redefined the elect christologically, so that God's faithfulness to Israel becomes subordinated to Paul's concern for the salvation of those in Christ, which also includes non-Jews. It should be noted, Das maintains, that when Paul indeed accounts for all the advan-tages of the Jewish people in Romans 9:1-5, he never states, as in the later Mishnah (*m. Sanh.* 10:1), that all Israel have a share in the world to come. Instead, the enumeration of Israel's advantages culminates with the Messiah. Moreover, the end of Romans 9:5 (*ho ōn epi pantōn theos eulogētos eis tous aiōnas*) should, according to Das, be taken as mod-ifying "Christ," thus creating an identification between "God" and "Christ." Refusing to accept Jesus as the Christ would accordingly amount to rejecting the Jews' own God. If Christ is the God who is above all, "then a failure to follow the law to Christ would be to fall into idolatry," Das concludes.[20]

With regard to Romans 11:26, Das finds that scholars have offered basically four interpretations. Some have argued for "a two-covenant solution": the Torah is for the Jews what Christ is for the non-Jews. However, Das states, Paul would not have called Jesus "the Messiah" in Romans 9:5 unless he did not also consider him a vital part of the Jewish heritage. Other scholars believe "all Israel" means an "Israel of faith," that is, a people of God that includes both Jewish and non-Jewish followers of Jesus. Das also rejects this suggestion: it is evident that Paul makes a clear distinction between "Israel" and the non-Jews throughout Romans 9–11. A third group of scholars maintains that "all Israel" really means the Jewish remnant mentioned in Romans 9:1-23 and 11:1-10. But, Das, asserts, "all Israel" in 11:25 stands in stark contrast to the "remnant" in 11:5-7, which renders this solution unlikely. Instead, Das finds the fourth alternative most convincing, according to which "all Israel," refers to a future mass conversion among the Jewish people. In short: those who presently are "enemies" will finally constitute "all Israel" and the law that until the coming of Christ had defined the elect no longer holds this function.

After an extensive discussion of the role of the sacrificial system in the Hebrew Bible, and possible allusions to this system of atonement in Paul's letters, Das is able to answer the question whether it is likely that Paul would have affirmed covenantal nomism's emphasis on atoning sacrifice. Sanders ascribed great importance to the sacrificial system in Judaism, as we recall. By means of atonement, the individual could restore a broken relationship with God. Das indeed recognizes that atoning sacrifices were an important institution within ancient Judaism. The question is whether Paul would have agreed. Several texts in Paul's writings allude to the sacrificial system, and many scholars believe that Paul thought of Christ's atoning ministry in terms of an atoning sacrifice. Das, however, argues that a better model for understanding Paul's explanation of Christ's saving work is an apotropaic ritual, that is, a ritual basically intended to ward off evil of some kind. Such rituals, Das states, involve a substitutionary representation, as in the case of the ritual at the Day of Atonement when an animal was driven out in the wilderness carrying away the sins of the people. In fact, Das maintains, Paul nowhere ascribes any salvific value to the atoning offerings in Judaism. When occasionally speaking of Christ in sacrificial terms, he is only illustrating the significance of *Christ's* saving work—not that of the sacrifices in and of themselves. Thus the atoning death of Jesus is effective in a way the sacrificial rituals in Judaism are not, according to Paul, Das concludes. This means that three vital features within Judaism—covenant, election, and sacrifices—are virtually nullified in Paul's mind.

Das now turns to the issue of whether Paul meant that the law required perfect observance. The crucial passage here is Galatians 3:10: "For all who rely on the works of the law are under a curse; for it is written, 'Cursed is everyone who does not observe and obey all the things written in the book of the law.'" While this passage traditionally has been taken as evidence that Paul really meant that the law requires perfect obedience, scholars, inspired by Sanders, have begun to finds other interpretations. According to Dunn, for example, perfect law observance is thought irrelevant since "works of the law" does not refer to the law in its entirety, but only to those aspects that distinguish Jews from non-Jews. Das, however, argues that Galatians 3:10 should be read against the background of deuteronomistic theology, especially Deuteronomy 27–30, where the connection between various curses and failure to observe "diligently . . . all the words of this law" (Deut 28:58) is a salient feature. Many Jews during the intertestamental period still believed they were under the curse of the exile, Das states—and Paul was one of them. His opponents in Galatia, however, comprising covenantal nomism, placed far more emphasis on the *blessings* bestowed upon Israel. From Paul's perspective, however, Israel's *inability in the past to avoid the curse of the exile* constitutes no ideal example for admonishing non-Jews to rely on the law, Das maintains, because the law evidently cannot be fulfilled and no one, whether Jew or non-Jew, can establish a right relationship with God through the law.

Jewish covenantal nomists are Paul's target also in Romans 2:17-29, Das states. While he argues that Romans 1:18-32 is not only directed toward non-Jews, as is the common view, but also toward Jews, he finds that Paul nevertheless introduces a new section in 2:17, which is specifically directed toward Jews. Paul is not attacking a legalistic Jew who is trying to earn his or her way into heaven, but a covenantal nomist, who believes that membership among the elect, God's chosen people, will guarantee a place in the world to come. Against this, Paul argues that Jewish identity is not enough, since if one transgresses the law, one's "circumcision has become uncircumcision" (Rom 2:25). He thus places Jews and non-Jews on equal footing—Jews have no advantage before non-Jews because of their special status as the chosen people. In this, Das asserts, Paul has departed from Judaism and has clearly moved away from covenantal nomism.

In Romans 3:27–4:8, Paul continues to confront Jewish claims on ethnic advantages because they are in possession of the law. In this passage too Paul insists that God will judge humanity equally accord-ing to their deeds, and this is also the problem—the law involves demands. Since not even Abraham and David were able to meet the standards of the law, God must justify the ungodly apart from the law, which opens a door to the salvation of the non-Jews. In this respect, the law has always pointed to the necessity of faith, having been emp-tied of any saving significance (Rom 3:21-26). All that remains of the law when grace has entirely been transferred to Christ is human achievement, Das claims. The demand of the law is further addressed in Romans 7. Contra Dunn, Das argues that Paul here elaborates on the law's function of placing a demand on people that they are unable to meet: "the failed daily struggle to do what the law requires leads to bondage and enslavement."[21]

Das's book is, of course, a tremendous defense of the traditional view of Paul. The most important aspects from the Reformation per-spective are all prevalent in Das's reading, albeit in a new, partly inno-vative way. However, Paul is clearly seen in contrast to Judaism and has moved beyond the most vital Jewish aspects of faith: the covenant, the election, and the atoning function of sacrifices. The law has no real function for Paul and represents only human achievements.

On the one hand, Das delivers a thorough critique of Sanders's emphasis on grace as the most important characteristic of ancient Judaism (though he agrees with Sanders that Paul was no covenan-tal nomist). On the other hand, it is primarily those scholars who have used Sanders's picture for creating a portrait of Paul that radi-cally differs from Sanders's who are criticized, in short: the advocates of "the new perspective on Paul." Thus, for example, while Dunn believes Sanders to be correct with regard to Judaism (Jews were in general covenantal nomists) and wrong with regard to Paul (who *was* a covenantal nomist), Das believes Sanders to be wrong about Judaism (Jews were indeed covenantal nomists but of another kind) and correct with regard to Paul (who was *not* a covenantal nomist). Whatever position one takes with regard to Paul and Judaism, Das's critique of Sanders is important and should be taken seriously.

Das constructs the relations between Paul and Judaism in a way that differs radically from both Sanders and the proponents of the new perspective on Paul. What Das finds wrong with Judaism is not that it was legalistic or that Jews were unilaterally occupied with works-righteousness, as was the common assumption in previous scholarship, but that Jews indeed embraced *a modified form of covenantal nomism.* While Sanders, in Das's view, overemphasized grace in Judaism, while disregarding those aspects in Jewish literature that certainly speak about merits or the connection between works and salvation, Das suggests a more nuanced picture: both aspects, grace and works, were prevalent in Jewish thinking. Some Jews erred in the same way Sanders did by putting too much stress on grace. Paul's newfound faith in Christ, however, compelled him to stress deuteronomistic theology to its extreme and led him to place the law in an entirely new setting in which it lost its importance.

Boasting in Christ—Simon J. Gathercole

In certain areas, Simon J. Gathercole's study, *Where is Boasting?* (2002), resembles Das's work, yet focuses on a more narrow aspect of Paul's theological outlook. Both scholars, however, focus on the issue of whether Sanders too simplistically pictured ancient Judaism as a religion of grace while downplaying the texts that reveal that Jews also, and perhaps even simultaneously, could think in terms of merits and works when reflecting on election, or more broadly, on salvation. Gathercole, Lecturer in New Testament at the University of Aberdeen, Scotland, has chosen a topic that has attracted rather few thorough treatments—boasting. Through the lens of the concept of "boasting"—which is rather generally recognized as connected to the doctrines of justification and salvation—Gathercole examines Judaism and Romans 1–5.

Because of the revolution that Sanders's *Paul and Palestinian Judaism* effected, scholars began to see Paul's talk about "boasting" in a new light, primarily because of its connection to other significant concepts that were affected by Sanders's revision, such as the doctrine of justification. Thus among the new perspective scholars, the idea that Torah observance represents a crucial criterion for acceptance at the final judgment is either completely denied or deemphasized, Gathercole asserts. The problem is, however, that such an approach is dangerously one-sided, and leads to serious distortions regarding the presentation of the relation between Paul and Judaism. In reality, Gathercole continues, "obedience as a condition of and basis for final vindication and salvation at the *eschaton* is fundamental to Jewish thought."[22]

This insight clearly affects the interpretation of Paul. For example, in the secondary literature, there is a considerable discussion of the meaning of Paul's expression "works of the law." We have briefly touched upon the problems involved in interpreting this phrase in connection with Dunn's and Gaston's work in the previous chapter and in Das's work in this chapter. Dunn, we recall, argues that "works of the law" specifically refers to those aspects of the Torah that distinguish Jews from non-Jews. The discussion concerns basically whether this is accurate, that is, is it correct that works of the law are identity markers, as the proponents of the new perspective argue, or does the phrase refer to something that has a functional role as a criterion for final salvation? With regard to "boasting," this is highly relevant, Gathercole asserts. If Paul simply uses "works of the law" for defining "Israel," then "boasting" in Romans can be understood as the confidence that membership in this group provides, thus only indirectly providing a basis for confidence of final salvation. However, if works of the law in some way are connected to God's reward for observing the Torah, resulting in eternal life at the *eschaton*, then boasting becomes directly connected to the idea of being justified through Torah observance. Although this position "has often had unfortunate connotations and therefore is hardly in vogue today, it does need to be reexamined," Gathercole states, and makes the addition that in his view, "there is a considerable amount of truth in it."[23]

With regard to methodology, Gathercole underlines that "any advance on the current state of play in Pauline scholarship will need to avoid the polemical formulations that have thus far characterized much of the debate."[24] This is, of course, an approach to be welcomed, and Gathercole is right in drawing attention to the fact that the discussion on Paul and Judaism has hardly benefited from the polarization of the discussion between proponents of the old and the new perspectives. In all likelihood *both* perspectives are in need of some correction. Gathercole's contribution to bring balance to the discussion involves, for instance, the ambition to cut through some of the emotive language often prevalent in the conversation and by trying not to force the pendulum to the opposite direction by means of polemic.

In the main part of book, Gathercole thus performs a careful analysis of a large number of texts from the Second Temple period, looking for an answer to the question of the basis of final salvation at the judgment. Since chronology is a crucial factor—some texts such as *4 Ezra*, for example, may have been affected by the fall of the temple—Gathercole deals almost exclusively with texts predating 70 CE. Later texts are used as supplementary and supporting evidence rather than as independent ones.

Gathercole first deals with the apocryphal and pseudepigraphal texts and finds ample evidence of images of final judgment, reward, or punishment for individuals. Even though some texts like Sirach, Tobit, and 1 Maccabees display no clear evidence of personal immortality, resurrection, or afterlife, there are nevertheless substantial discussions of deeds and rewards in connection with the ethical concerns of the authors, Gathercole states. In these texts, the reward of obedience is not eternal life but prolonged life and prosperity. Other texts, such as the *Testament of Job*, the *Sibylline Oracles*, the *Psalms of Solomon*, 2 Maccabees, and *1 Enoch*, which indeed picture a future age involving punishment and reward after death, clearly envisage obedience as a vital basis for receiving eternal life, albeit in different ways. "All these different portraits," Gathercole concludes, "highlight the fact that God is portrayed as saving his people at the *eschaton* on the basis of their obedience, as well as on the basis of his election of them."[25]

Turning to the Qumran literature, Gathercole argues against Sanders's view that the phrase "works of the Torah" simply refers to deeds carried out in response to God's grace. This view, however, only represents one side of the coin. In *Miqṣat Ma'aśê ha-Torah* (4QMMT), Gathercole claims the expression primarily refers to deeds done in obedience to the totality of the Torah and is as such already anticipated in the Hebrew Bible, where the verb "to do" frequently is connected with the noun "Torah." Thus the phrase "works of the Torah" has its "roots firmly established in the Hebrew Bible, and the noun phrase we see in Qumran and Paul is a very natural development."[26] As for the future soteriology, one important theme in the Qumran writings is (as in the apocryphal and pseudepigraphal texts) that *the present Torah observance will be rewarded at the judgment.* This theme certainly exists side by side, or rather in combination, with other models, such as national-political interpretations, and implies "a considerable future dimension in the theology of the group that is often considered to have the most 'realized' eschatology of all the Jewish groups of which we have evidence."[27]

A Jewish eschatological framework is also prevalent in the New Testament, Gathercole asserts. In the Gospel of Matthew, many examples can be found that clearly demonstrate that the author adhered to the idea of a reward for deeds and a judgment according to works (for example Matt 9:41), sometimes in a soteriological context (for example Matt 16:24-27), even though these are balanced by passages that emphasize election and grace (for example Matt 25–27, 19:25-26). In John's Gospel, no polemics against works are to be found, although the author has reinterpreted "doing" in a very specific way: the work required for eternal life is interpreted as believing in Jesus (John 6:26-29). In James's letter, the issue that has created most problems is the fact that James seems to affirm that a person is justified by works (Jas 2:22a). This, however, is not a problem, Gathercole asserts, since it only shows that James stands in continuity with his Jewish background: "works have a genuine instrumental role in eschatological justification for the believers James is addressing."[28]

The same is true with regard to Paul, according to Gathercole. In Romans 2, we find both an expression of the early Jesus movement's theology of judgment according to works and the same theology in contemporary Judaism. It is clear, Gathercole maintains, that Paul's dialogue partner in Romans 2 believed in a final judgment according to works. Paul, however, makes no attempt to question this theology; indeed "he cheerfully affirms it."[29] Now Paul certainly construes "obedience" differently, since with Paul, "works" should not be understood in terms of works done in obedience to the Torah. Paul never uses the Torah for the purposes of parenesis, which might be explained by his radical statements regarding the temporariness of the Torah, Gathercole argues. It is rather the christological nature of Paul's ethics that leads him to exhort his readers to imitate Christ. Thus, the model for Christian obedience is the burden borne by Christ—believers follow Christ by bearing one another's burdens.

Paul hence shows continuity with Jewish tradition in regarding obedience to be a vital criterion for the judgment, and discontinuity with
regard to the character of obedience, Gathercole concludes. Thus it is
not entirely clear what the common ground between early Christianity
and early Judaism is. "It is not that both consist in initial grace that
fully accomplishes salvation, followed by works which are evidence
of that; rather, both share an elective grace and also assign a determi-
native role to works at final judgment."[30]

Before turning to boasting in Romans 1–5, Gathercole reviews a
number of Jewish texts to see whether Jewish confidence is oriented
toward eschatology and whether Jews express confidence in relation to
God or to non-Jews. According to a common view within traditional
scholarship, Paul regarded doubts about salvation as the most significant problem within Judaism. The new perspective scholars, on the
other hand, claim that Judaism was not characterized by fear and that
Jews based their confidence in the final salvation on the grace of God,
not on their works. Gathercole's analysis reveals that both positions are
in need of significant correction. In certain texts from the Second
Temple period, the Jewish people are pictured as a holy, pious, and obedient nation, which also translates into the individual level—references
to perfect obedience in a variety of forms are numerous. This, Gathercole
claims, seriously calls into question the idea of doubts about salvation
found in previous scholarship. However, in this respect, the new
perspective also has seriously gone astray by excluding such texts as
Gathercole has analyzed and which show that "Jews represented themselves as obedient, virtuous people both in relation to gentiles *and*
before God."[31]

Finally, Gathercole reaches the point where his analysis of Jewish
texts will shed light on Romans 1–5. First, he points out that Paul has
already interacted with a *Jewish* interlocutor in Romans 2:1-16. This is
an important standpoint as some scholars, like Stanley Stowers and
Neil Elliott (whose recent work on Romans will be examined in the
next chapter), maintain that Paul introduces a Jewish interlocutor only
in Romans 2:17. Moreover, Gathercole claims that this Jew not only
represents one individual, as, for instance, a Jewish teacher, which is
sometimes suggested, but the Jewish people as a whole. Thus the sins
enumerated in 2:21-22 represent the sins of Israel as a nation. Now this

representative of the Jewish people is not only sinful but also *unrepen-tant and in effect an apostate,* Gathercole states. In Romans 2:4, Paul describes this assumed Jewish dialogue partner as someone who does not realize that "God's kindness is meant to lead you to repentance." Thus Paul is, according to Gathercole, denying that the Jewish inter-locutor is repentant of his sin, which means that Paul explicitly denies the validity of this representative of Israel to claim the title "Jew." In this, Gathercole asserts, Paul's accusation bears resemblance to com-ments in some strands of Jewish literature where disregard for the Torah is interpreted in terms of apostasy. In agreement with many other Jews, the Jewish interlocutor holds on to a doctrine of final salvation according to works. This Jewish confidence in the covenant presup-poses an assurance of obedience to the covenant, Gathercole says. It is this assurance of obedience that Paul criticizes in 2:1-5, 2:21-24, and 3:10-20.

Moreover, against Dunn and Wright, who believe that "justification by works of the Torah" refers to national privilege and exclusivism, Gathercole defends an anthropological standpoint. In Romans 4:2, Paul summarizes a Jewish expository tradition, Gathercole states, which asserts that Abraham was justified through works. In 1 Maccabees 2:52, for example, the author claims that "Abraham [was] found faithful when tested," implying that Abraham's obedience was not just an indi-cation of membership in the covenant, but that Abraham and conse-quently also Israel were justified through obedience, that is, works. This is exactly the point where Paul disagrees with his Jewish contempo-raries—human obedience without transformation in Christ can never be the basis for justification: Abraham is the model of faith and the Torah is also centered in faith. Thus Abraham, being an ungodly idol-ater, was justified without works on the basis of faith. The same soteri-ological pattern is thus applicable for the Jewish people, who are Abraham's descendants, Gathercole asserts. However, "Jewish thought made the mistake of conforming Abraham to its own soteriology based on commutative justice rather than conforming its own pattern to that of Abraham."[32]

This means that Paul is not only involved in defining the conditions under which non-Jews might be included in the covenant, which propo-nents of the new perspective often point out. Rather, Paul's discussion with the Jew in Romans 2 and his interpretation of Abraham's justification in Romans 4 show that Paul is concerned about the conditions under which sinful Israelites are accepted by God. In Romans 3:28, Paul argues against the view that works of the Torah lead to justification, not because this would lead to the exclusion of non-Jews—but to the exclusion of everyone—even Israel as a nation. Paul's doctrine of justification by faith concerns humanity in general, Gathercole maintains. Paul opposes Jewish boasting "in God" (Rom 2:17), because the Jew has an unrepentant heart, and even though he calls himself a Jew, in reality he is not. The Jewish confidence in salvation at the *eschaton*, based on election and obedience, is thus fundamentally unjustified. In Paul's mind, there is only room for boasting in Christ.

Gathercole's study has the same basic setup as the two previous works we have dealt with in this chapter. On the one hand, we find a thorough critique of some of the most fundamental aspects within the new perspective on Paul; on the other hand, the author suggests a new interpretation, which in all essentials represents a confirmation of the traditional perspective. Admittedly, Gathercole, in conformity with Das, also questions some important cornerstones within the traditional paradigm and even acknowledges some of Sanders's basic revisions. Judaism was not legalistic, Gathercole claims, nor was works-righteousness the most fundamental characteristics of ancient Judaism. He even problematizes the use of such terminology because of its connotations. As was the case with Das, Gathercole's critique of Sanders and the new perspective on Paul is important and every Pauline scholar needs to address the possibility that Sanders might have overstated his case. Gathercole shows convincingly that ancient Jews found no problem in combining two elements that from a Reformation perspective give rise to the most serious cognitive dissonance: grace *and* works.

With regard to his analysis, however, it is hard to avoid the impression that it is exactly such cognitive dissonance that is the motivating force behind his work. What Paul finds wrong with Judaism, according to Gathercole, is precisely that the Jews worshipped a God who both honors Torah observance and blots out transgressions according to his "steadfast love" and "abundant mercy" (Ps 51:1). That may very well be the case, but it could also be that the Protestant

dichotomy between grace and works has so permeated Western thinking that we are almost unable to see things from a different angle. As
we will see at the end of the review of the magisterial work of Stephen
Westerholm below, perhaps not even Sanders was able to free himself
from thinking in Lutheran categories.

The Explicitly Lutheran Paul—Stephen Westerholm

Stephen Westerholm, Professor of Biblical Studies at McMaster University, Canada, opens his study, *Perspectives Old and New on Paul* (2004),
with an account of four portraits of the "Lutheran Paul," where, interestingly enough, the fourth-century theologian, Augustine, appears as
the first representative. This is not as strange as it may first appear—the
great theologians of the Reformation all depended heavily on Augustine,
and Westerholm is, of course, right in claiming that Augustine is history's
most influential reader of Paul. Together with Augustine, and irrespec-
tive of minor disagreements among them, Luther, Calvin, and Wesley
are used for creating what Westerholm labels "a composite picture of
the 'Lutheran' Paul."[33]

Westerholm finds that all these "Lutheran" readers are in agreement
about five significant areas: (1) human nature has been corrupted and
humans are thus incapable of pleasing God; (2) humans must be justified by divine grace and not by works; (3) humans have no reason whatsoever to boast in the presence of God; (4) those justified by faith must
nevertheless produce good works as believers; and (5) believers are
delivered from the condemnation of the law, while God's Spirit enables
them to some extent to fulfill the moral demands. Regarding two
areas—whether sins remain a reality in the lives of believers, and to
what extent divine grace is considered to be "the irresistible source of
the believer's faith"[34]—Westerholm finds more difference of opinion
among his "Lutheran" readers. On both these topics, it is Wesley who
represents a deviant position. While Augustine, Luther, and Calvin all
appreciate the ongoing struggle with the flesh in the lives of the believer,
Wesley claims that a justified believer *cannot commit voluntary sin.*
Likewise, while Augustine's, Luther's, and Calvin's understandings of
the relationship between divine grace and salvation lead them to the
conclusion that God has predetermined who will become a believer,

Wesley emphatically stresses that God made humans moral agents, allowing them to determine their own destiny.

Having thus defined some important characteristic features of the "Lutheran" Paul, Westerholm proceeds by posing the question of whether these features owe more to Augustine and Luther than to Paul himself as many recent scholars have suggested. In part two of the book, Westerholm summarizes a large number of contributions to Pauline scholarship during the twentieth century, focusing on areas pertinent to the specific subject under discussion. This overview is a gold mine for anyone interested in Pauline scholarship and could indeed be recommended as an introduction to the present study.

In summarizing the main points of the critique of the "Lutheran" Paul, Westerholm first notes that numerous aspects of the "Lutheran" Paul were questioned long before Sanders introduced the term "covenantal nomism." Both William Wrede and Albert Schweitzer, for example, downplayed the doctrine of justification, and as we noted in chapter 4, Krister Stendahl did the same in the late 1950s. However, if Paul, in accordance with first-century Judaism, believed in the primacy of grace over works—thus, in reality, in covenantal nomism, as suggested by, for example, Dunn and Wright, what did Paul really find wrong with Judaism? Here Westerholm points to Räisänen's view that Paul wrongly attributed to Judaism the idea of pursuing righteousness through works and Sanders's suggestion that Paul really found nothing wrong with Judaism—except, of course, that it is not Christianity. As we also have seen, scholars associated with the new perspective (Dunn and Wright, for example) have suggested that Paul only reacted against nationalistic pride and Jewish ethnocentrism. Thus in the view of these scholars, Jewish legalism did not exist, and justification by faith cannot accordingly constitute Paul's response to it.

Westerholm points, furthermore, to the fact that Sanders and Wright, among others, connect righteousness or justification to the covenant—it is primarily *a membership term*. The works of the law are in the view of critics of the "Lutheran" Paul not good deeds performed in order to gain acceptance by God, but specifically those aspects of the law that created a barrier between Jews and non-Jews. Thus the doctrine of justification has nothing to do with sinners finding favor with

God, but on what terms non-Jews can belong to the people of God. Westerholm concludes:

> The issue that divides the "Lutheran" Paul from his contemporary critics is whether "justification by faith, not by works of the law" means "sinners find God's approval by grace, through faith, not by anything they do," or whether its thrust is that "Gentiles are included in the people of God by faith without the bother of becoming Jews."[35]

This conclusion is rather to the point, and in the third part of the book, Westerholm offers his view on the matter. By way of introduction, he discusses Paul's use of the concepts "righteousness," "law," and "grace." As for "righteousness," the intention is to scrutinize the common suggestion from new perspective scholars that the term primarily is covenant language and Sanders's idea that it is "transfer terminology" in Paul, but not in Judaism. In order to come to grasp with the well-known problem of translating the Greek *dikaio*-words, Westerholm simply invents a set of new hybrid words—"diakiosness," and "dikaiosify." In the ordinary sense, the various *dikaio*-words belong to Paul's general moral vocabulary, Westerholm states, and simply denote "what one ought to do and what one has if one has done it."[36]

However in Romans 5:9, Westerholm finds another mode of the *dikaio*-words. In Romans 5:7, Paul states that "indeed, rarely will anyone die for a righteous person." Here Paul uses the word *dikaios* in the ordinary sense, Westerholm claims, but in 5:9 Paul must refer to something else. Paul writes: "now that we have been justified [*dikaiosified* in Westerholm's terminology] by his blood, will we be saved through him from the wrath of God." When contrasted with Romans 2:13 ("it is not the hearers of the law who are righteous in God's sight, but the doers of the law who will be justified"), where those "*dikaiosified*" are recognized by God as *dikaios* because of their deeds, it becomes evident that the "sinners" (Rom 5:8) in 5:9 are "*dikaiosified*" in another sense, not because of what they have done (because they are *sinners*), but through the blood of Christ. This is Paul's "extraordinary" use of the concept, Westerholm argues, referring to Romans 4:6 as a summary of what is meant: "So also David speaks of the blessedness of those to whom God reckons righteousness [*dikaiosynēn*] apart from works."

Now, the problem, Westerholm continues, is that Pauline texts *never* link *ðikaio*-terminology with *covenant* terminology, while the critics of the "Lutheran" Paul constantly make such a connection. By studying the use of "righteousness" in the Hebrew Bible and in the Septuagint, Westerholm reaches the conclusion that "for a signifi-cant strand of Hebrew literature, then, what human beings . . . ought and ought not to do is discussed using the language of righteousness in a completely *non*covenantal framework."[37] He thereby refutes the claim from new perspective scholars that *ðikaio*-terminology, when understood in a Hebrew rather than in a Greek way, is covenantal itself. Thus with regard to Paul, Westerholm maintains that "'right-eousness,' by definition, represents what 'sinners,' *as* 'sinners,' lack and need. It is *not*, by definition, that from which Gentiles, *as* Gen-tiles, are excluded."[38] As for Sanders's idea of *ðikaio*-terminology as "transfer" terminology, that is, connected to the process in which people who do not belong to the people of God *become* the people of God, Westerholm admits that such a connection is prevalent with Paul, although never disconnected from its ordinary link to right and wrong deeds: "Jews did not (generally) think they were sinners," Westerholm concludes, "whereas for Paul such a declaration was an essential part of Christian salvation."[39]

As for Paul's use of "law" (*nomos*), Westerholm asserts that Paul occasionally uses it to refer to the Bible or more specifically to the Pentateuch as, for example, in Romans 3:21b: God's righteousness is attested "by the law and the prophets." However, in the beginning of the verse ("apart from law, the righteousness of God has been disclosed"), it is evident that Paul refers to the law in a narrower sense: to the pre-scriptious of the law. Thus in Galatians 3:17 and 19, Westerholm main-tains, the law given after 430 years was not the Pentateuch as whole but "the sum of specific divine requirements given to Israel through Moses."[40] This means that the emphasis in Paul's use of "law" is on the *Sinaitic legislation*—commandments in need of being fulfilled. In this respect, the word *nomos* is fully in line with the Hebrew usage of the word *torah*, Westerholm claims.

Because of this distinction between "law" meaning "Scripture" and "law" meaning "the Sinaitic legislation," one cannot simply apply what Paul says about Scripture to the Sinaitic legislation. Paul surely believed that the Scriptures witnessed to faith but found no problem in contrasting faith with the Sinaitic legislation, or in short, with works. Between these two concepts, work and faith, there exists in Westerholm's view a stark contrast. The simple reason is that the law is based on a different principle than faith, one that requires deeds, which is why it cannot lead to justification. The law's fundamental principle rests on the fact that the one who "does the works of the law will live by them" (Gal 3:12). Transgressions, however, bring the curse, and since no one is able to "obey all the things written in the book of the law" (Gal 3:10), only faith-righteousness, introduced as an emergency measure, can deal with the curse of the law and human transgressions. Faith and law are hence exclusive alternatives. Such a contrast, Westerholm asserts, would have been unthinkable for Paul's Jewish contemporaries, who regarded the Torah as God's gift, given by grace.

Now this view is repeatedly challenged in contemporary scholarship, Westerholm notes (as we have). In critical discussion with Sanders, Gaston, and Dunn, he refutes Sanders's suggestions that righteousness based on the law is open only for Jews and that the fault of the Jews is that they have tried to establish "their own righteousness" (Phil 3:9) not available to non-Jews. Westerholm also refutes Dunn's idea that the Jews were occupied with creating a barrier between Israel and the nations. Gaston's idea that "the works of the law" refers to "works which the law does" (cf. chapter 4), Westerholm finds interesting, but since it is clear that Paul's expression *can* refer to "works demanded by the law," and because Gaston's suggestion does not explain why Paul supports his claim that no one can be justified through the law by referring to the fact that Abraham was *not* justified by works, Westerholm also refutes this alternative.

Westerholm's discussion of grace is mainly limited to a discussion of Sanders's view that the positions of *Paul and Palestinian Judaism* on grace and works were one and the same. Westerholm admits that scholars who argue that Jews earned their salvation may have imposed Lutheran categories foreign to Judaism. However, when scholars, supporters, and critics alike suggest that first-century Jews were all "good Protestants,"[41] it becomes evident that Sanders, who is believed to have refuted Lutheran readings, strangely has become the advocate of precisely such a view. The fault is partly Sanders's own, Westerholm states. In his effort to "destroy the view of Rabbinic Judaism which is still prevalent in much, perhaps most, New Testament scholarship,"[42] Sanders's polemical ambition has created a certain amount of discrepancy between simplified slogans and a more nuanced discussion certainly prevalent in Sanders's work. A careful reading of Sanders shows, however, that not even his own analysis leads to the conclusion that "salvation is always by the grace of God" in Judaism,[43] Westerholm argues.

Westerholm asserts that the heart of Sanders's claim that salvation is by grace is the idea that God's election of Israel provided the basis for Israel's salvation. Since the election, according to Sanders, is an act of divine grace and membership in the people of God is equivalent to possessing salvation, salvation is thus dependent on God's mercy rather than human achievement. However, even Sanders admits that a common theme in rabbinic literature is that God actually found *some* merits with the people of Israel, either in the past or in the future, on which he based his decision to choose Israel. It thus appears that Sanders's thesis of the total gratuity of the election and that salvation is always by the grace of God is not entirely correct.

The problem is, Westerholm states, that whereas the rabbis were unaware of the Lutheran problem of works-righteousness, Sanders, who aims at refuting a Lutheran understanding of ancient Judaism, still argues in Lutheran categories. "The point to be made," Westerholm concludes, "is that we do Judaism neither justice nor favor when we claim that it preached 'good' Protestant doctrine on the subject of grace and works."[44]

Westerholm's critique should, however, not be understood as a complete refutation of the new view of Judaism as suggested by Sanders. Quite the contrary, Westerholm believes that much credit must be given to Sanders for having rectified the previous caricature of ancient Judaism. Sanders has

> assembled abundant evidence from rabbinic literature in which it is clear that salvation was not believed to be earned by individual Israelites apart from divine grace. If by "legalism" we mean the conviction that it was, then Judaism was not legalistic.[45]

What Westerholm does refute is the claim that ancient Judaism taught that humans cannot contribute *anything* to their salvation (which they would have if they preached good Protestant doctrine):

> Sanders has shown that Judaism did not generally believe that salvation was earned from scratch by human deeds of righteousness; the point is well taken, but it by no means differentiates Judaism from the classical opponents of "Lutheran" thought.[46]

Thus on the relationship between works and grace, ancient Judaism "seems to differ little from that of Pelagius, against whom Augustine railed, or that of the sixteenth-century church, upon which Luther called down heaven's thunder,"[47] Westerholm concludes. This is, of course, the decisive point, Westerholm maintains, which makes it impossible to accept for any adherent of the Lutheran Paul.

In the remaining part of the book, Westerholm lays out his view of Paul—a view that is indeed Lutheran. With regard to Romans, for example, Westerholm states, with frequent allusions to the new perspective scholars, that the doctrine of justification by faith

> is indeed the divine response to the dilemma posed, not by the earlier exclusion of Gentiles from the covenant, but by God's demand of righteousness from all human beings, none of whom is righteous (2:6-13; 3:9-20). The works (or works of the law) by which no flesh can be declared righteous (3:20, 28) are not the boundary markers that distinguish Jews from Gentiles, but the righteous deeds that God requires of all human beings. Jews continue to pursue righteousness through such works (9:32); this pursuit Paul finds misguided, not because the law does not demand works (cf. 2:13; 10:5), but because no one *is* righteous, and God has provided for the righteousness of sinners, through Christ, by faith. Justification is thus a gift of grace, received through faith, not gained by works. Received in this way, it excludes the possibility of human boasting.[48]

Westerholm's book is, of course, a splendid defense of a Lutheran reading of Paul. Through careful and detailed exegesis, the traditional view of Paul is outlined in critical discussion mainly with the proponents of the new perspective on Paul, who clearly are Westerholm's main targets, as is evident from the quotation above. Regrettably, Westerholm does not engage in a serious discussion with scholars advocating an even more radical new perspective on Paul. Of the representatives of a radical new perspective on Paul dealt with in this book, only Gaston appears in the body type; Stowers once, in a footnote; Nanos and Tomson do not appear at all. In all essentials, Westerholm's book represents a highly contentious objection to the Sanders-Dunn-Wright new perspective.

Perhaps this is quite natural: Dunn's and Wright's reading of Paul represent one *theological strategy* to deal with Sanders's new view of Judaism. For example, Dunn "saves" Paul for Luther by creating an identification between the Protestant doctrine of grace and Judaism. Both Paul and first-century Judaism are thus seen as representing covenantal nomism, which is the reason why Paul, in Dunn's view, did not oppose Judaism in general. "Justification by faith," in Dunn's view, means "that God accepts persons without reference to whether they have been born into a particular race, or not."[49] Admittedly, Dunn believes that justification also means that God justifies "the sinner,"[49] but even so it is evident that Dunn's Lutheranism implies a certain hermeneutical redefinition of the doctrine of justification by faith, which cannot easily be harmonized with an orthodox Lutheran standpoint. This seems to be what lies behind Westerholm's critique of the "new perspective on Paul."

Westerholm questions Sanders's reading of the rabbinic material, arguing that not even Sanders's analysis leads to the conclusion that Palestinian Judaism *never* contrasts works with merits or faith with grace. His own solution opens the possibility of maintaining a traditional Lutheran view. Westerholm's critique of Sanders is, however, well founded and should thus be taken seriously. It is hard to disregard the fact that Sanders sometimes promises somewhat more than the sources permit. No doubt this can partly be explained, as Westerholm does, by Sanders's ambition to destroy the caricature of Judaism then prevalent within the scholarly community. It is equally true that Sanders also imposes Lutheran categories upon the description of ancient Judaism. This too can certainly be explained by taking his target group into consideration: scholars advocating a Lutheran reading at the expense of the Jews.

In this respect, Westerholm, like many other contemporary Lutheran scholars, differs somewhat from the classical proponents of the Lutheran paradigm. He has indeed accepted Sanders's fundamental findings—ancient Judaism was *not* legalistic. This insight, however, has very little impact on his results. He still reaches the traditional conclusion that Paul represents a significantly different perspective than first-century Judaism. Jews still observing the Torah, for instance, are misguided in Paul's view, according to Westerholm. The medieval conflict between, in effect, a Semipelagian standpoint and a Lutheran is anticipated already in the first-century conflict between Judaism and Paul. Thus at the end of the day, this is what Westerholm finds wrong with Judaism—it is not Lutheranism, and a Lutheran reading of Paul appears fully possible also in the post-Sanders era.

Conclusion

The most striking common denominator in the works reviewed in this chapter is the relationship between exegesis and normative Protestant theology. This is most prominent in the works of Thielman and Westerholm, but also in the case of Das and Gathercole; it is not a far-fetched conjecture that their scholarly efforts are aimed at confirming a rather traditional Protestant interpretation of Paul. Historically, the bonds between normative theology and New Testament scholarship have been strong. In fact, the discipline originated within the church to stand in the service of the church. The increasing emphasis on the biblical text during the Reformation further established this relationship. During the Enlightenment, scholars for the first time began working from perspectives other than distinctly Christian, even though they can hardly be labeled secular. The alternative perspectives were indeed aimed at challenging traditional Christian theology, but the points of departure were regularly within the religious realm—often deism in combination with the most recent philosophical trends.

The radicalism of these contributions was sometimes significant and caused reactions from scholars who wanted to defend the teaching of the church. As we recall from chapter 2, the Old Tübingen School represented one such an attempt to create a synthesis between the scientific developments and New Testament exegesis. The nineteenth-century history of religions school is another example of adaptation to a new epistemological situation, as is Rudolf Bultmann's hermeneutical program of *demythologizing* the New Testament. Thus for historical reasons, New Testament exegesis has a long tradition of connections between church and academia, and many of the problems within the discipline are still defined by issues raised by contemporary Christian theology. With regard to Paul, this predominantly means Protestant theology. The extent of this dependence on Protestant theology is, for example, evident in the fact, pointed to above by Westerholm, that even Sanders, who aimed at criticizing Lutheran influences, still works with Lutheran categories.

It is also apparent from the fact that while most scholars within the traditional fold willingly admit that Sanders was right in stating that ancient Judaism was not legalistic or unilaterally preoccupied with works-righteousness, the influence of this insight on their results is minimal. Rather, scholars working from within a confessional paradigm usually reach confessional results, *despite Sanders*. Having said that, it is important to state clearly, as has been repeatedly done in this chapter, that much of the critique of Sanders from the traditional perspective is worth taking seriously. However, it is equally true that taking such critique into consideration does not necessarily lead to a traditional portrait of Paul. In order to reach such results, the individual scholar has to share other basic assumptions also, which leads to the question of whether confessional legitimation through academic scholarship is an appropriate way of developing the discipline. Before we address this conflagrant issue in the concluding chapter, we will see how the study of Paul and his relationship to Judaism is affected by cross-disciplinary interaction with other perspectives.

BREAKING BOUNDARIES

In this chapter, we are going to examine monographs that stand as representatives of the most recent trends within Pauline studies. In addition, we will take a brief look at another expression of the recent interest in Paul that cannot be said to belong to New Testament scholarship. The phenomenon we will address in the first section below rather belongs to *the reception* of Pauline scholarship—in this case, more specifically—the use of Paul in radical contemporary secular philosophy.

With regard to proper Pauline studies in this chapter, the difference from the ones we have previously dealt with is that the scholars in this chapter have to some extent moved beyond the Paul–Judaism complex of problems. That is to say, solving the overarching Paul–Judaism problem does not constitute the dominant issue that is being addressed. Rather, the common denominator in these studies is a clear ambition to move beyond even the radical new perspective on Paul. Thus in this chapter we concentrate on Pauline scholars for whom a radical approach to Paul constitutes *the normal point of departure*—not the result—or scholars who approach Paul from a completely different angle leading to new results with regard to Jewish–non-Jewish interaction in antiquity.

In this respect, they certainly belong to the wide tradition of Pauline scholars who have criticized the traditional paradigm. For that reason they could very well have been included in the section on the radical new perspective in chapter 5. Moreover, apart from their radical position in relation to the Paul–Judaism problem, these scholars also work from well-defined and specific methodological points of departure and to some extent, their results also amount to important critical questions even for adherents of a radical new perspective on Paul. But before we engage in scholarship that truly can be said to break boundaries, we will take a look at what secular philosophers make of Paul.

Paul and the Philosophers

The wide-ranging return of religion within some strata of contemporary philosophy has led to a new interest also in Paul, especially among some radical atheistic philosophers, such as Giorgio Agamben, Alain Badiou, and Slavoj Žižek.[1] In general, since Friedrich Nietzsche's showdown with the apostle at the end of the nineteenth century,[2] philosophers have expressed little interest in Paul. However, during recent decades, Paul has been revived in philosophical discourses, and this new interest certainly involves many aspects worthy of note. Our focus in this area, however, is restricted to the relationship between the different pictures of Paul as presented by New Testament scholars and his appeal in contemporary philosophy. In short, is the recent development in Pauline studies also reflected within these philosophical discourses? In this respect, the work of the Jewish philosopher of religion Jacob Taubes (1923–1987), Professor of Judaism and Hermeneutics at the Free University of Berlin, constitutes the natural point of departure. In the following, we will concentrate on Taubes and Badiou, who are exemplars of two opposite approaches to contemporary Pauline scholarship among recent philosophers.

Taubes, who has served as a source of inspiration for both Agamben and Badiou, differs nevertheless in several respects from the philosophers mentioned above. While neither Agamben, Badiou, nor Žižek are interested in Paul as a religious thinker, it is clear that Taubes approaches Paul from within Jewish tradition. It is also evident that Taubes is in close contact with those traditions of Pauline scholarship that aim at localizing Paul within Judaism, which seems rather natural considering the fact that Taubes for many years was a close friend of Krister Stendahl. Taubes's view of Paul is clearly expressed in *The Political Theology of Paul*, a book comprising recorded lectures that were delivered in Heidelberg in 1987 and published posthumously in German 1993, with the English translation published in 2004.

Paul is for Taubes clearly a Jew who has not broken with Judaism. Introducing his fundamental view of the apostle, Taubes states that the reason he has entered into "the business of gathering the heretic back into the fold" is that he regards him "as more Jewish than any Reform rabbi, or any Liberal rabbi," he has ever heard "in Germany, England, America, Switzerland, or anywhere."[3] In agreement with Stendahl, he regards Paul's experience on the road to Damascus as a calling, not a conversion, from Judaism to Christianity. Paul was thus a Jew, but, of course, a Jew with a special mission—to the Gentiles, whom Taubes says were recruited from those non-Jews who previously had been attached to the synagogue. In anticipating (as we soon will see) the later rise of political readings of Paul, Taubes claims that Paul's gospel, at least as presented in Romans, *is a political declaration of war on the Caesars*. In a highly controversial interpretation of the concept of *nomos* (law) in Romans, Taubes connects Paul's anti-imperial gospel with his view of the law, which is also part of Paul's political theology. Paul's critique of the law, Taubes maintains, has nothing to do with the traditional opposition between faith and works-righteousness but is rather "a critique of a dialogue that Paul is conducting not only with the Pharisees—that is, with himself—but also with the Mediterranean environment."[4] Echoing Nietzsche's critique, Taubes claims that Paul approaches the issue of the law by answering with a protest, with a transvaluation of values: "It isn't *nomos* but rather the one who was nailed at the cross by *nomos* who is the *imperator*."[5] Paul, according to Taubes, thus opposes every use of the law, whether by theocratic or imperial rulers, as a power for dominating others. In this way he challenges both the imperialism of the Roman Empire and Israel's self-understanding of being an ethnic community under the law. Paul's alternative is, according to Taubes, the formation of a new kind of community of solidarity, the creation of a new people, consisting of Jews and Gentiles, independent of the law and centered around the Messiah.

This is the decisive aspect of Paul that constitutes the foundation for Taubes's suggestion of how to use Paul in contemporary political theologies. It may be tempting for oppressed groups to emphasize the revolutionary side of Paul, but considering Paul's (according to Taubes) general antinomistic gospel, no one should be able to use him for legitimizing an oppressive political theology. Paul's "negative theology" undermines completely any law's function as an ordering power since no earthly institutions of power can represent the Messiah. Taubes's interpretation of Paul's view of the law, however, does not imply that Taubes sides with those New Testament scholars who advocate the traditional opposition between Judaism and Christianity. Quite the contrary, Taubes's lectures are full of critiques of the traditional readings of Paul. The reason Paul criticized the law, Taubes believes, can be found within Jewish tradition itself as one expression of many Jewish attempts to achieve freedom from the law.

A rather different reading of Paul is found in the French philosopher Alain Badiou's book, *Saint Paul: The Foundation of Universalism* (2003), originally published in French in 1997. In contrast to Taubes, Badiou is not interested in Paul as a religious thinker. "Basically," he states in the prologue, "I have never really connected Paul with religion."[6] Badiou is rather interested in the potential of Paul for creating a political philosophy aimed at criticizing globalization and capitalism. However, in agreement with Taubes, Badiou indeed considers Paul to be a revolutionary thinker, but for different reasons.

Badiou's own philosophical thinking emphasizes the contrast between *the order of things* in an ontological sense (which Paul was not interested in, according to Badiou) and the contingent, unpredictable *event*. This latter aspect is what makes Paul such a revolutionary thinker, Badiou claims, because Paul attaches no importance to "the order of things," only to "the event"—the resurrection of Christ. The idea of Christ's resurrection is a notion completely impossible for modern human beings to adhere to, Badiou states, and is to be regarded as Paul's radical innovation. However, even though Badiou does not regard religion as an area in which truth-events can occur, it is clear that Paul meant that truth is not dependent on objective circumstances (the order of things) but on a single event. This shows, Badiou maintains, that Paul believed in the importance of the singular event, in contrast to the order of things, and this is the reason why Badiou claims Paul to be "one of the very first theoreticians of the universal."[7]

Against the particularizing cultural relativism Badiou finds in the wake of capitalism, leading to a fragmentation of identities, he presents the idea of a "singular universality" as a way out of this situation. This, he maintains, is what Paul gives voice to in Galatians 3:28: "There is no longer Jew or Greek, there is no longer slave or free, there is no longer male and female; for all of you are one in Christ Jesus." Thus ethnicity, social position, and gender no longer define the identity of the Christian but his or her belonging to Christ: "what matters, man or woman, Jew or Greek, slave or free man," Badiou states, "is that differences *carry the universal that happens to them like a grace.*"[8]

It is clear, however, that Badiou is quite influenced by the traditional perspective on Paul. While his book contains no references to Pauline scholars, one of only two books suggested for further reading is Bornkamm's *Paulus* (*Paul*). Thus it is no wonder that the traditional dichotomy between Judaism and Christianity functions as a natural point of departure for Badiou, even though this opposition is interpreted as a fundamental contrast between the event and the order of things (which is profoundly different from Bornkamm's view). Yet, it is rather uncontroversial for Badiou to assume that Paul "emphasizes rupture rather than continuity with Judaism,"[9] and that Paul ceased observing the law, because such "communitarian marking (circumcision, rites, the meticulous observance of the Law)" has been rendered indifferent by the "postevental imperative of truth,"[10] that is, the Christ-event. Thus Ola Sigurdson is probably correct in stating that "Badiou's interpretation of Paul looks a lot like the interpretation that was put forward by the existential interpretation of the famous Lutheran New Testament scholar Rudolf Bultmann."[11]

In summing up the relationship between New Testament scholarship on Paul and recent philosophical discourses it can be said that the bipolar nature of Pauline scholarship is also detectable in the recent philosophical approaches to Paul. Taubes is undoubtedly closest to a new perspective on Paul, even though the opposition between Judaism and Christianity is also, to some extent, apparent in his reading of Paul. With Taubes, it is rather the tendency to locate Paul within Judaism that connects him to the new perspective. Giorgio Agamben is also more connected to the new perspective than to traditional Pauline interpretations. His commentary on Romans, *The Time that Remains* (2005, Italian original 2000), is dedicated to Jacob Taubes, and is in several respects clearly influenced by Taubes's work. Thus in Taubes's and Agamben's interpretations, the dichotomy between Paul and Judaism is, at least, somewhat mitigated. As noted above Badiou, on the other hand, seems more connected to the traditional, Lutheran scholarly tradition. The same is true regarding Slavoj Žižek, whose reading of Paul is heavily influenced by the French psychoanalyst Jacques Lacan.

Even though the recent philosophical interest in Paul probably represents a movement independent of the exegetical discussion, it is interesting to note that a similar polarization between a traditional perspective and a more progressive one is clearly detectible also in radical philosophical readings of Paul, which ultimately aim at developing a secular political-philosophical critique of Western society. The focus on the political potential in Paul's writings, however, is one common trait that creates a kind of connection between radical philosophy and radical exegesis that could serve as a common ground for a fruitful dialogue between the two disciplines. With regard to radicalism, some strains within Pauline scholarship still seem to be ahead of the philosophers. Regrettably, even the most radical philosophical readings of Paul do not build on the most radical portraits of the apostle within New Testament scholarship, and one cannot help wondering about what the results would have looked like if they had. To some of these radical interpretations of Paul—postcolonial, political, feminist, and even queer readings—we are now going to turn.

Postcolonial Approaches

Concurrent with the emerging interest in the Jewishness of Paul, as a result of E. P. Sanders's revised picture of ancient Judaism, another kind of deconstruction process began to influence the academy — postcolonialism. As an academic field of specialization, postcolonialism has its roots in the creative literature of the former (and in some cases, present) colonies of the Western empires that specifically dealt with the experience of living under imperial rule or under the process of decolonization.[12] Originally, the word "postcolonial" was, in fact, used in a restricted sense referring to a specific period in history, that is, the period immediately following the process of decolonization in the Western empires.

During the subsequent development, postcolonialism has, however, evolved into a dehistoricized perspective used in a variety of academic disciplines such as "postcolonial studies," "postcolonial criticism," or "postcolonial theory."[13] Far from being monolithic, postcolonialism today denotes a multitude of approaches basically aimed at analyzing situations where one social group has dominated another in a colonial or postcolonial context.

Postcolonial perspectives have gradually made their entrance in the field of biblical studies and have influenced many areas, not only historical studies, but also hermeneutical approaches dealing with the role of the Bible in contemporary society—for example, how the Bible has been, and is, used in the service of Western imperialism. In combination with feminist and gender-critical approaches, postcolonial perspectives have proven especially helpful in unmasking underlying power structures in the dominant Western readings of the Bible.

With regard to Pauline scholarship, postcolonial perspectives seem quite natural given the fact that Paul's writings (as the rest of the New Testament) undeniably originated in an imperial context. Furthermore, as Richard Horsley (who is one of the earliest voices to bring postcolonial questions to bear) has pointed out, "Western Christianity's cooptation of Paul is surely European Christianity's and established biblical studies' paradigmatic essentialization, individualization and depoliticization of the Bible."[14] Indeed, the traditional bipolar construction of Paul's relation to Judaism is, from a postcolonial perspective, one result of this process of "essentialization, individualization and depoliticization." Horsley continues: "Paul's letters must be the prototypical case of a history that was submerged by the West despite the fact that it was already clearly written and widely available for reading."[15] Unveiling this process by taking Paul's imperial context into consideration certainly leads to new interpretations on Paul, which challenge not only the traditional Lutheran view, but also the so-called new perspective on Paul. As we will see below, "the doctrine of righteousness by faith alone" is not a salient feature in postcolonial approaches to Paul.

Neither Plight Nor Solution—Neil Elliott

Neil Elliott, who has taught biblical studies at Metropolitan State University and United Theological Seminary, has dealt with the political context of Paul and underlying anti-Jewish currents in New Testament scholarship already in his two previous monographs, *The Rhetoric of Romans* (1990) and *Liberating Paul* (1994). In his third book,

The Arrogance of Nations (2008), he takes both these aspects one step further in a highly interesting new reading of Paul's letter to the Romans.

Elliott's picture of Paul differs significantly from most previous interpretations mainly because of his persistence in stating that the themes that dominate Romans are first and foremost *political topics*. Whereas most traditional readings of Romans have identified the so-called doctrine of justification by faith (Rom 1:17) as the center of the letter, formulated as a principle of salvation in sharp contrast to Jewish legalism and works-righteousness (cf. Käsemann in chapter 3: Paul's *antijudaistische Kampfeslehre*), Elliott refutes any perspective that focuses on the salvation of the individual. Paul, Elliott claims (referring to Romans 1:18-32), "does not seem to be setting up a depiction of a (human) plight awaiting a (divine) solution."[16] Instead, Elliott states, "Romans is Paul's attempt to counteract the effects of imperial ideology within the Roman congregations."[17]

Thus Elliott rejects not only the traditional, Lutheran readings of Paul (which indeed emphasize faith in opposition to Jewish works-righteousness) but also the suggestion from new perspective scholars that Paul opposed, not Jewish legalism, but Jewish ethnocentrism (cf. Dunn and Wright in chapter 4). The problem with previous attempts to understand Paul's message in Romans, Elliott states, is the general inability to appreciate the imperial context, to which in his view Romans constantly refers.

Scholars generally agree that Paul reaches an emotional climax in Romans 9–11, but fail to draw the correct conclusions from this observation, Elliott maintains. Governed by preconceived theological presumptions on the nature of the letter, scholars often read Romans as a series of proofs of the thesis presented in 1:16-17. According to Elliott, however, Romans 1–8 should not be regarded as the doctrinal core of the letter "but as an argumentative preparation for the appeal in the later chapters that reaches its rhetorical climax in 9–11."[18] Thus instead of pursing the idea of the Christian church's supremacy over Israel, of Christian identity over Jewish identity or of grace in contrast to law, Elliott suggests that Romans "confronts both the 'boast' of supremacy over Israel and, by necessity, the attitudes in the wider cultural environment that nourished that boast."[19] Taking the "wider cultural environment" into account, according to Elliott, means recognizing precisely *the imperial context.*

Drawing from rhetorical and postcolonial criticism in dialogue with insights from classical studies, Elliott presents a rather unique and indeed highly controversial reading of Romans. Elliott finds one of the first implications of a political dimension in the letter in Romans 1:5. While the phrase *hypakoēn pisteōs* often has been translated "the obedience of faith" (so NRSV), Elliott argues that the word *pistis* (the Greek word used in the phrase above) normally carries the meaning of "faithfulness," involving loyalty and steadfastness—not "belief." Paul is thus involved in securing "faithful obedience among the nations." According to Elliott, the passage should be understood against the fact that the Roman emperor was involved in the same process: empires, ancient and contemporary, are constantly involved in "winning the hearts and minds" of conquered peoples.[20]

Now, in the case of the Roman Empire (and indeed of many modern empires, as Elliott makes quite clear), the fact that the growth of the empire was a result of brutal coercive force meant that the empire was in constant need of legitimizing this state of affairs. This was done by creating an effective imperial ideology that, for example, presented Augustus as a sacred figure, a savior whose destiny was to rule the world and to conquer proud nations. In this way, conquered nations, now as "Romans," were invited to partake in this divinely ordained destiny.

The public interaction between the dominant and the subordinate classes took place in what Elliott labels "the public transcript."[21] Building on the work of the political scientist James C. Scott, Elliott identifies three discursive arenas in which the imperial ideology was interpreted in different ways. In the "public transcript," the imperial ideology was expressed through assigning specific roles to the weak and dominant respectively according to the mythology created to legitimize the current ideology. However, both the powerful and the subordinate also gave expression to opinions hidden from the public sphere. As for the powerful, dominant class, this could mean occasionally giving voice to the real motives behind their oppression of the subordinate classes: greed leading to exploitation and an ideology that emphasized the inevitability of ruling by brutal force.

A "hidden transcript" also existed among the subordinate. For obvious reasons, open protests were rare—and doomed—as the Jewish revolt of 66–70 CE clearly demonstrates. Instead, subordinate groups had to rely on strategies of indirection, disguise, and anonymity. For this reason, protests from rebellious groups never appear on the surface level in the sources but are hidden, veiled, even encoded. In the case of Romans, we find Paul using words with strong political implications. Titles like "Christ" (*Christos*) and "son of God" (*huios tou theou*) were titles also claimed by the Caesars. Thus when applying these and other titles to Jesus in Romans 1:1-5, Paul clearly confronts the imperial ideology by encouraging the Roman community, as part of the nations, to enter into a completely different realm of dominion. Not the dominion of Caesar, but of the true ruler of the world—"Jesus Christ our Lord."

One example of how, according to Elliott, Paul moves in the "hidden transcript," delivering a massive (but hidden) critique of the Roman Empire, is Romans 1:18-32. From a traditional Lutheran perspective, this section has usually been taken as evidence of the fallen nature of humanity, or more specifically, of the non-Jews (the Jews are usually considered to get their share in Romans 2:17-24). As noted above, Elliott does not consider this passage to describe the universal plight of humanity. He draws attention to the fact that Paul presents the situation in Romans 1:18-32 as a direct result of divine intervention: "God gave them up in the lusts of their hearts to impurity, to the degrading of their bodies among themselves" (Rom 1:24). Elliott shows that "morality" was an important feature of Roman imperial ideology and that beginning with Augustus, the emperors were pictured as representing the embodiment of divine justice. According to the Roman historian Suetonius, however, the real situation seems to have been rather different. In his biography of the emperors, probably originally called *De vita duodecim Caesarum libri VIII* ("The Eight Books on the Lives of the Twelve Caesars"), written in the beginning of the second century, Suetonius presents, for example, Gaius (Caligula) as an utterly immoral, cruel, lustful, arrogant ruler, prone to every perversion known to mankind. When compared to Suetonius's presentation of Gaius, Paul's description of "the wrath of God" in Romans 1:18-32 seems to indicate that he in fact *has the Caesars themselves in mind*, Elliott argues. While we cannot be sure that Paul intended his audience to think specifically of Gaius, Elliott continues, it is quite likely that they made the connection between Paul's wording and members of the imperial house. Thus "Paul's rhetoric impels his hearers to choose between the justice he represents and the rampant injustice that already stands under the wrath of God."[22]

The reason why Paul was forced to confront Roman imperial ideology is that the non-Jews in the Roman congregations had been influenced by it, causing them to look down on their Jewish brothers and sisters in Christ. The historical context is as follows: in 49 CE, the Roman Emperor Claudius expelled the Jewish population, including Jesus-believing Jews, from the city of Rome. Five years later, they were allowed to return at the mercy of Claudius's successor, Nero. According to Elliott, "mercy" is the key word here. In compliance with imperial ideology, mercy, *clementia*, was the exclusive privilege of those who enjoyed absolute power exercised toward unworthy subjects as an undeserved favor, thus emphasizing the moral standard of the ruling power. Thus the natural way of looking at the returning Jews from a non-Jewish, Roman perspective would be "not only as the wretched and broken people that they appeared, but as the undeserving beneficiaries of imperial largesse, troublemakers who had escaped being held accountable for their misdeeds."[23] This is the situation Paul addresses in the stylized conversation in Romans 2–3.

As we noted in chapter 4, when dealing with Stanley Stowers's work, Romans 2:17-24 has traditionally been seen as Paul's frontal attack on Judaism aimed at showing that the Jews are in no better standing than the non-Jews presented in Romans 1:18-32. In a critical dialogue with Stowers, Elliott argues that the section certainly aims at establishing the fact that Jews and non-Jews are on equal standing before God, but not in the way that is usually assumed. It is hard to believe that any Jew would disagree with Paul regarding the fact that Israel is accountable before the God of Israel, Elliott claims. Contra Stowers, Elliott argues that the person Paul addresses in 2:17-24 is not "bragging about what [he] does not truly possess."[24] From Romans 9:4-5 it is evident that Jews really do possess these things:

> They are Israelites, and to them belong the adoption, the glory, the covenants, the giving of the law, the worship, and the promises; to them belong the patriarchs, and from them, according to the flesh, comes the Messiah, who is over all, God blessed forever. Amen.

Furthermore, it should be noted that Paul's interlocutor never admits to having broken the law. Paul, so Elliott argues, asks his Jewish dialogue partner a set of hypothetical questions: "do you not teach yourselves?" . . . "do you steal?" . . . "do you commit adultery?" . . . "do you rob temples?" But he does not wait for the answer in order to deliver a guilty verdict as was the case with the people referred to in 1:18-32: "Therefore you have no excuse, whoever you are, when you judge others; for in passing judgment on another you condemn yourself, because you, the judge, are doing the very same things" (Rom 2:1). *If* the Jewish interlocutor had been found guilty of these transgressions in 2:17-24, *then* "the name of God is blasphemed among the Gentiles because of you." But, Elliott states, Paul's target is not the Jews: his point—"addressed to the non-Judean audience—is that Jewish scriptures establish God's claim on the whole world, not just upon Judeans. All the world—not just the Judeans—is accountable to God."[25] It is, in fact, the non-Jews in the Roman congregation who need to be informed that Jews *do not* presume on God's grace and mercy to give free rein to their sins.

In the following section Paul makes his point. Again, in critical dialogue with Stowers, Elliott suggests a new reading of Romans 3:1-9. In contrast to Stowers, who takes 3:1, 3, 5, 7, 8, and 9 as *objections* from the Jewish interlocutor, Elliott suggests that they are *Paul's leading questions,* answered by his fictive Jewish dialogue partner. It is worth quoting his reading of the passage:

3:1	Paul's leading question	Then what advantage has the Judean? Or what is the value of circumcision?
3:2	Interlocutor's response	Much in every way. For in the first place, the Judeans were entrusted with the oracles of God.
3:3	Paul	What if some were unfaithful? Will their faithlessness nullify the faithfulness of God?
3:4	Interlocutor	By no means! Although everyone is a liar, let God be proved true. . . .
3:5	Paul	But if our injustice serves to confirm the justice of God, what should we say? That God is unjust to inflict wrath on us? (I speak in a human way.)

3:6	Interlocutor	By no means! For then how could God judge the world?
3:7, 8	Paul	But if through my falsehood, God's truthfulness abounds to his glory, why am I still being condemned as a sinner? And why not say (as some people slander us by saying that we say), "Let us do evil so that good may come"?
	Interlocutor	Their condemnation is deserved!
3:9a	Paul	What then? Do we have any defense (against God's judgment)?
3:9b	Interlocutor	No, not at all; for we have already charged that all, both Judeans and Greeks, are under the power of sin. . . .[26]

From this point of departure, Romans 3:1-9 functions as a confirmation of Paul's view outlined earlier in the letter: Jews do not enjoy certain privileges because of their standing before God. To expect God to leave sins (*if* committed) unpunished would be to question the justice of God. The Jewish interlocutor agrees with Paul that the Jews do not enjoy a special privilege over against the nations that exempts them from God's judgment. In this respect, Jews and non-Jews have identical standing before God.

However, what the non-Jews in the Roman congregations had been led to believe, Elliott argues, is that the present situation of the Jews of Rome, after the return from the exile, reflected the (divine) empirical hierarchy of rules and ruled. The mercy of the gods could clearly be determined from facts on the ground, since many Jews probably appeared broken and wretched as undeserving recipients of Nero's mercy. In this respect, the Roman congregations had again begun to think in imperial categories, confusing imperial justice with the justice of God. Paul's intention, however, is to counteract this tendency. What the non-Jews have to realize is that in the same way God will deal with sins among the Jewish people, he will certainly deal with sins among the nations. The present "justice," exercised through brutal imperial power, will in the future be replaced by the true justice of God. Thus what Paul aims at in Romans, Elliott argues, is to make a distinction between the present and the future. This is ultimately what establishing "faithful obedience among the nations" (Rom 1:5) is really about.

As such, Romans 2–3 hence anticipates the argument in 9–11. Traditionally, these chapters have been taken as evidence of the failure of Israel and the rise of the non-Jewish church, through the distinction between the "true" and "false" Israel. Such a typological reading misconstrues Paul's argument, according to Elliott, who argues that Paul in this section makes a distinction between present and future conditions. The tension is not between "who is in and who is out," Elliott states, but "who is in *now*, and who is destined to be in *soon*."[27] While it may be tempting to consider the broken people returning from exile as evidence that God has abandoned his people and chosen a new people in their place, Paul's intention is precisely to draw attention to the distinction between the *appearance* that God's word has failed and the *reality* that it has not (Rom 9:6). The present conditions are—despite appearances— in accordance with God's plan for saving both Jews and non-Jews. To assume otherwise (as the non-Jews of the Roman congregations have) would amount to accepting the *imperial justice*. Paul's aim, however, is to convince his (non-Jewish) audience that the course of history has not reached its final climax at the mercy of the emperor but still awaits the future divine justice.

Elliott's book is another excellent example of the relation between the overarching approach being used and the outcome of a study. Reading Paul, as Elliott does, from a political perspective apparently leads to a significant change in the interpretation of the whole letter. Quite obviously, his reading of Paul represents an important challenge to the traditional interpretations of Romans, where the salvation of the individual has been the focus because of the importance given to the doctrine of righteousness by faith alone. Taking Paul's imperial context into consideration implies a radical shift of focus from the individual to the collective. We have already seen a similar development with some of the other proponents of a radical approach to Paul (chapter 5). According to Elliott's analysis, Paul was not involved in a theological revision of the salvation of humanity that involved a profound critique of Judaism. Instead, his aim was to defend the precedence of Israel against a profound critique from Jesus-believing non-Jews, which in a remarkable way anticipates the subsequent development in early Gentile Christianity. We have previously noted a similar interpretation in the work of Mark Nanos (chapter 5). Thus Elliott's approach highlights the complex of problems related to "identity" and "ethnicity." Far from constituting one homogeneous group, the early Jesus movement, as Elliott's study strongly suggests, was made up of two groups — Jews and non-Jews — and many of the tensions within the movement can be explained by this state of affairs. Also this aspect has been emphasized in the studies we dealt with in chapter 5.

Finally, Elliott's study, of course, challenges normative theology as well. If "the counteracting of imperial ideology" rather than the doctrine of righteousness by faith was the center of Paul's theological thinking, at least in Romans, the church would need to hermeneutically relate to this shift of focus. Elliott has already initiated such a process by a parallel, analogical reading from a Marxist perspective in which he compares the situation in antiquity to contemporary correlates. Here he outlines a theology of liberation based on a historical portrait of Paul. Thus the political context of Paul is indeed here to stay as an inevitable perspective to consider along with other approaches. Perhaps it will also prove to be a viable theological alternative for the contemporary church.

Paul and the Feminists

As is the case with postcolonialism, feminism denotes a wide range of theories, political movements, and philosophical discourses focusing on gender differences and the historical reality of male dominance over women. The roots of feminist theory are thus to be sought primarily in political movements emerging during the nineteenth century, struggling for women's rights and liberation from various forms of oppression. Simone de Beauvoir's *Le Deuxième Sexe* of 1949 (*The Second Sex*, ET 1973) is commonly regarded as introducing feminism as part of the philosophical discourse. However, it was not until the 1970s that feminist perspectives became established at the university level. Today, feminist perspectives have a natural position within academia and aim at analyzing gender inequality, gender politics, power relations, and sexuality, often in close contact with other disciplines, such as postcolonialism, economics, anthropology, literary criticism, psychoanalysis, and biblical studies. Within the field of biblical studies, feminist perspectives constitute a specific set of conceptual tools developed for analyzing and unmasking the male-dominated political, religious, and social power structures at various levels. The general theoretical diversity of feminism is, of course, reflected also within biblical studies.[28]

The Feminist Paul—Kathy Ehrensperger

In Kathy Ehrensperger's study on Paul, *That We May Be Mutually Encouraged* (2004), the new perspective on Paul also constitutes a natural point of departure, not a view that primarily has to be defended. Rather, Ehrensperger, Senior Lecturer in New Testament Studies at the University of Wales, explores how feminist interpretations may be affected by the recent change within Pauline scholarship. Ehrensperger points out that while there have been significant transformations in the fields of Pauline studies, feminist theologies, and theologies dealing with the Holocaust, these transformations have had little impact outside the boundaries of the respective discipline. This is to be regretted, Ehrensperger claims, since relating these three perspectives to each other would "lead to illuminating and fruitful interactions and new insights for each of these theologies and would prove especially relevant for understanding Paul from a radically new perspective."[29] For example, such an interdisciplinary enterprise could lead to the creation of a new view of Paul, beyond traditional, malestream scholarship's reconstruction of Paul as the founder of the law-free church, but also beyond "traditional feminist scholarship's image of [Paul] as the father of misogyny and dominating power," Ehrensperger states.[30]

Thus in the first part of her book, Ehrensperger studies the presuppositions behind any interpretation—hermeneutics. Her point of departure is the general observation that interpretive acts are involved in the process of creating meaning. This process, however, is not static but changes over time also within the same cultural context. The Reformation, for example, resulted in a shift from "hegemony to diversity," Ehrensperger states, since people suddenly were confronted with differing versions of truth. The ambition to liberate people from church domination during the Enlightenment can be seen as an attempt to deal with this post-Reformation trauma. The Enlightenment, however, created a new totalitarian system: "despite the Enlightenment's liberationist point of departure, to free people from church domination, its project of rationality quickly developed into a new instrument of domination," Ehrensperger states.[31]

During the postwar era, different postmodern approaches emerged in sharp opposition to the prevalent objectivistic paradigm. This development resulted in a more complex view on the notion of interpretation and constituted the basis of the contemporary situation, which is characterized by diversity and a highly problematized concept of truth. Within the fields of theology and religious studies, this development paved the way for the emergence of different perspectives challenging the dominant discourse. This is the context of the rise of post-Shoah perspectives, feminist interpretations, and the emerging trend within Pauline scholarship to read Paul against a Jewish framework.

Feminism and feminist theology have contributed significantly to this shift from hegemony to diversity, Ehrensperger maintains, for example, by making visible that the interpretive prerogative traditionally has rested with European, white men. Feminist theology was originally born out of the struggle to overcome the oppression of women resulting from a general male domination and is therefore closely associated with visions of equality, justice, and liberation. However, in spite of this general liberationist tendency within feminist interpretations of the Bible, Jewish feminists, working during the 1970s, made Christian feminists aware of the inherent anti-Jewish traditions prevalent in many feminist theological concepts. Thus a scholarly tradition that focused specifically on liberation, equality, and justice as a result of a conscious "hermeneutics of suspicion" could still retain traits that were part of precisely such an oppressive discourse as feminist theology aimed at criticizing. Common anti-Jewish features were, for example, the idea of Judaism as the antithesis of Christianity, a tendency to consider Jewish images of God as inferior to Christian images of God, and a reappearance of the old accusation that the Jews murdered God, Ehrensperger states.

More recently, however, feminist scholars have increasingly become aware of the problem of anti-Jewish influences, which has resulted in an increasing interest in Paul, who, until lately, has been a rather neglected figure in feminist scholarship. In a first wave of feminist readings of Paul, the apostle was judged mainly by his "varied and contradictory statements about women,"[32] Ehrensperger states. Certain feminist scholars still adhere to this view and regard Paul as being inspired by Platonic dualism, as the one who did not see men and women as equals in Christ—as Jesus is assumed to have done. According to these scholars, Paul had indeed overcome Jewish particularism by founding Christianity as a new universal religion, but he also began to betray the ethics of the original Jesus movement, which regarded men and women as equals. Other scholars, Ehrensperger states, have more seriously tried to read Paul against the background of first-century patriarchal structures and from a Jewish perspective. This approach has resulted in the conclusion that there may be "more relevance in Paul for feminist theology than might be obvious at a first glance."[33]

Thus it is evident that feminist theory and feminist theology have introduced new paradigms demonstrating a sensibility about the diverse nature of the process of interpretation and about the fact that there is more than one universal perspective to take into consideration. In an attempt to demonstrate how the recognition of contextuality and diversity have affected the interpretation of Paul, Ehrensperger turns to the issue of contradictions in Paul, a problem we have dealt with previously when studying the work of Heikki Räisänen in chapter 4. Traditionally, scholars have tried to resolve this problem from the dominant epistemological system prevalent in Western society. The fundamental assumption has often been that Paul was a logical, rational thinker. According to Ehrensperger, however, most scholars have failed to appreciate that Western rationality is just one way to perceive life and reality and is heavily influenced by Greco-Roman philosophy. Instead, she indicates two alternative systems of interpretation: Jewish biblical interpretation, and modern feminist interpretation.

The Greek philosophical influence on Western thinking led to the ideal of establishing the one and true meaning in a text, Ehrensperger argues, which has had devastating consequences for women and Jews in particular. In contrast to the Greek matrix for establishing one singular truth, Jewish biblical interpretation rather aimed at finding different, sometimes contradicting, meanings in the text. This is, according to Ehrensperger, quite natural since the biblical text is in itself polytonic. The tensions and contradictions in the Hebrew Bible do not imply that the redactors were unaware of such tensions and contradictions, but are "an intended symphony for theological reasons,"[34] Ehrensperger argues.

In fact, the Hebrew Bible pleads for theological pluriformity, which is the reason why we find this realized in rabbinic literature. Feminist perspectives have originated from the experience that the dominant Western discourse hardly is value-free or objective. On the contrary, a white, masculine elite has almost exclusively dominated it. Thus feminist theory originally emerged as a tool to analyze deeply rooted patterns of thought with the clear ambition to change the situation for oppressed women. In the following argument, Ehrensperger gives ample examples of feminist theorists who have dealt with issues of particularity, identity, diversity, and relationality, and their impact on feminist theological interpretations. According to Ehrensperger, these aspects are crucial for the process of developing alternative theological discourses.

In the second part of the study, Ehrensperger turns to the question of how the changing perspectives in feminist theologies and Pauline studies can relate to and illuminate each other. As we noted in chapters 4 and 5 in this book, E. P. Sanders's *Paul and Palestinian Judaism* resulted in a major paradigm shift in Pauline studies and led to various attempts to overcome the opposition between Paul and Judaism. Some scholars, however, felt that the old dichotomy between Jewish particularism and Christian universalism was still prevalent in the so-called new perspective on Paul, and have (as we have seen in chapter 6) brought Pauline scholarship significantly beyond the new perspective in several decisive ways. Ehrensperger clearly belongs to this recent trend of Pauline scholarship, and by critically reviewing research that emphasizes a variety of contextual aspects, she presents an image of Paul that in all essentials moves beyond the traditional image of him. From a "beyond the new perspective" approach,[35] Paul can be seen as fully rooted within Judaism, a religious tradition from which he had no intention to separate. His thinking was hence rooted in the Tanakh and his arguing was halakic (as shown by Peter Tomson). Even though he, like his contemporaries, was influenced by Hellenism, this did not affect his Jewish identity. Moreover, in relation to non-Jewish followers of Jesus, Paul emphasized that oneness in Christ does not imply that ethnic identities are eradicated, but that Jews and non-Jews constitute a unity in that diversity.

By turning to Paul in recent feminist scholarship, Ehrensperger focuses on interpretations of Paul that seem to have taken over hermeneutical patterns from the very same tradition they aim at criticizing, thus reiterating the picture of Paul as an anti-Jewish misogynist. For example, in Elisabeth A. Castelli's contributions to *A Feminist Commentary* (vol. 2 of *Searching the Scriptures*, 1994), Ehrensperger finds that the ideology Castelli presupposes for her reading of Romans "especially of chapters 8 and 9–11, has significant similarities to the image of Paul in the aftermath of the Protestant Reformation and its emphasis on the dualistic opposition of 'law and gospel.'"[36] Moreover, "the presuppositions behind her exegetical comments have close similarities to traditional malestream interpretations of Paul and their inherent anti-Judaism."[37] Thus Ehrensperger states, Castelli has failed to take into account what she in the beginning of her essay declares as most relevant for feminist exegesis, namely: "to examine critically the ideology that underwrites the text."[38]

Aiming at disclosing the underlying, unconscious assumptions in this and similar studies, Ehrensperger poses the question of what the result would be if feminist interpretations of Paul were based on the new view of Paul instead of on the traditional one. In an analysis of Romans 14–15, where she combines the new picture of Paul with three key issues (universalism/particularism, hierarchy/mutuality, sameness/diversity) recently emphasized in feminist approaches, Ehrensperger shows how it is possible to present Paul as *a source of inspiration for feminist perspectives.*

In Romans 14–15, Paul explicitly addresses practical issues that have come up in the community. Still, these chapters are closely linked to the central issue of the letter and serve as an excellent example of the particularity of Paul's theology. The precise identity of the groups addressed in this section of the letter is hard to determine, according to Ehrensperger, but the context (matters related to food, drink, and certain days) suggests that Jewish matters are at stake. Thus Paul most likely addresses non-Jewish followers of Jesus, within or at least with links to the synagogue. It is clear that Paul attached great importance to the quality of the relationship between Jews and non-Jews within this community, and the labels he uses for identifying them, "the weak" (Rom 14:1) and "the strong" (Rom 15:1), show that inequalities in power relations are involved. However, Paul addresses the strong far more than the weak in these chapters and asks them to change their behavior in relation to the weak while he never demands that the weak should change their opinions. This, Ehrensperger says, "indicates a theology of mutuality and accommodation rather then of hierarchical dualism."[37] This could be interpreted as indicating several things: that Paul regards the strong as much more in need of being addressed; that the strong are more responsible for causing the conflict, according to Paul; that he considers them to be in a more powerful position; or that the practices of the strong rather than the opinions of the weak are a threat to the "oneness in Christ."

Romans 14–15 is closely linked to Romans 9–11, Ehrensperger states, where Paul also deals with the relation between Jews and non-Jews. The strong are those who have forgotten that the gospel is first to the Jew and also to the Greek (Rom 1:16), that the Jews were "entrusted with the oracles of God" (Rom 3:2), and that God's gifts and calling are "irrevocable" (Rom 11:29). Consequently, Romans 14–15 is not merely an appendix to the more theological chapters, "but the concrete testing ground of what otherwise would be a purely theoretical faith."[40] Contrary to what is often assumed, we find in Romans 14–15

> a Paul who actually is strongly opposing tendencies of the strong dominating the weak in the Christ-believing communities of Rome. Here Paul is clearly advocating the right of people who are different to remain different: he is advocating diversity rather than uniformity in Christ. He is emphasizing a crucial aspect of faith, that people who are different must respect and support each other mutually in their abiding differences. In Christ, they do not have to overcome differences. Instead, they are a presupposition for real unity.[41]

Thus Paul's theological thinking emerges from practical, everyday issues, and in dialogue with specific Christ-believing communities, he focuses on the relational nature of faith and pays special attention to the need for mutual respect and equality. He also shows an awareness of power issues in relationships and recognizes the need to respect those in weaker positions. Finally, he stresses the need for diversity rather than sameness. Accordingly, these aspects resemble some key matters addressed in feminist theology, and while Paul's problems in Romans are not identical with those issues feminist theologians struggle with, the way he approaches the situation in Rome can still be of interest for contemporary feminist theologians. Ehrensperger concludes that a serious dialogue between the radical perspective and post-critical approaches can be stimulating and lead to whole new fields of research.

Ehrensperger's study covers a wide range of areas and could for that reason just as well have been presented in the next section. The main topic dealt with, however, is the relationship between Pauline studies and *feminist interpretations*. One important aspect that is underscored in Ehrensperger's work is the incredible influence of the traditional perspective on Paul. Even a hermeneutical tradition specifically focused on revealing patterns of domination and hidden power structures failed, at least initially, to unmask the underlying and dominating theological assumptions upon which the traditional image of Paul rests. While the recent development within feminist scholarship demonstrates a significant improvement with regard to anti-Jewish currents, Ehrensperger's approach underlines the importance of interdisciplinary cooperation. All too often, different strands, even within the same scholarly tradition, are hopelessly out of step with closely related disciplines. As is evident from Ehrensperger's hermeneutical experiment, the project of relating various, seemingly incompatible disciplines to each other can lead to highly interesting and unexpected results. Another study that further highlights the importance of interdisciplinary approaches is Davina C. Lopez's rather unique work on Paul and the Gentiles, to which we now will turn.

Multi-Disciplinary Approaches

Paul, the Mother of Effeminized Gentiles—Davina C. Lopez

At the recently rediscovered Sebasteion at Aphrodisias in Asia Minor, excavators found an image of a man and a woman carved in stone. The man is pictured almost naked, except for a military helmet and a cloak. At his feet lies a woman with her right breast exposed, pressed against the ground by his knee, her hair being held, as it seems, by his left hand. An inscription identifies the couple: the man is Emperor Claudius; the woman is Britannia, conquered and vanquished at the feet of the ruler of the Roman Empire. This picture is taken as the point of departure in the highly interesting monograph, *Apostle to the Conquered* (2008), by Davina C. Lopez, Assistant Professor of Religious Studies at Eckerd College.

Lopez's study is an excellent example of the emerging interest in cross- and multidisciplinary readings of Paul. The theoretical model she has developed, *gender-critical reimagination*, not only includes an extension of the source material through the inclusion of visual representations, but also draws from empire-critical, postcolonial, feminist, and queer approaches. All these perspectives are brought together in a synthesizing model aimed at exposing "the situatedness, biases, and veiled objectivism of traditional scholarly exegetical approaches to the New Testament."[42] The application of the model can be illustrated by Lopez's own demonstration of how the different theoretical perspectives complement and interoperate with one another in the interpretation of the picture of Claudius and Britannica:

> If we (can) read for gender alone, we see a female body violently situated under a male body. If for queerness, we see both a female body in forced hierarchical relationship to maleness, as well as an unruly Amazonian type of gender transgression held in check by the forces of male power and, perhaps, an anxiety about penetration. If we think about empire and religion, we see a divine emperor "sacrificing" and taming an inferior woman's body; we also see this relief as part of an imperial cult complex, where provincials would go to worship. And if postcolonial analysis is brought to bear on this relief, perhaps we see a representative of the central colonizing power defeating a colonized borderland, forcing her into "civilization."[43]

It is evident, Lopez argues, that each of these perspectives emphasizes different aspects of the image, revealing its complexity. However, none of the relationships between Claudius and Britannica can be properly understood without attention being brought to the other aspects. This insight has a direct bearing on the main problem Lopez wants to address: Paul's relationship to the Gentiles.

Traditionally, "the Gentiles" in the New Testament have been interpreted almost entirely as a theological category, without any real

connection to social, economic, and political factors in the Roman
Empire, Lopez asserts. Within New Testament scholarship, the terms
ethnos, ethnē, are usually defined in relation to Jews and signify, in
short, people who do not adhere to Judaism. While this usage of the
term finds some support in Jewish writings (where *ethnos, ethnē* often
refer to the "other"), defining "Gentiles" only from what they are not
(Jews) prevents scholars from asking questions about who the
Gentiles really were. Interestingly enough, the Gentiles, who lack any
real substance of their own, are at the same time at the center of Paul's
mission. "Even relatively recent New Testament scholarship," Lopez
states, "that affirms Paul's thoroughgoing Jewishness does not ask the
question of who, precisely, the Gentiles are outside of a construct
dependent on differences from Jews."[44] This is basically the issue
Lopez wants to address: who exactly are the Gentiles and why is it so
important for Paul that they relate to Jews? Is it likely that they saw
themselves as non-Jewish heathens?

From Lopez's gender-critical reimagination perspective, other
aspects of Gentile identity suddenly come to life. Could it be, Lopez
asks, that Paul confronts an imperial ideology that is set out to incorpo-
rate all nations into the Roman family? From such a perspective, the
relations between Jews and Gentiles change in a decisive way, since
both Jews and the Gentiles (Paul's intended audience) belong to ethnic
groups that have been conquered by Rome. Paul's mission to the
Gentiles thus becomes *a mission to the conquered nations,* among whom
Britannica is one. Now, since the dichotomy between Rome and the
nations is expressed through hierarchical gender constructs (as in the
case of Claudius and Britannica), revealing the underlying ideology
becomes highly interesting, especially when the various sources are
interpreted from a perspective that involves theoretical tools aimed at
focusing on precisely such aspects.

In an illuminating analysis of several kinds of visual representations,
such as statues, coins, and reliefs, Lopez shows that the visual traditions
used in promoting Roman imperial ideology consistently present conquered nations in the form of women's bodies. Images of maleness dominating femaleness can be found in the city of Rome as well as in the largest
imperial cult complex ever found, the Sebasteion in Aphrodisias in Asia
Minor, which suggests that such power relationships were communicated

throughout the Roman Empire, either in the form of female bodies forced to subjection or, occasionally, as feminized men, deprived of their masculinity. Thus the public exposure of images depicting Roman men conquering female nations served to legitimize Roman territorial expansion, imperial domination, and patriarchal gender constructs. "Roman identification of the nations as outsiders, as that which must be penetrated in order to maintain peace, is a critical element in this broader, gendered, imperial imagery of the natural cosmic and colonial order of things," Lopez concludes.[45] Thus the Roman imperial world order is expressed as a gendered world order and the peace Rome offers can only be realized through patriarchy: "feminine submission stabilizes Roman masculinity."[46]

Turning to literary sources, Lopez demonstrates how this gendered hierarchical attitude toward the nations is expressed in literature from around the same time as the New Testament was written. From texts written by authors dealing with the mytho-historical origin of Rome (Dionysius of Halicarnassus, Livy, Virgil), it is clear that the theme of maleness dominating femaleness is a recurrent theme. Foreign nations are characterized as female and in need of incorporation into the Roman family—or else subject to destruction. The project of uniting the whole world under Roman dominion is clearly expressed as a divinely ordered mission, already revealed in the stories about Romulus and Remus, who are predestined to build the city that will rule the cosmos forever. This is also expressed in the well-known story of the "rape of the Sabine women," which connects the conquering of neighboring women to the origin of Rome precisely in terms of maleness dominating femaleness.

Thus through different forms of media—literature, inscriptions, visual representations, and carefully designed public manifestations—the fate of the nations was effectively communicated in highly gendered constructs in which sexual violence and military violence were presented as thoroughly intertwined. This, Lopez states, is the ideological and political context of Paul and leads to a rather different understanding of Paul as an apostle to the conquered nations.

"Paul," Lopez says, "also uses gendered language to navigate, critique, and re-imagine the very same patriarchal structure that so many have used him to affirm and propagate."[47] Her analysis of Paul's conversion, however, leads to a significantly different result compared to what is usually assumed in traditional Pauline scholarship. Paul's conversion,

Lopez states, implies that the apostle identifies with the other feminized nations. According to Roman imperial ideology, the emperor and positive values like self, the gods, civilization, and victory, were connected to the upper position in visual representations, whereas "barbarians," the outsiders, the godless feminized nations occupied the lower position. Thus the gendered status hierarchy in Roman imperial ideology was clearly visually expressed by a bipolar scheme, as in the depiction of Claudius and Britannia, where subordination is represented in spatial terms. At the core of this ideology, we recall, is the idea that Rome, representing maleness, conquers feminized nations, thus bringing stability and civilization to the world.

Lopez argues that before his so-called conversion, Paul shared this ideology. In Galatians 1:13-14, Paul describes his life before his encounter with the risen Christ:

> You have heard, no doubt, of my earlier life in Judaism. I was violently persecuting the church of God and was trying to destroy [*eporthoun*] it [*autēn*]. I advanced in Judaism beyond [*hyper*] many among my people of the same age, for I was far more zealous for the traditions of my ancestors.

Paul himself claims that he, before his conversion, belonged to the persecutors, thus living a life defined by upward mobility. The verb *portheō*, which Paul uses in the imperfect in Galatians 1:13, is frequently used in texts outside of the New Testament where it denotes "total destruction of a collective entity, usually a city or the countryside, in military conflict; it is also used as a participle in that regard (e.g., 'ravager')."[48] Interestingly enough, the word *ekklēsia*, translated as "church," is feminine (which is why the pronoun, *autēn*, also takes this form). Paul is thus persecuting God's *ekklēsia*, trying to annihilate *her*. He has moved above (*hyper*) his fellow Jews. In reality, Paul reproduces the same ideological configuration as the Romans, Lopez states, which means that he behaves in a way that resembles that of a Roman soldier, equating God's approval of Judaism with the ability to conquer, thus demonstrating freedom, maleness, and penetration as the means by which the feminized nations (= the *ekklēsia* consisting of Jews and members from the nations) are being conquered. Paul was, in short, in his former life "reproducing the very same power structure that the Roman metanarrative portrays as natural," Lopez concludes.[49] It is this way of relating to the world that changes when God reveals to Paul that he is called to the nations.

Paul's allusion to the calling of Jeremiah in Galatians 1:15-16 is by no means accidental, Lopez states, since Jeremiah too was called to "the nations" (Jer 1:5). Likewise, in Isaiah God designates Israel as the servant who will teach the true way as a "light to the nations" (Isa 49:6). In the prophetic literature of the Hebrew Bible, the idea that Israel and the nations should not be opposed to one another is common. This idea is linked to the notion of a common genealogical heritage of all nations in Genesis 10 and the blessing of Abraham in Genesis 12. Thus all the nations have a common origin and will eventually be reconciled with Israel. This vision of Israel's role in the salvation of the world would also have been completely in line with the traditions of the fathers, Lopez maintains; Israel's mission was not to persecute the nations, "but to reincorporate them and make justice with them, to turn them from idolatry and toward a relationship with the one imageless God."[50] This means that Paul's perception changes in a dramatic way when he realizes that his "earlier life in Judaism" (Gal 1:13), which in all essentials was in accordance with Roman imperial ideology, is not in accordance with the true mission of Israel. In order to become an apostle to the nations, *Paul must adopt the subordinate position among the other defeated nations*, which means taking on another identity, in fact, a change from masculinity to femininity. There is, according to Lopez, ample evidence of this transformation in Paul's letters.

Paul's statement in 2 Corinthians 11:23-27, for example, points to a life of penetrated, defect masculinity, Lopez argues. Paul mentions that he has been flogged and suffered various hardships. Bodily trauma, such as whipping, beating, and flogging, were commonly associated with slaves, hardly with masculine Roman war heroes. Paul frequently identifies with the defeated and the weak at the bottom of the worldwide power structure. Or put differently: instead of siding with Claudius, the converted Paul now has taken on the role of Britannica. In Galatians 4:19, Lopez states, the defeated Paul transforms into the sufferings of a woman in labor, thus in reality into a "mother." This transformation is implied in other texts as well: in 1 Thessalonians 2:7,

Paul speaks about his "tenderly caring for her own children"; in 1 Corinthians 3:1-2, he describes his Corinthian brothers as his children who are fed "with milk, not solid food." This is fully in accordance with the prophetic tradition, Lopez says, where Israel and the nations are commonly personified as women suffering birth pains during the time of exile, which, however, led to restoration. Paul is thus transformed from conquering male, to defeated male, to laboring mother, and his/her birth pains are the symbol of a new creation of different relationships between Jews and other defeated nations, pointing to the restoration of humanity under the one God in sharp contrast to the violently established peace of Caesar.

This, however, does not imply that Jews and the nations become the "same," even though both Jews and Gentiles are placed together at the bottom in relation to the Roman Empire. It does, however, imply that Paul aims at establishing a sense of solidarity between the Jews and the nations. In Christ, both groups participate in the new creation while maintaining physical differences. As sons (and thus heirs) of Abraham, all nations, that is, both Jews and Gentiles, are blessed, regardless of differences or location. This perspective has far-reaching consequences for the interpretation of the Sarah-Hagar allegory in Galatians 4:21–5:1. This text, which traditionally has been taken as evidence of the sharp opposition between Judaism and Christianity, is really about another kind of opposition, Lopez suggests, namely the one between the covenant of Caesar (leading to slavery) and the covenant of God (leading to freedom). Hagar represents the allegorical personification of Jerusalem taken captive with her children enslaved with her—not however enslaved by the Torah, as is usually assumed, but by Rome. Thus in reality, Hagar represents the imperial co-option leading to *a separation from the Torah forced by Jewish adherence to the Roman world order.* Thus Paul can no longer be seen as an enemy of Judaism, Lopez concludes, but must be seen as an enemy of Roman imperial order, an enemy "not of the local synagogue, but of the worldwide drive toward civilization/slavery."[51] As the apostle to the conquered, he envisions another faith of the nations, not enslavement by the father of the fatherland (Caesar) but the freedom of the father of the promised land.

Lopez's gender-critical reimagination clearly puts most Pauline scholarship on its head. By emphasizing other power structures than the ones that have usually been paid attention to, she is able to present a rather unique interpretation that appears as a challenging alternative to the traditional, idealistic perspectives on Paul. However, Lopez's interdisciplinary reading of Paul against the background of Roman imperial ideology also constitutes an important critique of both the radical new perspective of Paul and empire-critical readings. Even among scholars who generally affirm Paul's thoroughgoing Jewishness, the identity of the Gentiles, apart from their relation to Jews, has seldom been problematized. Also the issues dealt with by the radical new perspective have been rather determined by the idealistic assumption within traditional scholarship. This is a quite natural process, but Lopez's study shows that time indeed seems apt for moving on into areas that have been underdeveloped. Likewise, imperial-critical approaches have certainly brought highly important insights into the field of Pauline studies. However, as Lopez remarks, empire-critical and postcolonial approaches have generally been rather undertheorized when it comes to the gendered texture of the discourse as a whole. The obvious strengths in Lopez's work are the inter-, multi-, and crossdisciplinary approaches, where different perspectives complement each other. As will be discussed more thoroughly in the next chapter, this is the way scholarship works in general—the uniqueness of Lopez's study is that so many perspectives are brought together in the same study. The approach, as such, promises much for the future.

Conclusion

In this chapter we have mainly dealt with scholars who are not primarily involved in the discussion of whether Paul broke with Judaism or not. For these scholars, Paul's Jewishness is the natural point of departure. This means that they all are in close contact with the radical new perspective on Paul, but instead of participating in the ongoing process of finding support for a Jewish Paul, these scholars are rather involved in developing the standpoints that have been outlined by the radical new perspective. This does not imply that there are watertight bulkheads between scholars from the radical new perspective and the ones dealt with in this chapter. It is rather that some scholars within the radical new perspective have moved beyond the basic issues that led to the formation of this scholarly tradition. One might say that within the radical new perspective, there are general agreements on some fundamental issues that are no longer considered to be in need of validation. What we, in fact, are witnessing, and what the works of these scholars indicate, is *the beginning of a formation of a scientific paradigm in which certain assumptions simply are taken for granted*. We will return to this aspect in the next, concluding chapter.

Accordingly, the fact that all scholars within this tradition share some essential perspectives means that scholars can concentrate on other areas. It is obvious, at least from the works examined here, that various power relations and issues of domination and subordination are regarded as especially important. This may partly be explained by the recent development of analytical tools and hermeneutical perspectives that are specifically suited for such analyses. However, the fact that the scholars examined here are drawn to these specific theoretical perspectives indicates an awareness of and an interest in hermeneutical and epistemological issues, which is also reflected in the methodological sophistication these studies display. At any rate, the works dealt with in this chapter clearly show that Pauline studies are involved in a constant process of development.

8

CONCLUSION—HISTORY AND PAUL

Now that we have completed our presentation of the historical development of Pauline scholarship leading up to the contemporary situation, characterized by a multitude of approaches to Paul, the time has come for some concluding remarks. The focus in this presentation has been Paul's relationship to Judaism, because this issue aptly frames the most important discussions of Paul since the emergence of New Testament studies as a scholarly discipline. In this concluding chapter, we will discuss the hermeneutical implications of the contemporary situation, taking its historical development into account. In short: what we will focus on is the issue of how to deal with a situation characterized by such diversity. On what grounds should we base our evaluation of the results of all the approaches to Paul? First, however, we will summarize the presentation in the previous chapters.

Paul—From Hegel to Žižek

The Early Church and the Reformation Period

From the early church, the Reformation churches inherited two problems: first, the theologized opposition between Judaism and Christianity, which originally had been part of the struggle of the non-Jewish part of the Jesus movement to become an accepted religion; second, the so-called Pelagian and Semipelagian controversies. In the writings of Augustine, the individual's relation to God became more and more accentuated. The question of sin and grace, and the relation between the respective roles of the individual and God in salvation, occupy the center of the stage in the Pelagian controversy, a complex of problems dominating the teaching on the function of grace in the Latin, Western church during the Middle Ages. With Martin Luther's solution to the problem—justification by faith alone—the conflict was brought to an end within the Lutheran churches. However, Luther's emphasis on justification by faith in contrast to works further underlined the difference between Judaism and Christianity. In Luther's theological system, the law lost almost all of its positive values with the result that the normal way for Jews to relate to God—through the Torah—became the fundamental human sin in Luther's theological construction: self-righteousness. In view of the influence that Luther's interpretation of Paul has had on Western civilization, it is probably not an understatement to claim that Luther invented one of the most successful theological ideas ever.

In Wake of the Enlightenment

As a result of the Enlightenment, a scientific biblical research tradition developed in the course of the nineteenth century that from more or less secular (or rather deistic) starting points strove to call in question ingrained patterns of thought. When it comes to the relation between Paul and Judaism, however, even the most radical scholarship from this period was often highly influenced by the Christian theological antagonism toward Judaism. The German scholar F. C. Baur, employing the methods offered by Hegelian idealistic philosophy, created what can be regarded as a scientific legitimation of the relation between Paul and Judaism. The research on Judaism pursued especially in Germany, deeply influenced as it was by the growing anti-Semitism in society, confirmed the antithetic relationship between Paul and Judaism that the church for a long time had presupposed, and which Luther had further explained theologically. Judaism was thus presented as a legalistic religion in which the individual strove to merit his or her justification by means of the fundamentally hopeless undertaking of trying to please God by keeping the law. The caricature of ancient Judaism constituted for a long time the normal point of departure for New Testament scholars trying to understand Jesus and Paul. As such, this perspective, of course, worked excellently. If Judaism really was characterized by dead legalism, this in itself can be a reasonable explanation as to why Paul criticized the law.

The interesting question is thus whether the late nineteenth-century understanding of Judaism was correct or not. Already in the beginning of the twentieth century, scholars had questioned the prevalent view of ancient Judaism. This criticism, however, was completely drowned out by the evolving Protestant research, and the image of Paul as the one who liberated Christianity from petrified Jewish legalism and narrow-minded particularism was carried forward in the twentieth century, not least by Rudolf Bultmann and his disciples, Günther Bornkamm and Ernst Käsemann. Because of their prominent positions at the universities and in the churches, they come to exert a considerable influence on generations of future scholars and theologians. In the middle of the century, the dichotomy between Paul and Judaism was hardly called into question and was the natural starting point for New Testament scholars.

From Stendahl to Sanders

After World War II, the situation gradually started to change. The realization of the role played by Christian theology in the Holocaust became for many an incentive for renewed theological reflection during the postwar era. The evolution of an organized Jewish-Christian dialogue and the establishing of the state of Israel in 1948 are other important factors contributing to an increased interest in understanding Judaism on its own terms. Some scholars, notably Krister Stendahl already in the 1960s, started to question the historical basis for the emphasis Protestant theology placed on, for instance, justification by faith and Paul's presumed break with Judaism. But even though individual scholars began thinking along new lines, inspiring others to view Paul from another angle, this was not yet time to speak of a real break-through in Pauline scholarship. The probable reason is that there was not yet any real alternative to the traditional image of Judaism. Dissenting opinions by individual scholars hardly constituted a threat, since the prevailing views were not generally called into question.

The situation changed radically only at the end of the 1970s when E. P. Sanders published his work, *Paul and Palestinian Judaism*. Sanders proved with extraordinary clarity that the traditional picture had arisen through the use of a selection of Jewish texts confirming the Lutheran image of ancient Judaism established long ago. Sanders, however, found an entirely different picture of Judaism. Judaism was, according to Sanders, characterized not by legalism but by *covenantal nomism*, that is, a specific relationship between the Torah and the covenant that God has made with the Jewish people. Observing the Torah is thus not a means for the Jew to merit justification, but the consequence of God, by grace, having chosen the Jewish people. God indeed punishes transgressions and rewards faithfulness, Sanders argues, but the important point is that a broken relationship with God can be restored by the atonement system the Torah offers.

Strictly speaking, Sanders's picture of Judaism is not new. Practically the same view that he emphasizes was pointed out already at the beginning of the twentieth century. The difference was that Sanders's book enjoyed a very widespread circulation. One of the reasons why his interpretation of Judaism became so generally accepted was that Sanders did not come to very far-reaching conclusions about Paul. Sanders is of the opinion that Paul did not adhere to the model of covenantal nomism, which in principle characterized all Jewish groups during the period from roughly 200 BCE to 200 CE. According to Sanders, Paul denied the importance of Jewish mainstays such as the covenant, the election, and the law. His main criticism against Judaism, Sanders says, was that God had chosen another way of saving humankind than by means of the Torah. The problem with Judaism was simply that it was not Christianity. Regarding Paul's relationship to Judaism, Sanders thus came to the same conclusion as most scholars at that time—Paul left Judaism—but according to Sanders, he did it for reasons others than those generally given. The anti-Jewish component thus became considerably toned down, while Paul still could be seen to be in opposition to Judaism.

New Perspectives on Paul

Initially, it did not seem as if Sanders's revision of Judaism would have any dramatic impact on Pauline scholarship. During the 1980s, however, scholars such as J. D. G. Dunn and N. T. Wright pointed out that Sanders had not fully understood the consequences of his own interpretation of Judaism with respect to Paul. Dunn, who coined the term "the new perspective on Paul," suggested, as did Wright, that Paul only opposed those aspects of the Torah that served as specific Jewish markers of identity, thus separating Jews from non-Jews. The problem, Dunn maintained, was not the Torah or covenantal nomism, but Jewish national righteousness. In the course of the ensuing decades, a large number of books and articles were published in which the authors made attempts to understand Paul from this new perspective. By redefining the problem of Paul's relation to Judaism, new perspective scholars brought other aspects of Paul's writings to the fore and the inherent anti-Judaism prevalent in the traditional opposition between Paul and Judaism was significantly downplayed—but not obliterated.

Radicalism and Reactions

Some scholars soon reached the conclusion that the new perspective had not gone far enough with regard to Paul's Jewishness. They pointed out that the traditional dichotomy between Judaism and Christianity and between Judaism and Paul still constituted an important fundament even within the new perspective. Thus instead of assuming that Paul opposed Judaism, scholars like Lloyd Gaston, Stanley Stowers, and Caroline Johnson Hodge all assume that Paul should be even more closely related to first-century Judaism than scholars from within the new perspective usually imagine. This change of perspective has indeed led to new, challenging results, and scholars working from a radical new perspective have reached fundamentally different conclusions than scholars before them. Within the radical new perspective, many of the established truths about Paul have thus been challenged, for instance, the idea that Paul ceased observing the Torah or that he created a new religion based on universalism instead of Jewish particularism.

The cornerstone in this perspective on Paul is the natural development of Sanders's revision of Judaism and the new perspective on Paul. If the old caricature of Judaism can be proven false and it can be assumed that first-century Judaism was not characterized by legalism and works-righteousness, it seems quite unlikely that Paul found reason to leave Judaism for Christianity. If the Torah was given by grace and contains a sacrificial system that makes it possible for the individual to atone for his or her sins, it seems, on the contrary, likely that Paul continued to express his relation to the God of Israel through the Torah, God's most precious gift to the Jewish people. From this point of departure, other factors must have led to the distressing conflicts within the early Jesus movement. This insight has led scholars to emphasize the ethnic and political situation within the Roman Empire. Thus radical new perspective scholars commonly deal with the relationship between Jews and non-Jews within the Jesus movement and their relationship to society as a whole, focusing on various power structures that may have affected these relationships. This has also led to a development with regard to the analytical tools used within the discipline. Postcolonial, feminist, and queer perspectives are nowadays commonly used for interpreting Paul.

The traditional Paul, however, is by no means dead, even though this perhaps could be expected after Sanders's presentation of Judaism as a religion of grace. In the wake of Sanders's *Paul and Palestinian Judaism,* scholars advocating a Reformation perspective in which Luther's doctrine of justification by faith still plays an important role have taken pains to find ways of retaining the fundamental opposition between Judaism and Christianity. Their position is quite clearly motivated by theological reasons, and the project as such—to prove that Luther or Calvin was right (or almost right)—suffers from an inherent anachronistic touch, difficult to understand for scholars who approach Pauline studies from other disciplines like Jewish studies or the history of religions. Nevertheless, in spite of the clear ambition of creating a synthesis between normative theology and New Testament studies, Reformation perspectives have also contributed important insights of great relevance for scholars belonging to more radical traditions. Scholars like Andrew Das, Simon Gathercole, and Stephen Westerholm have pointed out that although Sanders was not completely wrong, he was not completely right either. As many from the Reformation perspective claim, Sanders probably overestimated the aspect of grace in ancient Judaism, while downplaying texts that imply that grace and works seem to have coexisted in Jewish thinking without giving rise to the degree of cognitive dissonance that such tension has created in post-Pelagian Christianity.

To conclude: Pauline studies today exist in a tension between a traditional Reformation perspective, ultimately aiming at legitimizing a neoorthodox standpoint, and methodologically sophisticated, radical attempts to understand Paul from other assumptions than the traditional ones. The increasing amount of studies within and even outside the field of New Testament studies (as in the case of secular philosophy) clearly demonstrates that the apostle to the Gentiles has not ceased to fascinate diverse audiences.

The Different Perspectives on Paul

Focusing on the major trends within current Pauline scholarship and bearing in mind that there are many examples of scholars who do not really fall into these categories, it nevertheless seems fairly correct to suggest that three different schools occupy the scene: 1) scholars who basically work from a traditional, Reformation perspective; 2) scholars who would define themselves as adhering to the new perspective; and 3) scholars who have moved beyond the new perspective into what we may call a "radical new perspective." These major traditions within Pauline scholarship are by no means homogenous. Scholars belonging to the same tradition may very well arrive at different interpretations of a given text or suggest even contradictory solutions to a certain problem. Accordingly, there is a significant diversity both within each of these schools and among the respective traditions. What defines these traditions is rather a general agreement on some basic shared perspectives.

With regard to the first two schools, issues pertaining to normative theology seem to constitute a considerable part of the ideological package. Within the traditional perspective, it is often clearly stated that the aim of the investigation is to confirm a Lutheran reading, or alternatively, the investigation deals with certain key themes important for Christian theology. Thus within the traditional perspective, the dichotomy between Judaism and Paul constitutes a seldom-questioned assumption. Still, as has frequently been pointed out, the critique of Sanders from contemporary representatives of the traditional perspective, for example, is highly relevant. Sanders's emphasis on the element of grace in Judaism constituted, of course, a serious challenge to the traditional perspective, as did his critique of Lutheran scholarship. It is thus only natural that scholars tried to find reasons to question his main thesis concerning Judaism and so they did. (Sanders's view of Paul was probably perceived as less threatening because Sanders too adhered to the idea that Paul broke with Judaism.)

In this regard, the new perspective differs significantly from the traditional perspective. Within the "new perspective," scholars willingly (and perhaps somewhat uncritically) accepted Sanders's view of Judaism *while questioning his image of Paul*. Also the new perspective can basically be considered a Christian confessional strategy to cope with Sanders's revision of Judaism, albeit using a different approach. While the traditional perspective (perhaps somewhat stubbornly) has held on to the Reformation perspective, the new perspective sought to solve the tension *by partly incorporating Judaism into Lutheranism*. Ancient Judaism was truly a religion of grace; Paul only opposed the nasty parts, those connected to national righteousness. Thus within the new perspective, classic Christian theological concepts, such as "the works of the law" and "justification by faith," are still considered meaningful within a Christian context—but are considerably redefined and filled with a new content. This, I believe, is why the fiercest battles have been fought between representatives of the traditional perspective and the new perspective.

While being neither neutral nor objective, the assumptions of the radical new perspective still differ significantly from the ones used within the traditional and the new perspective. Within the radical new perspective, I dare say, scholars are not primarily involved in the process of confirming or developing a specific Christian contemporary theology, partly because quite a few scholars within this tradition would not define themselves as Christians. Christian scholars within this tradition may indeed have a theological agenda, but this seems to be secondary, although one should bear in mind that the radical new perspective ultimately is a reaction against the Reformation perspective's theological view of Paul. Yet for many within the radical new perspective, it is precisely the confusion between normative theology and science that has given rise to the suspicion that the traditional portrait of Paul may be misconstrued. This implies that a certain hermeneutical sensibility is perhaps more developed within this tradition, and suggests that scholars are dependent on other hermeneutical traditions than scholars from the traditional perspective. While the concept of truth within the traditional perspective to a significant degree is determined by theological factors, scholars within the radical new perspective seem more connected to hermeneutical traditions that emphasize diversity in interpretation. Still, ideological factors that may affect scholars within the radical new perspective are, for instance, involvement in Jewish-Christian dialogue and a general consciousness about the connection between the traditional anti-Jewish theology of the church and the Holocaust, in some cases leading to a wish to contribute to the development of theological alternatives.

To conclude: there is evidently a strong connection between the overarching perspective shared among scholars within each of these schools and the results that are produced. Within the traditional perspective, the normal assumption is that Paul opposed Judaism, whereas within the radical new perspective, scholars read Paul assuming that he did not break with Judaism. This may not be as strange as it first appears, and may even have to do with how science generally works. This we will dig into somewhat more deeply.

Paradigms and Scientific Revolutions

In 1962, Thomas S. Kuhn (1922–1996), then Professor of the History of Science at the University of California, Berkeley, published his work *The Structure of Scientific Revolutions*. In this, his most influential work, he suggests that scientific evolution does not develop continuously, but that different *scientific paradigms* succeed one another and drastically change a certain scientific field. A *paradigm* is made up of the sum of theories and methods used within a certain field and leads to the establishment of a kind of scientific, conceptual worldview, which Kuhn called *normal science*. Within the paradigm of normal science, where most research is carried out, scholars work without directly questioning the overall framework of interpretation. Rather there is a tendency to focus on *confirming the predominant paradigm*. A distinct norm for which solutions to a given problem are acceptable is established. In this way, certain expectations regarding the results of an investigation also arise.

Kuhn's idea of normal science and paradigms may help us understand why the starting point of traditional scholarship was the assumption that Paul stood in opposition to Judaism, and why scholars working in this dominant paradigm have arrived at so similar general conclusions, regardless of the methods employed. The traditional view of Paul can be considered the normal scientific paradigm determining the boundaries of scholarship on Paul and which scholars have taken pains to confirm. Through those research traditions and established social networks, new scholars have been trained to see matters in the manner that is considered scientifically and, equally important, *socially accepted* (scholars sometimes need jobs). Particular observations that seemingly confirm the overall pattern are being emphasized, whereas those that do not fit, so-called *anomalies*, are explained away. In the case of Paul and Judaism, matters have been further complicated by normative theology. The theologically motivated picture of antagonism between Paul and Judaism has played a crucial role for the rise of the dominant scientific paradigm and probably also for its power to dominate the field for such a long period. The confusion of scientific perspectives and normative theology has probably also functioned as a reciprocal legitimation of the respective perspectives.

What we now experience when the dominant, traditional Reformation paradigm is challenged by radically different perspectives could, using Kuhn's terminology, be defined as the beginning of *a scientific revolution*. Kuhn insists that scientific evolution does not occur in a cumulative manner, in which small progressive stages are added to one another, but that evolution takes place by scientific revolutions. When an increasing number of observations cannot be explained by means of the current paradigm, scholars start producing new, radical ideas, perhaps even paying attention to research previously not accepted because it fell outside the prevailing paradigm. In the course of this process, which gradually leads to the established paradigm being replaced by another one, *different perspectives clash with each other.* It is perhaps here we can find one explanation as to why Paul can be understood in such different ways: the conflicting paradigms are part of a rather natural process that will eventually lead to the establishment of a new dominant paradigm.

Knowing the Truth

Kuhn may thus explain why conflicting paradigms coexist and why scholars representing different worldviews reach conflicting results. However, what is not explained by Kuhn's idea of scientific revolutions is why scholars sharing the *same* worldview also disagree on the interpretation of, in this case, Paul. This rather has to do with the general conditions for studying history. In the following, we will discuss the process of interpretation and pose the question if it is possible to determine whether one interpretation is to be preferred over another. In short: is it possible to know the truth about Paul?

The Framework of Interpretation

The fact that the same text can be given so many different meanings, of which we have seen ample evidence in this book, not only indicates that there may be a wide scope for interpretation, but also that it is fully possible to completely misunderstand the author's intention.

In the 1879 novel *The Red Room*, written by Swedish author August Strindberg, there is a good example of how easy it is to miss the intended meaning if necessary background information is missing. On page 2, Strindberg describes how the main character, Mr. Falk, enters the garden and goes for a walk. Strindberg continues: "Far below him rose the clamour of the newly awakened town." It appears that this scene took place early in the morning, an impression that is further strengthened by the description of how Falk "turned into the wind, unbuttoned his overcoat and took several deep breaths that seemed to refresh both his lungs and his mind." This is, however, a completely erroneous conclusion. If we turn to page 1, we find that the opening sentence of the novel begins with the words: "It was an *evening* early in May" (my emphasis). This piece of information completely changes the meaning of the phrase on page 2. Only when the temporal interpretation is ruled out, we understand that Strindberg uses the word "awakened" in a figurative sense — Stockholm, at the turn of the century, was a city in the process of being industrialized and it is probably this development to which the author refers — "the steam cranes whirred, the bars rattled, the steamers steamed."

In course of a normal reading, we would probably have retained in our memory that the time of the day was already given on the preceding page and found another interpretation of the phrase in question quite natural. *The problem when reading texts from antiquity, such as the New Testament, is that we are not quite sure what was said on page 1.* In the case of Paul, we are thrown into a world of ideas constituting the natural background for the original readers, but which is only partially known to us. Each attempt to understand what Paul meant must also include a reconstruction of the symbolic world to which the texts refers.

Unfortunately, our ability to enter into the world of Paul and his contemporaries is quite restricted. A whole range of basic facts and circumstances are indeed entirely uncontroversial and can probably with a high degree of probability be considered as safe knowledge. One serious concern, however, is that the reconstruction of the background of Paul's thinking places us in exactly the same interpretive quandary as the interpretation of Paul himself. In order to understand the world in which Paul lived, we must turn to other texts, archaeological remains, and as we have learned, visual representations, leading us into an endless maze of further interpretive problems.

Moreover, Jewish sources from this period are rather meager, which means that scholars often use the rich source material from the third century CE and onwards for reconstructing Paul's thinking. However, this literature stems from a rather different period in Jewish history. Paul lived in an era when the temple was still standing, the sacrificial cult was practiced, and Jerusalem was the natural center of Judaism, while rabbinic Judaism evolved as a result of the fall of Jerusalem and the destruction of the temple. The rabbis strove to create a new form of Judaism no longer centered on the temple but on the sacred text. Thus it is not entirely clear to what extent this form of Judaism can contribute to Pauline studies.

While we know quite a lot about the general social, political, and religious conditions in the Roman Empire, we know much less about the relationship between cult and society in the everyday life of the individual. What was it like for an inhabitant in a Greco-Roman city to live outside the established religious system? How was a person with a divergent religious behavior regarded, a person who because of his or her commitment to the Jesus movement no longer could partake in the religious festivals the majority considered crucial for the well-being and continued existence of the entire city? The answer to these and many other questions, *highly relevant for the study of Paul,* are not known to us. This means that the interpretive framework created in order to understand Paul, *and on which our interpretations are entirely dependent,* consists of incomplete reconstructions based on a variety of assumptions. Consequently, if there is a measure of insecurity already built into the system that is supposed to serve as the point of departure for the interpretation, the result cannot be regarded as an absolute and definitive reconstruction, but rather a tentative construction.

So how can we know when we have found the truth? From these points of departure, it is quite obvious that there is no way of knowing for sure whether the interpretation of a text from antiquity represents what the author intended or not. It is possible that there are interpretations of Pauline texts that entirely correspond to Paul's intention, but we can never know this for sure, and there really is no way of finding out. Thus it is important to bear in mind that when someone claims to have found the original or the one and only true meaning in a text, he or she represents an interest group. When it comes to ideas of what Paul really said, there are plenty of them.

Finding Truth through Diversity

The insight that the process of gaining knowledge about the past through the interpretation of various ancient sources is complex is not to say that historical truth does not exist—only that it is hard to find. Paul was a real person and meant to communicate something quite specific through his writings. The fact that it is hard to know what he meant to say, what he believed, and what he expected from those he communicated with does not imply that every solution to these problems is equally historically likely. Embracing the self-consuming subjectivity of radical postmodernism will not help us get closer to the historical Paul. What we *can* learn from the postmodern project is that the symbolic universe of the interpreter affects the interpretation and that there is a strong connection between specific assumptions and the result of a historical investigation.

Once we have dismissed the quest for the absolute, historical truth in the biblical texts as a methodological impossibility, what remains are numerous interpretations more or less plausible. The degree of probability depends on a number of factors, but the most important one is the overarching perspective the scholar adheres to, *the paradigm* that determines which questions are relevant to ask and what answers are scientifically and socially acceptable. Almost equally important is *the interpretive framework* understood as the sum of all theories and presumptions (more or less valid) included in the interpretation and on which the interpretation is based. Is a certain (re)construction built on relevant and correct historical information that can be sufficiently verified, or at least, sufficiently argued for? Finally, of course, the internal coherence of a certain interpretation must be considered. It is important to realize that it is possible to criticize a certain interpretation on each one of these levels. Thus it is possible to disagree with a certain scholar with regard to the first level, that is, one might adhere to a different paradigm, but still find the interpretation as such coherent, although disagreeing with the result. Or one can be in complete agreement with the fundamental perspective (the paradigm), and with the interpretive framework, but still consider the conclusions to be wrong, thus disagreeing with the result.

With regard to the various approaches to Paul that we have encountered it should be noted that the traditional perspective and to some extent also the new perspective are so closely related to normative theology that it is problematic to criticize the overarching paradigm from normal scientific points of departure. The issues that are seen as relevant and acceptable are bound up with rather specific interpretations of Christian theology in which the opposition between Paul and Judaism, between Judaism and Christianity are important. Truth is to some extent bound up with religious belief, which is always complicated. Thus the amalgamation of normative theology and historical scholarship is, in my view, problematic. It is legitimate to question whether it is justifiable from the perspective of the science of history to build scholarship upon religious notions. Rather, it seems to me that the relationship between science and normative theology should be reversed. Thus instead of letting a theological paradigm determine New Testament scholarship, normative theology should be inspired by new insights in the field and develop new theologies. A similar hermeneutical program has already been suggested by Heikki Räisänen in his 1990 monograph, *Beyond New Testament Theology*, and is scarcely controversial any longer. Admittedly, the new perspective on Paul represents such an effort to some degree, but the traditional paradigm, perhaps unconsciously, still plays an important role.

The problem with the traditional paradigm is that it originally emerged *as a theological solution to a theological problem*—the relationship between the respective roles of the individual and God in salvation. The idea of an absolute opposition between Paul and Judaism is a theological consequence of a certain theological problem. Thus considering the history of the development of the idea of the absolute opposition between Paul and Judaism, especially the confusion between science and normative theology, I find it highly unlikely that the traditional perspective on Paul qualifies as a valid point of departure for modern Pauline scholarship in close contact with other disciplines within the broad tradition of humanities. The truth about Paul, I would assume, lurks somewhere within the radical new perspective.

Exactly what this truth about Paul looks like is difficult to say. We have seen examples of scholars who all have dismissed the traditional view of Paul's relationship to Judaism and who are working from other points of departure. Nevertheless their results differ, sometimes substantially, from each other. All these interpretations constitute coherent constructions against the background of circumstances in antiquity, which are relatively well investigated. But who presents the real Paul? The question is probably wrongly posed: perhaps it is precisely in the multitude of these various interpretations that we may glimpse a blurry and elusive portrait of Paul. The general hermeneutical limitations when it comes to knowledge about the past make it crucial that we appreciate the multitude of interpretations. Scholars do not deal with the same problem from the same points of departure using the same perspectives. Thus different interpretations deal with different aspects of Paul, which together make up a more complete image of the apostle.

Occasionally, one individual scholar may apply several approaches simultaneously, as in the case of Davina Lopez, whose study demonstrates how various approaches may interact in creating a complex image of Paul. This, I assume, is ultimately the way Pauline scholarship will develop. Through the interaction of various parallel and even contradictory interpretations, a new dominant paradigm will perhaps eventually emerge, built on other aspects than the dichotomy between Paul and the Judaism he was born into. Such a perspective may prove highly interesting also for those interested in developing the theology of the Christian church, which in several ways seems to be in need of being rescued from itself. In this respect, radical Pauline scholarship may provide an interesting starting point.

NOTES

Chapter 1

1. See, for example, E. P. Sanders, *Jesus and Judaism*, 23–58.
2. Räisänen, *Paul and the Law*, 3.
3. All scripture citations are from the New Revised Standard Version unless otherwise indicated.
4. Cranfield, *Romans*, 2:22-24. See also Fitzmyer, *Romans*, 79, who believes Paul wrote Romans both as an introduction and in order to deal with certain problems in the community.
5. See, for example, Bornkamm, *Paulus*, 63–111, idem, "Paul's Last Will."
6. See, for example, Klein, "Paul's Purpose"; Wedderburn, *Reasons*.
7. Zetterholm, "Missing Messiah," 43–45.
8. See the discussion on Paul's so-called opponents in Nanos, *Irony*, 75–199.
9. On Jewish privileges, see for example Tellbe, *Synagogue and State*, 37–50.
10. Young, *Jewish Theologian*, 1.
11. Horsley and Hanson, *Bandits*.
12. On the relation between the classical prophets and Paul's self-understanding, see Sandnes, *One of the Prophets*.
13. Stendahl, *Paul*, 7–23.
14. Zetterholm, *Formation of Christianity*, 93–94.
15. On Jewish views on non-Jews, see for example Donaldson, "Proselytes"; idem, *Paul and the Gentiles*, 51–78.
16. See, for example, Fung, *Galatians*, 110–11; Taylor, *Paul, Antioch and Jerusalem*, 123–39.
17. See, for example, Slee, *Church in Antioch*, 17–23, 28–29, 42–52; Dunn, "Incident," 31–37; Betz, *Galatians*, 104.
18. Sanders, *Practice and Belief*, 214–30.
19. Hayes, *Gentile Impurities*, 45–67.
20. Ibid., 54–58, 66–67.

21. Cf., however, Esler, *Galatians*, 93–116.
22. Nanos, "Peter's Eating."
23. On this passage, see Nanos, *Mystery*, 184.
24. Cf., however, Johnson, *1 and 2 Timothy*, 55–97, who maintains a Pauline authorship for the Pastoral Letters.

Chapter 2

1. On Baur's life and theological development, see Harris, *Tübingen School*; Hodgson, *Historical Theology*.
2. Schäfer, *Judeophobia*, 197–211.
3. Ibid.
4. Beard, North and Price, *Religions of Rome*, 1:245–312.
5. Tellbe, *Synagogue and State*, 34–35.
6. Harland, *Associations*, 213–28.
7. Barclay, *Mediterranean Diaspora*, 48–60.
8. On non-Jewish interest in Judaism, see also Murray, *Jewish Game*, 11–27.
9. On various non-Jewish attitudes to Judaism, see Cohen, *Beginnings*, 140–74.
10. Schäfer, *Judeophobia*, 210.
11. Meier, *Marginal Jew*, 3:622–26; Guillaume, "Miracles," 21–23; Hammer, "Elijah and Jesus," 210–13.
12. Meier, *A Marginal Jew*, 2:315; Sanders, *Jesus and Judaism*, 218–21.
13. Ibid., 220–21.
14. Zetterholm, *Formation of Christianity*, 193–202.
15. On laws regarding idolatry, see Tomson, *Paul and the Jewish Law*, 151–86.
16. On Paul's view of "idol offerings," see Zetterholm, "Purity and Anger," 11–16; Tomson, *Paul and the Jewish Law*, 187–220.
17. See, for example, Overman, *Matthew's Gospel*; Sim, *Gospel of Matthew*.
18. On the separation between Judaism and Christianity, see Zetterholm, *Formation of Christianity*.
19. On Christian anti-Semitism and early Jewish-Christian relations, see Gager, *Origins of Anti-Semitism*; Klein, *Anti-Judaism*; Ruether, *Faith and Fratricide*; Sanders, *Schismatics*; Segal, *Rebecca's Children*; Simon, *Verus Israel*; Taylor, *Anti-Judaism*; Zetterholm, *Formation of Christianity*.
20. On Augustine and Pelagius, see Brown, *Augustine*, 340–53.
21. For introductions to rabbinic literature, see for example Holtz, "Back to the Sources"; Safrai, "Literature of the Sages"; Stemberger, *Talmud and Midrash*.
22. Baird, *History of NT Research*, 2:222.

Chapter 3

1. For an overview of Bultmann's theology, see Fergusson, *Bultmann*.
2. For an overview of theological liberalism, see Baird, *History of NT Research*, 2:85–136.
3. Stendahl, "Introspective Conscience," 207.
4. Barclay, *Mediterranean Diaspora*, 105–6.
5. Feldman, *Jew and Gentile*, 153–58; Schäfer, *Judeophobia*, 93–105.
6. See Rubin, "Decircumcision."
7. Thiselton, *First Corinthians*, 551.
8. Barclay, *Mediterranean Diaspora*, 322.
9. Fish, *Text in This Class*, 307–8.
10. See Vanderkam and Flint, *Meaning of the Dead Sea Scrolls*, 351–52.
11. Montefiore, *Judaism and St Paul: Two Essays*, 7.
12. Schechter, *Aspects of Rabbinic Theology*, 4, 18.
13. Moore, *Judaism*, 3:151.
14. Moore, "Christian Writers," 252.
15. Ibid., 253.

Chapter 4

1. Simpson and Weyl, *Story of ICCJ*, 117.
2. *Theology of the Churches*, 6.
3. Abbott, "Documents," 666.
4. Ibid., 664.
5. On the history of *Nostra Aetate*, see Miccoli, "Sensitive Issues," 135–66.
6. Fergusson, *Bultmann*, 145; Martin, "Käsemann," 500; Morgan, "Bornkamm," 439.
7. On Stendahl's view on Rom 9–11, see also *Final Account*, 33–44.
8. Sanders, *Palestinian Judaism*, 19.
9. Ibid., 180.
10. Ibid., 75.
11. Ibid., 423.
12. Räisänen, *Paul and the Law*, 1.
13. Ibid., 264.
14. Ibid., 4.
15. Ibid., 15.
16. Ibid., 168.
17. Ibid., 188.
18. Ibid.
19. Ibid., 201–2.
20. Ibid., 265.
21. Dunn, "New Perspective," 97.

22. Ibid., 100.
23. Ibid., 101.
24. Ibid., 114.
25. Dunn's view of Paul's relation to Judaism has, of course, been developed in a number of other articles and books. The most important ones can now be found in a convenient collection; see Dunn, *New Perspective*. See also idem, *Theology of Paul*, esp. 334–89.
26. Stendahl has later commented upon the fact that he has been thought to have advocated a "two-covenant model," and seems to argue that such a label does not really correspond to what he wanted to express in his early work on Paul; see Stendahl, *Final Account*, x.
27. Wright, "Paul of History," 63.
28. Ibid.
29. Ibid., 65.
30. Wright, *Paul: In Fresh Perspective*, 6.
31. Ibid., 6.
32. Hays, *Echoes of Scripture*.
33. Wright, *Paul: In Fresh Perspective*, 24.
34. Ibid., 34.
35. Ibid., 37.
36. Ibid., 57.
37. Ibid., 86.
38. Ibid., 113.
39. Ibid., 135.
40. Ibid., 161.
41. See for example Dunn, "Paul's Conversion," 93.

Chapter 5

1. Gaston, *Paul and the Torah*, 2.
2. Ibid., 3.
3. Ibid., 17.
4. Ibid., 134.
5. Ibid., 79.
6. Tomson, *Paul and the Jewish Law*, xiv.
7. Ibid., xiii.
8. Ibid., 1.
9. Ibid., 18.
10. Ibid., 16.
11. Ibid., 52.
12. Ibid., 65.
13. Ibid., 86.
14. Ibid., 220.

15. Ibid., 269.
16. Stowers, *Rereading Romans*, 7.
17. Ibid., 21.
18. Ibid., 145.
19. Ibid., 192.
20. Ibid., 304.
21. Cf. Isa 59:20, 21; 27:9; Jer 31:33, 34.
22. Stowers, *Rereading Romans*, 329.
23. Ibid., 310.
24. For a summary of some of the main arguments, see Nanos, "Jewish Context."
25. Nanos, *Mystery*, 5–6.
26. Ibid., 72.
27. Ibid., 143.
28. Ibid., 237.
29. See also Nanos, "Inter- and Intra-Jewish Political Context."
30. Johnson Hodge, *If Sons, then Heirs*, 4.
31. Ibid., 11.
32. Ibid., 9.
33. Ibid., 59.
34. Ibid., 80.
35. Ibid., 83.
36. Ibid., 106.
37. Ibid., 129.
38. Ibid., 148.
39. See ibid., 117–25.

Chapter 6

1. Thielman, *From Plight to Solution*, 25.
2. Ibid., 27.
3. Ibid., 29.
4. Ibid., 36.
5. Ibid., 45.
6. Ibid., 49.
7. See Westerholm, *Israel's Law*, 201–5, or idem, *Perspectives*, 433–37.
8. Hübner, *Law*, 36–42.
9. Räisänen, *Paul and the Law*, 62–64, 200–202.
10. Thielman, *From Plight to Solution*, 53.
11. Ibid., 59.
12. Ibid., 120.
13. Ibid., 49.
14. Das, *Paul*, 7.

15. See, for example, *Jub.* 6:14; 50:10-11.
16. 1QS 7.22-27.
17. Ibid., 29.
18. Ibid., 36.
19. Ibid., 69.
20. Ibid., 101.
21. Ibid., 228.
22. Gathercole, *Where is Boasting?*, 13.
23. Ibid., 14.
24. Ibid., 20.
25. Ibid., 90.
26. Ibid., 93.
27. Ibid., 111.
28. Ibid., 118.
29. Ibid., 124.
30. Ibid., 135.
31. Ibid., 194.
32. Ibid., 251.
33. Westerholm, *Perspectives*, 88.
34. Ibid., 96.
35. Ibid., 257.
36. Ibid., 272.
37. Ibid., 288.
38. Ibid., 291.
39. Ibid., 295.
40. Ibid., 299.
41. Westerholm refers, for example, to an article by Dunn ("Justice of God," 8) where he states that the "Judaism of what Sanders christened as 'covenantal nomism' can now be seen to preach good Protestant doctrine: that grace is always prior; that human effort is ever the response to divine initiative; that good works are the fruit and not the root of salvation."
42. Sanders, *Palestinian Judaism*, xii.
43. Ibid., 297.
44. Westerholm, *Perspectives*, 351.
45. Ibid., 350.
46. Ibid., 351.
47. Ibid., 351.
48. Ibid., 400.
49. Dunn, "Justice of God," 15.
50. See for example Dunn, *Theology of Paul*, 386.

Chapter 7

1. For more extensive treatments of Paul in philosophical discourses, see Langton, "Approaches to the Apostle Paul"; Martin, "Promise of Teleology"; Sigurdson, "Reading Žižek Reading Paul."
2. On Nietzsche's critique of Paul, see Sigurdson, "Reading Žižek Reading Paul," 215–18.
3. Taubes, *Political Theology of Paul*, 11.
4. Ibid., 25.
5. Ibid., 24.
6. Badiou, *Saint Paul*, 1.
7. Ibid., 108.
8. Ibid., 106.
9. Ibid., 35.
10. Ibid., 23.
11. Sigurdson, "Reading Žižek Reading Paul," 222.
12. Edward Said's *Orientalism* (1978) is perhaps the most best known post-colonial literary work and has indeed been of great influence. However, creative works of literature relating to postcolonial cultures and societies can, of course, be found throughout the nineteenth century.
13. For a short introductions to postcolonial criticism, see for example Sugirtharajah, *Postcolonial Criticism*, 11–42; Lazarus, "Introducing Post-colonial Studies," 1–16.
14. Horsley, "Submerged Biblical Histories," 162.
15. Ibid. As an introduction to postcolonial perspectives in Pauline studies, see also the collection of articles in Horsley, "Paul and Empire."
16. Elliott, *Arrogance of Nations*, 77.
17. Ibid., 158.
18. Ibid., 20.
19. Ibid., 20.
20. Ibid., 25.
21. Ibid., 30.
22. Ibid., 83.
23. Ibid., 100.
24. Ibid., 103.
25. Ibid., 101.
26. Ibid., 105–6.
27. Ibid., 115.
28. For a comprehensive introduction to feminist biblical interpretation (with an extensive bibliography), see Phillips, "Feminist Interpretation."
29. Ehrensperger, *Mutually Encouraged*, 1.
30. Ibid., 1.
31. Ibid., 9.
32. Ibid., 40.

33. Ibid.
34. Ibid., 63.
35. This term was introduced by W. S. Campbell in a seminar paper, "The Interpretation of Paul: Beyond the New Perspective," given at the New Testament Postgraduate Seminar, Oxford, 2001.
36. Ehrensperger, *Mutually Encouraged*, 164.
37. Ibid., 168.
38. Ibid.
39. Ibid., 183.
40. Ibid., 184.
41. Ibid., 199.
42. Lopez, *Apostle to the Conquered*, 7.
43. Ibid., 16–17.
44. Ibid., 5.
45. Ibid., 55.
46. Ibid., 54.
47. Ibid., 119.
48. Ibid., 129.
49. Ibid., 133.
50. Ibid., 135.
51. Ibid., 167.

BIBLIOGRAPHY

Ancient Sources

Bibles, apocrypha, and pseudepigrapha

The Holy Bible . . . New Revised Standard Version. Nashville: Thomas Nelson, 1989.

Novum Testamentum Graece. Edited by B. and K. Aland, J. Karavidopoulus et al. 27th ed. Stuttgart: Deutsche Bibelgesellschaft, 2001.

The Old Testament Pseudepigrapha, vol 1: Apocalyptic Literature and Testaments. Edited by J. H. Charlesworth. New York: Doubleday, 1983.

The Old Testament Pseudepigrapha, vol 2: Expansions of the 'Old Testament' and Legends, Wisdom and Philosophical Literature, Prayers, Psalms, and Odes, Fragments of Lost Judeo-Hellenistic Works. Edited by J. H. Charlesworth. New York: Doubleday, 1985.

Jewish-Hellenistic literature

Josephus
Josephus. Translated by H. St. J. Thackeray et al. 10 vols. Loeb Classical Library. Cambridge: Harvard University Press, 1926–.

Philo
Philo. Translated by F. H. Colson and G. H. Whitaker. 10 vols. Loeb Classical Library. Cambridge: Harvard University Press, 1929–.

Rabbinic literature

Exodus Rabbah
Midrash Rabbah: Translated into English with Notes, Glossary and Indices. Edited by H. Freedman and M. Simon. 3rd ed. 10 vols. London: Soncino Press, 1983.

Mishnah
Mishnah: A New Translation with a Commentary by Pinhas Kehati. 21 vols. Jerusalem: Eliner Library, Education for Torah Education and Culture in the Diaspora, 1994–96.

Tosefta
The Tosefta: Translated from the Hebrew. Edited by J. Neusner and R. S. Sarason. Translated by A. J. Avery-Peck, R. Brooks et al. 6 vols. Hoboken: Ktav, 1977–86.

Christian literature

Augustine
The City of God against the Pagans. Translated by W. M. Green. 7 vols. Loeb Classical Library. Cambridge: Cambridge University Press, 1957–.

Eusebius
The Ecclesiastical History. Translated by K. Lake. 2 vols. Loeb Classical Library. Cambridge: Cambridge University Press 1926–.

First Clement
The Apostolic Fathers. Translated by B. D. Ehrman. 2 vols. Loeb Classical Library. Cambridge: Harvard University Press 2003–.

Ignatius
The Apostolic Fathers. Translated by B. D. Ehrman. 2 vols. Loeb Classical Library. Cambridge: Harvard University Press 2003–.

Melito of Sardis
On Pascha and Fragments: Texts and Translations. Edited by S. G. Hall. Oxford: Clarendon Press, 1979.

Classical literature

Celsus
De medicina. Translated by W. G. Spencer. 3 vols. Loeb Classical Library. Cambridge: Harvard University Press, 1935–.

Dio Cassius

Dio's Roman History. Translated by E. Cary. 9 vols. Loeb Classical Library. Cambridge: Harvard University Press, 1914–.

Suetonius

Suetonius. Translated by J. C. Rolfe. 2 vols. Loeb Classical Library. Cambridge: Harvard University Press, 1913–.

Papyri and epigrapha

Corpus inscriptionum judaicarum: Recueil des inscriptions juives qui vont du IIIe siècle avant Jésus-Christ au VIIe siècle de notre ère. Edited by J. Frey. Vol 2. Rome: Pontificio istituto di archeologia Cristiana, 1952.

Corpus papyrorum judaicorum. Edited by V. Tcherikover and A. Fuks. 3 vols. Cambridge, Mass.: Harvard University Press, 1957–64.

Monumenta Asiae Minoris Antiqua, vol. 6: *Monuments and Documents from Phrygia and Caria.* Edited by W. H. Buckler and W. M. Calder. London: Society for the Promotion of Roman Studies, 1939.

Modern Works

Abbott, W. M., ed. *The Documents of Vatican II.* New York: Guild Press, 1966.

Badiou, A. *Saint Paul: The Foundation of Universalism.* Stanford: Stanford University Press, 2003.

Baird, W. *History of New Testament Research,* vol. Two: *From Jonathan Edwards to Rudolf Bultmann.* Minneapolis: Fortress Press, 2003.

Barclay, J. M. G. *Jews in the Mediterranean Diaspora: From Alexander to Trajan (323 BCE–117 CE).* Edinburgh: T & T Clark, 1996.

Baur, F. C. "Die Christuspartei in der korinthischen Gemeinde, der Gegensatz des petrinischen und paulinischen Christenthums in der ältesten Kirche, der Apostel Petrus in Romans" ["The Christ Party in the Corinthian Church . . . "], *Tübingen Zeitschrift für Theologie* 4 (1831): 61–206.

———. *Paulus, der Apostel Jesu Christi: Sein Leben und Wirken, seine Briefe und seine Lehre: Ein Beitrag zu einer kritischen Geschichte des Urchristenthums.* Stuttgart: Becher & Müller, 1845. ET: *Paul, the Apostle of Christ: His Life and Works. His Epistles and Teachings.* Peabody, Mass.: Hendrickson, 2003.

———. *Symbolik und Mythologie, oder die Naturreligion des Altertums* ["Symbolism and Mythology or Nature Religion in Antiquity]. Stuttgart: Metzler, 1824–25.

————. *Vorlesungen über neutestamentliche Theologie* ["Lectures on New Testament Theology"]. Leipzig: Fues, 1864.

Beard, M., J. A. North, and S. R. F. Price. *Religions of Rome,* vol. I: *A History.* Cambridge: Cambridge University Press, 1998.

Beauvior, S. de. *Le deuxième sexe.* Paris: Gallimard, 1949. ET: *The Second Sex.* Translated and edited by H. M. Parshley, with an introduction by M. Crosland. New York: Knopf, 1993.

Betz, H. D. *Galatians: A Commentary on Paul's Letter to the Churches in Galatia.* Philadelphia: Fortress Press, 1979.

Bornkamm, G. "The Letter to the Romans as Paul's Last Will and Testament," in *The Romans Debate: Revised and Expanded Edition,* ed. K. P. Donfried. Peabody: Hendrickson, 2001, 16–28.

————. *Paulus.* Stuttgart: Kolhammer, 1969. ET: *Paul.* Translated by D. M. G. Stalker. Minneapolis: Fortress Press, 1995.

Bousset, W. *Die Religion des Judentums im neutestamentlichen Zeitalter* ["The Judaic Religion in the New Testament Era"]. Berlin: Reuther & Reichard, 1903.

Brown, P. *Augustine of Hippo: A Biography; A New Edition with an Epilogue.* Berkeley: University of California Press, 2000 [1967].

Bultmann, R. *Das Urchristentum im Rahmen der antiken Religionen.* Zürich: Artemis, 1949. ET: *Primitive Christianity in Its Historical Setting.* Translated by R. H. Fuller. Philadelphia: Fortress Press, 1980.

————. *Die geschichte der synoptischen Tradition.* Göttingen: Vandenhoeck & Ruprecht, 1921. ET: *The History of the Synoptic Tradition.* Translated by J. Marsh. Oxford Blackwell, 1972, © 1963.

————. *Theologie des Neuen Testaments.* Tübingen: Mohr, 1948–53. ET: *Theology of the New Testament.* Translated by K. Grobel. 2 vols. New York: Scribner, 1951–55.

Cohen, S. J. D. *The Beginnings of Jewishness: Boundaries, Varieties, Uncertainties.* Berkeley: University of California Press, 1999.

Cranfield, C. E. B. *A Critical and Exegetical Commentary on the Epistle to the Romans.* Edinburgh: T & T Clark, 1990 [1975].

Das, A. A. *Paul, the Law, and the Covenant.* Peabody: Hendrickson, 2001.

Donaldson, T. L. *Paul and the Gentiles: Remapping the Apostle's Convictional World.* Minneapolis: Fortress Press, 1997.

————. "Proselytes or 'Righteous Gentiles'? The Status of Gentiles in Eschatological Pilgrimage Patterns of Thought," *Journal for the Study of the Pseudepigrapha* 7 (1990): 3–27.

Dunn, J. D. G. "The Incident at Antioch (Gal 2:11-18)," *Journal for the Study of the New Testament* 18 (1983): 3–57.

———. "The Justice of God: A Renewed Perspective on Justification by Faith (The Henton Davies Lecture, Regent Park College, Oxford, January 1991)," *Journal of Theological Studies* 43 (1992): 1–22.

———. "The New Perspective of Paul," *Bulletin of the John Rylands University Library of Manchester* 65 (1983): 95–122.

———. *The New Perspective on Paul.* Grand Rapids: Eerdmans, 2008.

———. "Paul's Conversion—A Light to Twentieth Century Disputes," in *Evangelium, Schriftauslegung, Kirche: Festschrift für Peter Stuhlmacher zum 65. Geburtstag,* ed. J. Ådna, S. J. Hafemann, and O. Hofius. Göttingen: Vandenhoeck & Ruprecht, 1997, 77–93.

———. *The Theology of Paul the Apostle.* London: T & T Clark, 2005 [1998].

Ehrensperger, K. *That We May Be Mutually Encouraged: Feminism and the New Perspective in Pauline Studies.* London: T & T Clark, 2004.

Elliott, N. *The Arrogance of Nations: Reading Romans in the Shadow of the Empire.* Minneapolis: Fortress Press, 2008.

———. *Liberating Paul: The Justice of God and the Politics of the Apostle.* Maryknoll, N.Y.: Orbis Books, 1994.

———. *The Rhetoric of Romans: Argumentative Constraint and Strategy and Paul's Dialogue with Judaism.* Sheffield: JSOT Press, 1990.

Esler, P. F. *Galatians.* London: Routledge, 1998.

Feldman, L. H. *Jew and Gentile in the Ancient World: Attitudes and Interactions from Alexander to Justinian.* Princeton: Princeton University Press, 1996.

Fergusson, D. A. *Bultmann.* London: Geoffrey Chapman, 1992.

Fish, S. *Is There a Text in This Class? The Authority of Interpretive Communities.* Harvard University Press: Cambridge, 1980.

Fitzmyer, J. A. *Romans: A New Translation with Introduction and Commentary.* New York: Doubleday, 1993.

Fung, R. Y. K. *The Epistle to the Galatians.* Grand Rapids: Eerdmans, 1988.

Gager, J. G. *The Origins of Anti-Semitism: Attitudes toward Judaism in Pagan and Christian Antiquity.* New York: Oxford University Press, 1985.

Gaston, L. *Paul and the Torah.* Vancouver: University of British Columbia Press, 1990.

Gathercole, S. J. *Where is Boasting? Early Jewish Soteriology and Paul's Response in Romans 1–5.* Grand Rapids: Eerdmans, 2002.

Guillaume, P. "Miracles Miraculously Repeated: Gospel Miracles as Duplication of Elijah-Elisha's," *Biblische Notizen* 98 (1999): 21–23.

Hammer, R. A. "Elijah and Jesus: A Quest for Identity," *Judaism* 19 (1970): 207–18.

Harland, P. A. *Associations, Synagogues, and Congregations: Claiming a Place in Ancient Mediterranean Society*. Minneapolis: Fortress Press, 2003.

Harris, H. *The Tübingen School*. Oxford: Clarendon Press, 1975.

Hayes, C. E. *Gentile Impurities and Jewish Identities: Intermarriage and Conversion from the Bible to the Talmud*. Oxford: Oxford University Press, 2002.

Hays, R. B. *Echoes of Scripture in the Letters of Paul*. New Haven: Yale University Press, 1989.

Heidegger, M. *Sein und zeit*. Halle: Niemeyer, 1927. ET: *Being and Time*. Translated by J. Macquarrie and E. Robinson. New York: Harper, 1962.

Hitler, A. *Mein Kampf*. München: Zentralvlg. der NSDAP, 1939. ET: *Mein Kampf*. With an introduction by D. Cameron Watt. Translated by R. Manheim. London: Pimlico, 1992.

Hodgson, P. C. *The Formation of Historical Theology: A Study of Ferdinand Christian Baur*. New York: Harper & Row, 1966.

Holtz, B. W., ed. *Back to the Sources: Reading the Classic Jewish Texts*. New York: Summit Books, 1984.

Horsley, R. A., ed. *Paul and Empire: Religion and Power in Roman Imperial Society*. Harrisburg: Trinity Press International, 1997.

———. "Submerged Biblical Histories and Imperial Biblical Studies," in *The Postcolonial Bible*, ed. R. S. Sugirtharajah. Sheffield: Sheffield Academic Press, 1998, 152–73.

Horsley, R. A., and J. S. Hanson. *Bandits, Prophets, and Messiahs: Popular Movements in the Time of Jesus*. Harrisburg: Trinity Press International, 1999.

Hübner, H. *Law in Paul's Thought*. Edinburgh: T & T Clark, 1984.

Johnson, L. T. *The First and Second Letters to Timothy: A New Translation with Introduction and Commentary*. New York: Doubleday, 2001.

Johnson Hodge, C. *If Sons, then Heirs: A Study of Kinship and Ethnicity in the Letters of Paul*. Oxford: Oxford University Press, 2007.

Käsemann, E. *An die Römer*. Tübingen: Mohr, 1980. ET: *Commentary on Romans*. Translated and edited by G. W. Bromiley. Grand Rapids: Eerdmans, 1980.

———. *Paulinische Perspektiven*. Tübingen: Mohr, 1980. ET: *Perspectives on Paul*. Translated by M. Kohl. 1st American ed. Philadelphia: Fortress Press, 1971.

Klein, C. *Anti-Judaism in Christian Theology*. Philadelphia: Fortress Press, 1978.

Klein, G. "Paul's Purpose in Writing the Epistle to the Romans," in *The Romans Debate: Revised and Expanded Edition*, ed. K. P. Donfried. Peabody: Hendrickson, 2001, 29–43.

Langton, D. R. "Jewish Philosophical and Psychological Approaches to the Apostle Paul: Spinoza, Schestov, and Taubes," *Studies in Christian-Jewish Relations* 2 (2007): 114–39.

Lazarus, N. "Introducing Postcolonial Studies," in *The Cambridge Companion to Postcolonial Literary Studies*, ed. N. Lazarus. Cambridge: Cambridge University Press, 2004, 1–16.

Lopez, D. C. *Apostle to the Conquered: Reimagining Paul's Mission.* Minneapolis: Fortress Press, 2008.

Luther, M. *Von den Jüden und iren Lügen.* Wittemberg: Hans Lufft, 1543. ET: *The Jews and Their Lies.* St. Louis, Mo.: Christian Nationalist Crusade, 1948.

Martin, D. B. "The Promise of Teleology, the Constraints of Epistemology, and Universal Vision in Paul," in *Paul among the Philosophers*, ed. J. D. Caputo and L. Martín Alcoff. Bloomington: Indiana University Press, forthcoming.

Martin, R. P. "Käsemann, Ernst," in *Historical Handbook of Major Biblical Interpreters*, ed. D. K. Mckim. Downers Grove: InterVarsity Press, 1998, 500–505.

Meier, J. P. *A Marginal Jew: Rethinking the Historical Jesus*, vol. two: *Mentor, Message, and Miracles.* New York: Doubleday, 1994.

———. *A Marginal Jew: Rethinking the Historical Jesus*, vol. three: *Companions and Competitors.* New York: Doubleday, 2001.

Miccoli, G. "Two Sensitive Issues: Religious Freedom and the Jews," in *History of Vatican II*, vol. IV: *Church as Communion: Third Period and Intersession, September 1964–September 1965*, ed. G. Alberigo. Maryknoll/Leuven: Orbis/Peeters, 2003, 95–193.

Montefiore, C. G. *Judaism and St Paul: Two Essays.* London: Goshen, 1914.

Moore, G. F. "Christian Writers on Judaism," *Harvard Theological Review* 14 (1921): 197–254.

———. *Judaism in the First Centuries of the Christian Era: The Age of the* Tannaim. 3 vols. Cambridge: Harvard University Press, 1927–30.

Morgan, R. "Bornkamm, Günther," in *Historical Handbook of Major Biblical Interpreters*, ed. D. K. Mckim. Downers Grove: InterVarsity Press, 1998, 439–44.

Murray, M. *Playing a Jewish Game: Gentile Christian Judaizing in the First and Second Centuries CE.* Waterloo: Wilfred Laurier University Press, 2004.

Nanos, M. D. "The Inter- and Intra-Jewish Political Context of Paul's Letter to the Galatians," in *The Galatians Debate: Contemporary Issues in Rhetorical and Historical Interpretation*, ed. M. D. Nanos. Peabody: Hendrickson, 2002, 396–407.

———. *The Irony of Galatians: Paul's Letter in First Century Context.* Philadelphia: Fortress Press, 2001.

———. "The Jewish Context of the Gentile Audience Addressed in Paul's Letter to the Romans," *Catholic Biblical Quarterly* 61 (1999): 283–304.

———. *The Mystery of Romans: The Jewish Context of Paul's Letter.* Minneapolis: Fortress Press, 1996.

————. "What Was at Stake in Peter's 'Eating with Gentiles' at Antioch?" in *The Galatians Debate: Contemporary Issues in Rhetorical and Historical Interpretation*, ed. M. D. Nanos. Peabody: Hendrickson, 2002, 282–318.

Overman, J. A. *Matthew's Gospel and Formative Judaism: The Social World of the Matthean Community*. Minneapolis: Fortress Press, 1990.

Phillips, V. C. "Feminist Interpretation," in *Methods of Biblical Interpretation: Excerpted from the Dictionary of Biblical Interpretation*, ed. J. H. Hayes. Nashville: Abingdon Press, 2004, 371–84.

Räisänen, H. *Beyond New Testament Theology: A Story and a Programme*. London: SCM PreRäisänen, H.ss, 1990.

————. *Paul and the Law*. Tübingen: Mohr, 1983.

Rubin, J. P. "Celsus' Decircumcision Operation: Medical and Historical Implications," *Urology* 16 (1980): 121–24.

Ruether, R. R. *Faith and Fratricide: The Theological Roots of Anti-Semitism*. New York: Seabury Press, 1974.

Safrai, S., ed. *The Literature of the Sages: First Part: Oral Torah, Halakha, Mishna, Tosefta, Talmud, External Tractates*. Assen: Van Gorcum, 1987.

Said, E. W. *Orientalism*. London: Routledge and Kegan Paul, 1978.

Sanders, E. P. *Jesus and Judaism*. Philadelphia: Fortress Press, 1985.

————. *Judaism: Practice and Belief 63 BCE—66 CE*. London: SCM Press, 1994.

————. *Paul and Palestinian Judaism: A Comparison of Patterns of Religion*. Minneapolis: Fortress Press, 1977.

————. *Paul, the Law, and the Jewish People*. Minneapolis: Fortress Press, 1985 [1983].

Sanders, J. T. *Schismatics, Sectarians, Dissidents, Deviants: The First One Hundred Years of Jewish-Christian Relations*. London: SCM Press, 1993.

Sandnes, K. O. *Paul One of the Prophets? A Contribution to the Apostle's Self-Understanding*. Tübingen: Mohr, 1991.

Schäfer, P. *Judeophobia: Attitudes toward the Jews in the Ancient World*. Cambridge: Harvard University Press, 1997.

Schechter, S. *Some Aspects of Rabbinic Theology*. London: Adam and Charles Black, 1909.

Schürer, E. *Geschichte des jüdischen Volkes im Zeitalter Jesu Christi*. Leipzig: Hinrichs, 1866–1890. ET: *The History of the Jewish People in the Age of Jesus Christ (175 B.C.– A.D. 135)*. Translated by T. A. Burkill et al. Revised and edited by G. Vermes and F. Miller. Edinburgh: T & T Clark, 1973.

Schüssler Fiorenza, E., A. Brook, and S. Matthews, eds. *Searching the Scriptures*, vol. 2: *A Feminist Commentary*. New York: Crossroads, 1994.

Schweitzer, A. *Von Reimarus zu Wrede: Eine Geschichte der Leben-Jesu-Forschung.* Tübingen: Mohr, 1906. ET: *The Quest of the Historical Jesus.* 1st complete ed. Edited by J. Bowden. 1st Fortress Press ed. Minneapolis: Fortress Press, 2001.

Segal, A. F. *Rebecca's Children: Judaism and Christianity in the Roman World.* Cambridge: Harvard University Press, 1986.

Sigurdson, O. "Reading Žižek Reading Paul: Pauline Interventions in Radical Philosophy," in *Reading Romans with Contemporary Philosophers and Theologians,* ed. D. Odell-Scott. London: T & T Clark, 2007, 213–45.

Sim, D. C. *The Gospel of Matthew and Christian Judaism: The History and Social Setting of the Matthean Community.* Edinburgh: T & T Clark, 1998.

Simon, M. *Verus Israel: A Study of the Relations between Christians and Jews in the Roman Empire (AD 135–425).* London: Vallentine Mitchell, 1996.

Simpson, W. W., and R. Weyl. *The Story of the International Council of Christians and Jews.* Oxford: International Council of Christians and Jews. Martin Buber House, 1995.

Slee, M. *The Church in Antioch in the First Century CE: Communion and Conflict.* London: Sheffield Academic, 2003.

Stemberger, G. *Introduction to the Talmud and Midrash.* Edinburgh: T & T Clark, 1996.

Stendahl, K. "The Apostle Paul and the Introspective Conscience of the West," *Harvard Theological Review* 56 (1963): 199–215.

———. *Final Account: Paul's Letter to the Romans.* Minneapolis: Fortress Press, 1995.

———. *Paul among Jews and Gentiles, and other Essays.* London: SCM Press, 1977.

Stowers, S. K. *A Rereading of Romans: Justice, Jews and Gentiles.* New Haven: Yale University Press, 1994.

Strauss, D. F. *Das leben Jesu, kritisch bearbeitet.* Tübingen: Osiander, 1835–36. ET: *The Life of Jesus, Critically Examined.* Edited and with an introduction by P. C. Hodgson. Translated from the 4th German ed. by G. Eliot. Philadelphia: Fortress Press, 1973.

Strindberg, A. *The Red Room: Scenes of Artistic and Literary Life.* London: Dent, 1967.

Sugirtharajah, R. S. *Postcolonial Criticism and Biblical Interpretation.* Oxford: Oxford University Press, 2002.

Taubes, J. *The Political Theology of Paul.* Stanford: Stanford University Press, 2004.

Taylor, M. S. *Anti-Judaism and Early Christian Identity: A Critique of the Scholarly Consensus.* Leiden: Brill, 1995.

Taylor, N. *Paul, Antioch and Jerusalem: A Study in Relationships and Authority in Earliest Christianity.* Sheffield: Sheffield Academic Press, 1992.

Tellbe, M. *Paul between Synagogue and State: Christians, Jews, and Civic Authorities in 1 Thessalonians, Romans, and Philippians.* Stockholm: Almqvist & Wiksell International, 2001.

The Theology of the Churches and the Jewish People: Statements by the World Council of Churches and Its Member Churches: With a Commentary by Allan Brockway, Paul van Buren, Rolf Rendtorff, Simon Schoon. Geneva: WCC Publications, 1988.

Thielman, F. *From Plight to Solution: A Jewish Framework for Understanding Paul's View of the Law in Galatians and Romans.* Leiden: Brill, 1989.

Thiselton, A. C. *The First Epistle to the Corinthians: A Commentary on the Greek Text.* Grand Rapids: Eerdmans, 2000.

Tomson, P. J. *Paul and the Jewish Law: Halakha in the Letters of the Apostle to the Gentiles.* Assen: van Gorcum, 1990.

Vanderkam, J., and P. Flint. *The Meaning of the Dead Sea Scrolls: Their Significance for Understanding the Bible, Judaism, Jesus, and Christianity.* New York: HarperSanFrancisco, 2004.

Weber, F. *System der altsynagogalen palästinischen Theologie aus Targum, Midrasch und Talmud* ["The Theological System of the Ancient Palestinian Synagogue Based on the Targum, Midrash, and Talmud"]. Leipzig: Dörffling & Franke, 1880.

Wedderburn, A. J. M. *The Reasons for Romans.* London: T & T Clark, 1988.

Westerholm, S. *Israel's Law and the Church's Faith: Paul and His Recent Interpreters.* Grand Rapids: Eerdmans, 1988.

———. *Perspectives Old and New on Paul: The "Lutheran" Paul and His Critics.* Grand Rapids: Eerdmans, 2004.

Wright, N. T. *The Climax of the Covenant: Christ and the Law in Pauline Theology.* Minneapolis: Fortress Press, 1992.

———. *Paul: In Fresh Perspective.* Minneapolis: Fortress Press, 2005.

———. "The Paul of History and the Apostle of Faith," *Tyndale Bulletin* 29 (1978): 61–88.

———. *What Saint Paul Really Said: Was Paul of Tarsus the Real Founder of Christianity?* Grand Rapids: Eerdmans, 1997.

Young, B. H. *Paul the Jewish Theologian: A Pharisee among Christians, Jews, and Gentiles.* Peabody: Hendrickson, 1997.

Zetterholm, M. *The Formation of Christianity in Antioch: A Social-Scientific Approach to the Separation between Judaism and Christianity.* London: Routledge, 2003.

————. "Paul and the Missing Messiah," in *The Messiah: In Early Judaism and Christianity*, ed. M. Zetterholm. Minneapolis: Fortress Press, 2007, 33–55.

————. "Purity and Anger: Gentiles and Idolatry in Antioch," *Interdisciplinary Journal of Research on Religion* 1 (2005): 1–24.

Žižek, S. *The Puppet and the Dwarf: The Perverse Core of Christianity.* Cambridge: MIT Press, 2003.

INDEX OF NAMES

INDEX OF PASSAGES

1 Corinthians